MILITARY WIVES

MILITARY WIVES

FROM THE FIRST WORLD WAR TO AFGHANISTAN

PENNY LEGG

For the unsung heroines, the military wives, and for Joe, Royal Navy Falklands veteran, my hero.

A donation from every copy sold will be made to SSAFA.

First published 2015

The History Press
The Mill, Brimscombe Port
Stroud, Gloucestershire, GL5 2QG
www.thehistorypress.co.uk

British Library Cataloguing in Publication Data.
A catalogue record for this book is available from the British Library.

ISBN 978 0 7524 9107 3

Typeset in Bembo 11.5/14pt by The History Press
Printed and bound in Great Britain by TJ International Ltd

CONTENTS

	Acknowledgements	7
	Foreword	9
	Introduction	10
	Author's Note	12
Prologue	*To Those Left Behind* by June Stead	13
1	The First World War and Beyond	15
2	Another World War	27
3	Post-war Britain	47
4	The End of the Twentieth Century	95
5	A New Beginning	125
	Epilogue	213
	The Final Word	215
	Bibliography	217
	Index	219

ACKNOWLEDGEMENTS

With a book like this it is very difficult to know where to start when it comes to saying thank you. So many people have helped me along the way and I hope I have remembered everyone. If I have missed anyone, please accept my apologies and sincere thanks.

Firstly, I must thank Sophie Bradshaw, general history & gift publisher and my commissioning editor, and Jo De Vries, senior commissioning editor at The History Press.

I couldn't have written this book without Jay Armstrong, Caroline, Lady Richards, Carol Backhouse, Jo' Ball, Lauren Bray, Kate Churchward, Gladys Curtis, Laura Delahay, Gail Douglas, Anthea Fillingham, Alis Glencross, Joy Hale, Sarah Hattingh, Barbara Hill, Phyllis Holroyd, Steffi Hughes, Fiona Jameson, Phyllida Joel, Sarah Kiff, Nicola Laing, Jade Leahy, Olive Leahy, Helen Malcolmson, Kelly Malster, Lorraine Matthews, Carol Musgrove, Irene Noyce, Margherita 'Rita' Woosnam, Liesel Parkinson, Sue Piper, Dr Jean Powell, Dr Clare Shaw, June Stead, Jean Weeks, Charlotte Woolrich and Kay Wylie. Thank you for the super chats, lovely coffee and cake and, above all, for trusting me with your stories.

I am indebted to Susanne Dawson for allowing me to use her mother Rose's story in this book, and for her help with admin during the production of this book.

With kind appreciation to: Maianna Moreau and Jenny Cuffe for allowing the use of material produced for the book, *This is my Home Now*; Iris Mardon, for allowing me to delve into her mother, Winifred Deahl's, wartime diary; Mike and Gill Holloway, for their continuing help and support; Jay Armstrong (www.jayarmstrong.co.uk) for permission to use the photograph of Kate Churchward and her family; James Marsh and the Marsh family for permission to use Edith Marsh's Second World War experiences; Pam Whittington, for the use of her poetry in this book, and for her valued friendship; Christopher and Eve Leahy, for not giving up the search and bringing me Lily Hannah's story; Wendi Friend, for excellent research and dogged determination; Roy and Lynn Lambeth, for allowing the Winter family First World War history to be told in this book; Eon Matthews, for his continuing staunch support and friendship. It is appreciated.

With grateful thanks to: Pauline and Simon Weeks, and Trish Simpson, for their help and assistance; John and June Curtis, for their support of this project; Ron Stead for encouragement and enthusiasm; Nicola Donoghue, for her admin support and long-distance assistance; Sarah Gomes, online officer at Charnwood LV (www.leicestershirevillages.com) for her assistance in making contact with a local photographer and Peter Smith, photographer, for permission to use his Anstey Church images. Thanks also to Dom, aka 'Bad CO', at www.rearparty.co.uk, Facebook friends who pointed the way when I got stuck, and Pip Legg, my four-legged old friend, who sleeps peacefully on my desk while I work.

Last as ever, but by no means least, my husband Joe, for being there.

FOREWORD

I am delighted and honoured to be asked to write the Foreword to *Military Wives: From the First World War to Afghanistan*. For too long the role of the military wife has been largely overlooked and misunderstood. Penny Legg, a naval wife, has taken up the challenge of researching the lives of military wives. She narrates their story through their own words: through the personal accounts of those who have lived and breathed the life. It is a fascinating and compelling read. I hope it leads to them receiving the recognition in Whitehall that good regiments, ships and air stations have always instinctively accorded them.

Few in society give much thought to the wife of a serviceman. Yet her role can be described as having 'operational importance'; if the wife and family of the serviceman deployed overseas are well cared for and happy, the better he can concentrate on the task in hand. In 1885, Sir James Gildea, the founder of SSAFA wrote to *The Times* on behalf of the wives and children of those on active service 'so they are not altogether forgotten, or that the cry of poverty and want be not added to that of suspense and anxiety'.

Perhaps the words 'suspense and anxiety' sum up why military wives deserve our respect and gratitude. Yet too often, in awe of the chain of command, wives lack confidence and fear stepping out of line. Indeed, they are often discouraged from voicing their anxieties. As mentioned in these pages, the inspirational Military Wives Choir has helped lift their self-esteem and has quite literally given wives a voice. For this reason I highly recommend this book which records the extraordinary lives of our brave and resilient military wives. In a world of emails and text messages this book leaves an important and lasting legacy; a tribute to the wives of our Armed Forces. As my husband would say, the indomitable spirit of Lady Sale lives on!

Caroline, Lady Richards

Wife of General Sir David Richards and the founder of the Afghan Appeal Fund: afghanappealfund.org.uk

INTRODUCTION

In 2011, I had the good fortune to be commissioned to produce a project I had been nurturing for some time – namely to save for posterity the experiences of British and Commonwealth military personnel who had all served Her Majesty Queen Elizabeth II in the sixty years of her reign. *Under The Queen's Colours* was the result, published in time for Her Majesty's diamond jubilee. The book raises funds for three service charities and was a lot of fun, if hard work, to put together. I got to meet many good people, hear about their experiences, laugh, cry and sigh with them. I was very grateful for the trust that these servicemen and women placed in me when they supported the project and it was a real privilege to get to know them.

When I was approached by my publisher and asked if I would like to produce a sequel, but this time looking at the experiences of the women married to the men in the military uniforms, I had no hesitation. I looked forward to hearing the opposite side of the coin, the women's story, which is so seldom heard. This book is the result. To produce it, I spoke to a number of ladies, all of whom had one thing in common – they were married to men in the British armed services at one time in their lives. I, too, was once a military spouse and I knew that there were stories to be told.

Marrying, or in this day and age, partnering, a member of Her Majesty's Armed Forces is not something that is undertaken lightly. Throughout history, it is the service personnel who put their lives at risk for monarch and country, and their loved ones who are left behind, to wait, hope and worry until they come back. If they don't return, life is never the same.

This book takes us back briefly to the First World War, when many women became fiancées but never wives. Their men were lost in a vicious war the like of which, it was hoped, would never be seen again. It was the war to end all wars and it took its toll on the British male military population, many of whom were conscripts.

Through the 1920s and 1930s women came to terms with their menfolk in peacetime military service, which sometimes brought its own problems, particularly as long separations, often for years at a time, were the norm.

Then came the Second World War, the war that struck terror into the hearts of all those who remembered the horrors of 1914–18. Gas masks, mass call-ups, women taking their men's places and make-do-and-mend were the order of the day.

The post-war era brought a plethora of small wars and crises – in Korea, Suez, Aden, Northern Ireland, the Falklands and the Gulf, until the twenty-first century arrived, and with it, Afghanistan. Throughout all, women have been behind their men, quietly getting on with their lives and giving the stability and domestic home life that balances the military discipline and frontline danger. These women have stood by men maimed and disfigured by war, whose minds and bodies will forever be tormented by experiences unimagined by most civilians. They put up with being left on their own, often for months at a time and often with several children, a home and a career of their own to look after. Nomads, they move from place to place, following their men, becoming adept at leaving their homes spotless for white gloved 'march outs' when moving on, fully able to change a fuse, unblock a sink or a toilet, be both mummy and daddy to a confused little one and yet still be a loving wife when the wanderer returns.

This book, which will help to raise funds for the Sailors, Soldiers, Airmen & Families Association (SSAFA), takes a behind-the-scenes look at life for military wives in the last 100 years. It seeks to show life, warts and all, for those unseen heroines, the military wives.

Penny Legg, 2015

AUTHOR'S NOTE

Time dims even the sharpest memory. Please bear with the story-teller if some of the details in these tales are not quite as posterity has recorded them.

PROLOGUE

TO THOSE LEFT BEHIND BY JUNE STEAD

A tear fell, then another
Into the sea to follow your calling
Once more you had left
For shores far away
Sailing into the sunset
Shipmates only for company

As I turned my back
One part of me died
But look, another part opens
For your sons now beckon
What's for dinner Mum?
Are my shorts washed?
Not a care in their world
'Cept stomach and footer

Your letter arrives
'Been to a banyan, it was good
Hope everything is fine with you'

No tears now, only tired eyes
Been up all night, two sick boys
Washing machine broke
Then telly broke

As navy wives we had no training
But jack-of-all-trades are we
Fix the window, mend the fuse
Car broken down – yet again

Ship due home, clean the house
Scrub the floors, polish the windows
New dress must have and shoes too

More tears are shed but tears of joy
For we are a family once more
Boys have their Dad
I have my mate, and, as he said before leaving
There is a silver lining

Would I swap my life for another?
Never,
I am a sailor's wife for ever

June Stead

1

THE FIRST WORLD WAR AND BEYOND

The big guns opened up from Calais …
It was a bit traumatic at the time …
Joy Hale

Much time has passed since the First World War. To us, looking back from the high-tech world of the twenty-first century, grainy, silent images of men and equipment moving jerkily around boggy trenches and over wasteland give a visual idea of the awfulness of battle, while well-tended war memorials, and cemeteries that dot both Britain and abroad are all that remain to give an indication of the scale of loss from the conflict. The last of the servicemen actually to take part in the war has passed away, and so, like all events, the 'war to end war' as H.G. Wells termed it, has slowly sunk into the pages of history.

When the men went to fight for king and country, the women were left to pick up the reins and keep the country going. More than a million women joined the work force between 1914 and 1918 (BBC). Many joined the Civil Service as typists or clerks. Others drove trams or other forms of transport. Some toiled in munitions or chemical factories, often working in hazardous conditions for long hours. All seized the opportunity to show that, although they were mere women, they could keep the country going in its time of need. In the process, they realised newfound independence.

Trying to find words left behind by military wives about their experiences of being married to a serviceman in this period has been a challenge.

Many letters home from the front to loved ones have survived the passage of time, but few letters from wives to their men arrived back to Blighty and then survived until the present. It is left to families to track down and record the details of their family history and, in so doing, to bring just a small idea of the life military wives lived a century or so ago.

❧ MARGARET WINTER ☙

There are no words left by Margaret, known as 'Maggie' to her loved ones. Her family have managed to trace the family tree and so know a little of her domestic life, and have documents and some letters that refer to her. The whole, meagre but fascinating, collection provides a small insight into what some military wives of the day had to deal with.

She was born Margaret Payne in 1884, and married William Dan Winter on 4 August 1907 in Southampton. She was the daughter of George Payne, a shipwright who did not live to see his daughter married, and he the son of Dan Winter, a carter. At the time of their marriage, 24-year-old William Dan was a baker journeyman and Maggie a tailoress. Of their four children, only one survived to adulthood. Little William Dan was born in 1909 and died a year later. In 1911, Emily Elizabeth Margaret was born, and it is through her that the family line ran forward. Her brother, Thomas, was born and died in 1913.

Then came the First World War, and baker William Dan found himself leaving Hampshire for the army and, eventually, the Western Front as Pte William D. Winter 32976, part of the 8th Lincolnshire Regiment. His war would eventually take him to the Arras Offensive and a fateful date with destiny.

Meanwhile, in 1915, Albert, known as 'Bertie', was born. This third son died tragically a week before his 1st birthday after falling into an open fire and dying of his injuries. Maggie was now alone with little Emily, known affectionately as 'Emmie'.

William Dan was stationed at Chiseldon, Swindon. In an undated letter sent to his sister before going to France in early 1917, he is clearly worried about his wife, 'I am sorry Maggie is no better. I pray to God that she will for I do not know what I shall do if she goes. I hope that she will be well when I comes back from the front … I wish they would let me home to see her once more.' Correspondence between William Dan and his oldest sister, Annie Drewett (*b*. 1870), dated 21 March 1917, sheds light on how Maggie was faring:

My Dear Sister

Just a few lines to you to say that I am very well at present. I can see by Maggie's writing that she is in a very bad state. I am glad that every-one else is very well at Shirley [Southampton] and little Emmie. I have wrote to Mr Payne, 30 Heysham Road [his father-in-law]. Dear Annie I hope that I shall come through alright. I pray every day and night to do so. I hope for Charlie's sight to come back [William Charles Drewett, Annie's husband] as much as for Maggie's health. If the worst do happen to her, I shall have one consolation – that I have always been a good hus-band to her and done my very best for her. God bless her. She have been a good wife to me. Dear sister did Ted tell you in his letter that he had one from me? It is a wonder Aunt Martha did not say something about my letter for it was a bit stiff. I told her I was surprised she have not been to see Maggie all the time she been ill after the kindness Maggie done for her Kate and it was like some people the more you done for them the less you get thought of and that Kate was not situated like Maggie and me, having to break our home up whereas she was living with her mother. Very likely the letter I sent pricked her conscience a bit. Dear Annie I am glad Maggie's mother sent Emmie a few things it will come in handy for her. Tell Emmie that her daddy thinks about her every day. We had a pleasant open air service Tuesday evening before I left for here and we had the hymns we sang when mother was buried and I asked for *God be with you till we Meet Again* for a farewell hymn. Dear Annie watch the papers for my number. I must close with love to all especially Emmie and Maggie.

From your loving Brother

WD Winter

I hope to see you all again soon. Kisses for my little Emmie and Maggie.

Margaret Winter died on 19 March 1917 of pulmonary tuberculosis. She was 33 years old. The telegram that Annie sent her brother to tell him of his wife's death did not reach him until 23 March 1917. He wrote to his sister immediately upon hearing the news:

My Dear Sister,

… I received your telegram today Friday 23rd Mar. I left the Base Mon 19th for to go up the line. I am not surprised to hear of Maggie's death. What she have suffered God alone knows. It is a happy release. I pray she is gone where our Dear Boys and our Dear Mother is which I know

she is and if I should get put under I hope to meet her up in heaven where there is no parting. Dear Annie take care of my little girl for me for she is the only one I have to live for. I hope to see her again one day. ... I have put the telegram in my C/O's hands and if I gets away it will be two or three days if I do not see to the Death Benefit from the Oddfellows. If anything happens to me that I get killed you will find it in the bottom drawer of the small chest in a sealed envelope with my will. You will know what to do. I know you will see she is buried decent. ... Dear Annie have a few memorial cards ... order a dozen. Dear Annie I am sorry she is gone but it is better so it was the Lords will did she die peaceful pray her soul at rest my burden is hard to bear but the good Lord can make it light. My trust is in him and he have made it light already. I think I have said all so I close with love to all especially Emmie from your loving and sorrowing Brother.
WD Winter

William Dan was not allowed home for his wife's funeral because he had too recently joined his unit. Sadly, the memorial cards he asked his sister to order for Maggie were eventually a joint memorial, as he was killed around 9–12 April 1917:

On the Resurrection morning
Soul and body meet again,
No more sorrow, no more
weeping,
No more pain.

On that happy Easter morning
All the graves their dead
restore,
Father, mother, sister, brother,
Meet once more.

★★★

Not long were they divided.

In Loving Memory
Of
William Dan Winter,
(8th Lincolns)
Who was killed in action
between the 9th and the 12th
of April, 1917,
★★★

ALSO, HIS DEAR WIFE.
MAGGIE,
Who died March 19th. 1917,
Aged 33 Years.

Annie raised Emmie. She married serviceman Horace Lambeth in 1945, thus becoming a military wife herself, and had two children, Leonard and Roy, both of whom survived.

🌿 MARGARET MIDDLETON-WEST 🌿

Sue Piper, who features later in this book, has the army in her blood. Both her grandfather and her father were officers in the Indian Army. We do not have her grandmother Margaret's words, but Sue recounts this story, which is an example of what military wives could expect during the First World War:

> My mother's father, Lt Col Stephen Middleton-West FRCS, IMS (Indian Medical Service), was a British surgeon in India with the Indian Army. During the First World War he was posted away. My grandmother, Margaret, was pregnant with my aunt. The lady of the guest house she was staying in turned her out when she found she was pregnant with no husband around! So, eventually, my grandmother travelled from Simla by train to the south of India. My aunt was born by then and spent the whole journey crying, apparently. My aunt wondered if that and the stress caused to my grandmother, was why she, my aunt, suffered from depression/anxiety/restlessness during her life.
>
> My grandparents eventually went to Burma as missionaries.

🌿 JESSIE MAUD WHITE 🌿

Jessie was born on 4 June 1876 and married a career sailor in the Royal Navy, William Henry Gibeon White on 28 January 1898. At the beginning of the First World War he was a chief petty officer. Their granddaughter, Joy Hale, has studied their family tree and this, combined with knowledge gained from the time, gives an insight into Jessie's life as a military wife.

Joy takes up the tale:

> Jessie's maiden name was Boryer. The family originally came from Plymouth and we think it possible that there was some sort of French influence. There might well have been. They might have been Boyer –

in those days they could not spell and they wrote down whatever they could pronounce.

The family moved to Portsmouth, where she was born, but she had three brothers and sisters born down in Plymouth. Her father, who was Warrant Officer Henry Robert Boryer, served in the Royal Navy until pension and then bought a pub in Emsworth, the Ship Inn, which is still there. It must have been a good thing to do, because two of his sons also became publicans.

Jessie was not very tall, about 5ft 5in. She was a very smart lady. She had worked as an apprentice milliner, which probably accounts for her knowing a little about clothes. She married at 22 and had my mother. Her husband being in the navy, in those days, they had very long commissions and were away for sometimes two and a half years or three years, she only had one more child, a boy, Gibeon Henry William (my uncle), after six years. Grandfather did the China Run. It was a long time. Endless. Life was hard but people stayed together.

She gave up millinery when she got married in 1898. Then my mother was born, so she looked after her. She had brothers and sisters and they all visited each other for cups of tea. She had one brother who went down and lived in Sittingbourne in Kent.

My mother was about 12 when my grandfather's brother and sister died quite quickly of tuberculosis. My grandmother was worried about my mother 'going into a decline', as they say. She sent her to Sittingbourne and she lived there for a year in the country air and atmosphere.

❧ WILLIAM ❧

Joy also tells us more about William:

My grandfather, William, was already in the navy when the war started. He did a six year apprenticeship and then went straight into the navy. He was a trained shipwright. He adored Jessie, as she was a bit of a tomboy. My uncle came along and he was very gentle. He fell when he was about 3 and broke his arm, and Jessie said that the sun never shone on him. He was cosseted because he had broken his arm.

My mother would miss her father terribly – the separations – but my grandmother had another sister whose husband was in the navy. He sadly went down with his ship at the Battle of Jutland, so they would have been commiserating with her and helping her. They all knew each other and all lived in Portsmouth.

Latterly, my mother and uncle always spoke about what a happy childhood they had. There was no poverty, as William and Jessie had been able to buy a house in a nice part of Portsmouth. They did not have a car, but then again, who did?

The big incident I remember from my mother and grandmother was that my grandmother, Jessie, was widowed right at the end of the war. Grandfather died, not in the war, but due to circumstances from the war and she qualified for a pension.

HMS Irresistible

My grandfather was in the war on HMS *Irresistible*, which was what they called a battle cruiser in those days. He was in the Battle of Gallipoli against Turkey and Russia and the ship was in the Dardanelles, which was a channel from the Aegean and the Sea of Marmaris. There was fighting on one side of Gallipoli and his ship was sunk by a mine. I think he survived, together with the ship's dog and quite a few of the crew [150 men were killed when the ship sank on 18 March 1915, after hitting a mine].

Subsequently, he came home and then he was in coastal forces and was stationed in Dover. Every now and again, when my grandfather came in to Dover, my mother and my nana, Jessie, and my uncle were able to go there and spend two or three weeks with him.

My mother used to tell me about how the big guns opened up from Calais. I think one was called 'Big Bertha'. They would always run and go in the shelters, which were in Dover Rocks in Dover Castle, and thereby survive. It was a bit traumatic at the time for them.

Butter Ration

They came through the war. My mother always remembered giving up the butter ration for my nana, because she did not like margarine.

So, my grandmother Jessie had quite a comfortable existence as a military wife. She would be living on a chief petty officer's pay, which would be good for those days, and living in their own home with the two children. If the war had not come along they might have gone abroad, because occasionally wives and families went.

His grave is actually in Milton Cemetery, I believe. It is a war grave, kept in nice condition.

Apoplexy

The story is that they went to a funeral at Milton Cemetery. There was a grave alongside the grave of the person whose funeral they had attended, newly dug ready for somebody. My grandfather said, 'Oh look, there is a grave there. Some poor bugger is going to go into that.'

It turned out to be him, because he died here in Portsmouth in the Sailors' Rest. We had a very big Sailors' Rest, which was near the town station. He was going back from leave and he didn't feel well. So he put himself in there for a night. His cabin was up the top of the building. In the morning, the room attendant went to get him up but could hear this very strong, heavy breathing. The management opened up and he was unconscious. They took him into the Royal Naval Barracks and he died. Apoplexy was the word they used. A stroke. He was a big man.

Jessie had a nice house in Kirby Road in Portsmouth. It was a biggish house. She had a good widow's pension. She was able to let some of the house and so she seemed to be comfortably off. She was a smart lady, a very nice cook and she seemed to have a boyfriend now and again. Someone usually with a car. As grandchildren we benefitted from that. My grandfather was only 45 when he died, so my grandmother was not old when she was widowed. She lived until she was 94. She did not remarry, but one of her gentleman friends used to come and visit two ladies she had let a room to. This gentleman subsequently became her partner. She did not marry, because she would have lost her pension. His name was William Hale. He had a nephew who lived in Lincoln and he used to come down and visit from time to time. In 1945, I married the nephew!

❧ LILY HANNAH PAYNE ❧

The author had the good fortune to bump into a family history researcher in the course of her work on this book. Wendi Friend had been working with the Leahy family in trying to trace information on a young man who was engaged to Lily Hannah Payne during the First World War. Subsequent to this meeting, two members of the family, Christopher, Lily's grandson, and Eve, his wife, were able to fill out more of Lily's story, and, finally, Lily's daughter, Olive, shed more light on this wartime romance and what happened to the pair. Many records were lost during the Second World War and so, at the time of writing, the family are still engaged in research.

Christopher begins the story:

> My grandmother grew up in a little village called Anstey, in North
> Hertfordshire. She was a school teacher in the village and was one of
> nine children. She was born Lily Hannah Cattley. She was engaged to
> Frederick Alexander Cook, who was named after his father, but every-
> one knew him as Alexander Cook. He was 20 when he was killed on
> Boxing Day, 1916.

Premonition

> She got the bad news. It turned out that Lily Hannah was also a friend of
> Ernest Payne, possibly having met both he and Alex when she was a land
> girl. Before he went off to war, Ernest had said to Alex, 'You won't marry
> Lily, but I will. You might be engaged to her, but you will not marry her.'
> It seemed to have been some kind of a premonition …

Wendi Friend came to assist the family, as they had been trying to find
details of Lily's fiancé without success. They had been under the mistaken
assumption that his name was Alexander Cook. Trips to cemeteries in
France drew a blank, but Wendi was able to find out why the family could
not find him. She takes up the story:

> He was born in Watford, Hertfordshire, on the war records, but on the
> 1911 census it showed he was born in Bishop's Waltham, Hampshire. We
> think he was born in Watford and then the family moved to Bishop's
> Waltham. His parents, Frederick William and Rosetta Cook, went on to
> have two more sons. We found that he is in Le Touret Military Cemetery,
> Richebourg-l'Avoué, Pas de Calais. He was a corporal and had been
> mentioned in dispatches. His Army Serial Number was 87427Y and he
> was part of the 5th Battalion, Royal Field Artillery.

Alex was a dispatch rider. His father was a domestic gardener. At 14 he was
described as the 'domestic garden boy'. He went to France on 27 July 1915.
In the same cemetery, buried next to him, is George Edward Kingsley
Bemand, second lieutenant, Royal Field Artillery, who also died on 26
December 1916. His name appears in both the University of London
Officer Training Corps (OTC) and the Roll of the Fallen, in which the
citation reads:

2nd Lt Royal Field Art attach trench mortar battery University College, son of Mr G. Bemand of Jamaica, killed in action on 26 Dec 1916 buried in La Touret.

Wendi says, 'He was one of the first black officers. We think he was Alex's commanding officer. University College London records George Bemand's death as killed by a shell near Bethune on 26 December 1916. Both were killed at the same time.'

Lily's daughter, Olive, takes up the tale:

When I was a little girl, I can remember one Boxing Day mum was very sad. I said, 'Mum, why are you so sad?'

She said, 'I was just thinking of my Alex.'

'Who was Alex?'

'He was the man I was engaged to be married to. He was killed on Boxing Day.'

I was sorry about it as she obviously adored him, the same as she adored my father. She went on to tell me that Alex was a gardener. I thought she said a head gardener at one of the big houses in Middlesex. I think dad worked with him. I imagined Alex to be older than he turned out to be. He could only have been a lad, as dad went to war when he was 17. He put his age up.

Granny Cook

We know that she used to go to Bishop's Waltham to visit Alexander's mother who was known as 'Granny Cook' but we don't know how she got there – by train? After Alex died, Granny Cook used to send boxes of flowers to Lily Hannah, because she had the most beautiful cottage garden. Inside, under the flowers, there was sometimes cash and it was always at a time when Lily Hannah was really desperate for money.

Alex's friend, Ernest Payne, spent the First World War in Darjeeling, India.

Mum must have continued to write to dad after losing Alex. When dad was coming back from India in 1919, he wrote to her [saying], 'Lily, I'm bringing the lace for your wedding dress and your bridesmaid's dresses – Indian lace'. That is what he did. Whether that was his proposal, I don't know, but they married in the June in the eleventh-century village church in Anstey. The wedding dress was later cut up to make dresses for my three elder sisters, Sylvia, Daphne and Patricia.

I remember asking my mother about my name, Olive, when I was little. I was the last, number eight, of the children, nine if you include the first stillborn child (Alexander, named after mother's Alex). The others all had pretty names, why hadn't I? Was I adopted? 'Of course not, why ever do you ask such a thing?' she said.

'My brothers and sisters have nice names and I haven't.'

'Olive Joy,' she said. 'What nicer name could you have? Olive for peace and Joy for love. What better?'

A few years ago, my brother Ray and I went to Anstey to see where our mother grew up. The first place we went to was the pub. We went in and the locals all stopped speaking and looked at us. Then one said, 'Lily Hannah!' to me. I am the image of her, apparently. We met one of Lily's cousins and went on to the church. It was such a lovely feeling. I don't remember being there before, but knowing that mum and dad got married there and that all four of their girls were christened there was nice.

❧ STELLA BAILEY ❧
— 1920S NAVAL WIFE

The author's grandmother, Stella May Bailey, died in 2000. However, she had spoken to the author on many occasions about her life as a military wife and some of her memories are given here.

Her husband, Frederick Walter Bailey, born in 1906, was a seaman in the Royal Navy, having run away to sea to become a boy sailor in 1921 at the age of 15. He served on a number of training establishments and ships in his twelve years of service, including HMS *Ganges*, HMS *Courageous*, HMS *Carlisle* (which was stationed in China for a number of years), HMS *Victory I* and HMS *Foxglove*.

They married in 1929, and Fred was invalided out of the navy while still a young man after falling overboard in China, into a Portuguese man o' war floating in the water by the ship. He damaged his leg in the fall, and that and the stings from the jellyfish put him in a Chinese hospital for several months.

Great Fun!
Stella said:

Fred and I were cousins. He was great fun. I remember being on the back of his bike and whizzing down the hill on it with him. His three spinster sisters were at the bottom and they looked down their noses at me for doing that.

I worked at the bank, checking banknotes, before I was married. Then Fred and I got married and things changed. Married women did not hold jobs then. I became a housewife.

You never had 'married quarters' in my day. We lived in digs, a single rented room to start with.

I waved my Fred off and did not see him again for two years. He went off on the China Run.

2

ANOTHER WORLD WAR

Make the most of what you have and get on with it.
Gladys Curtis, Second World War military wife, on how she got
through the war years.

Britain was at war again. Men were either volunteering for war service or were being called to arms. Once again, the country's women were stepping in to take the place of their menfolk.

Winifred Deahl, although not a military wife, still found that it was she who had to keep the family café in Southampton afloat during the crisis. She was worried about getting provisions for the business, as her diary entry for 1941 shows:

Wednesday 28 March
Meat rations went down to 1/- per head per week instead of 1/2d per head.
   Went to the food office about some cooking fats for the business. Meat has been cut again for the business.

Meanwhile, military wives were coping as best they could in the national emergency.

🎋 GLADYS CURTIS 🎋

Gladys had been married to Leslie Curtis for a year when the Second World War broke out. Born during the early part of the First World War, and not recognising her father when he came home, she was soon to experience the pain of separation that had been her mother's lot:

First World War Legacy

My mother was a military wife. She was apprenticed to a milliner before she married but didn't work after her marriage. My father was in the Royal Artillery as a gunner. He was in France for a long time in the First World War. They used gas in those days. I don't know too many details about it but he was in a gas attack. He used to get lots of spots on his hands, and I can remember them talking – they didn't talk to us children like they do today, children were seen and not heard – saying it was some of the gas that was left in his system. Still, he lived until he was 85, so it didn't do him a lot of harm.

I was only 3 when the war ended. I have been given the impression that I was a bit off with my dad. He was a stranger. He came home when the war ended and I wouldn't have much to do with him.

Meeting Les

My husband, Les, was from Southampton, as am I. We both belonged to what today would be called a youth club. When we were in our teens we went along. I was about 17 when we met. He was born in May 1915 and me in September 1915. My in-laws had a shop in Shirley. A fruit and flowers shop – a family business.

His life was queer because he never had any money. The family as a whole did very well. They lived on the premises, in the flat over the shop. All the bills were paid by mum and dad. They even bought him his clothes. When I met him, in 1932, I had about 2s pocket money a week, but he didn't have any money. Anything he wanted, he just went to dad and said. If he wanted to buy something it came out of the till. When we got engaged, he said to his dad, 'Can I have a wage?'

'What do you want a wage for?'

'Well, I might want to have some money.'

'Your mother and I buy everything for you, you don't need money.'

They wouldn't give him a wage. We wanted to save up to get married. Eventually, his father came around and he gave him 10s [50p] a week. It was a lot of money then. It wasn't until we were married that he had a proper wage and then it was £3 a week. He had a mortgage on £3!

I gave up work the week before we got married, in 1938. In September 1938 we were married, September 1939 war was declared and in November 1939 Jonathan [known as John] was born. So we had just one year of married life.

I was very naïve in those days. Not worldly wise at all. I was 23. We led a very sheltered life. You lived at home with your parents until you were married. We were engaged to be married, but we weren't allowed to go on holiday alone together. We did go away – we had family friends in Dartmouth, on the coast, who had a pub and we went there for a holiday. Of course, we had separate rooms. Then we were watched to make sure there was no hanky-panky! Girls today would be horrified.

Les, the Volunteer

When the war started, Les volunteered. As a child he'd had diphtheria twice, which was very unusual, and it had left him, so the medical profession said, with a weak heart. When he was at school he was not allowed to play football.

When war came he hated the thought of actually going to war. He wasn't a bit belligerent, but he was worried that if he waited until he was conscripted, he would be put in the army infantry and given a bayonet and sent to the front. He couldn't imagine sticking a bayonet into someone. He couldn't bear the thought. He thought that if he volunteered they would give the volunteers more choice of where they went.

I remember his dad saying, 'Don't worry, they won't take him with his heart. If they take him into the services they will give him a job in an office, not to worry.' He went for his interview and came home, went for his medical and they passed him, A1!

I was worried. I didn't want him to go. I listened to my father-in-law and so I thought that he would be around, it would not make any difference. John was a tiny baby, a weakly baby, and he was in hospital. He'd been there for two months, from when he was 2 months old. The day before he came out of hospital, my husband got his calling-up papers and he went off to be in the army. He was taken on to be a driver. He loved driving. He was attached to the medical corps and became an ambulance driver, which was a bit ironic as he couldn't stand the sight of blood!

I was more concerned with John. He was 8lb when he was born and when he came out of hospital at 4 months, he weighed 6lb. He was a bag of bones, he was my first child and I was terrified. No husband around either. The hospital consultant that I saw said that I had better bring him home now.

'I don't think I can look after him.'

'Oh, yes, you will. He'll be safer at home with you rather than in hospital in wartime with germs. If he catches anything, he won't live. He has no stamina. You want to keep him wrapped in cotton wool. Don't let anybody who has a cold near him.'

There was me, scared stiff.

I coped. I got over it. Thousands of people, everyone, had a tough time. It was the worst time in my whole life financially, and I am nearly 100 now. When I lived at home with my parents, there was not a lot of money, but they had enough and I was happy. I was okay when I got married because my in-laws had a bit of money, but there was a period when I was getting little money, just army pay, and there was hardly enough money to pay the bills.

I was a bit naïve. I had never had to do things. I had no experience to cope on my own. Then, suddenly, I was on my own with not much money coming in and a poorly baby. My mother still lived in Southampton then, but eventually moved. She was the other side of Southampton and we didn't have any phones or anything. Everything was chaotic. It was hard. I lived in Millbrook and the shop was in Shirley, opposite Woolworth's.

I spent my days looking after John; he was so weak. People would look at him and say, 'Oh, I don't think he will last very long'. He was christened at hospital before my husband left because we didn't think he was going to last. For two months I went back to work. The dairy I had once worked at was short staffed as people had been called up. They asked me if I would go back. It was in the same area as the hospital so I could nip up whenever I wanted to. I couldn't do anything. They wouldn't allow me to pick him up. So I could only go and stand and look at him in the cot – this bag of bones.

For the first week he was home from hospital I had to put him in his pram and take him up to the hospital for the nurse to dress the wound. From Millbrook to Shirley is half an hour's walk. We had no car. There they made a fuss of him, and after I had done this for about a week the consultant decided it would be better if I did it myself. They didn't put any stiches in. He had this great big cut, he still has the scar. He had reflux and was bringing food back and it was not going into his stomach. He would throw it all up.

This little boy did not have any flesh on him at all. He looked like he would break if you touched him and he had this great big gash in his tummy and I had to clean it and put a fresh dressing on it. That used to take me nearly all the morning. We had a great big dining room with a suite that was really huge. I used to pull the table out and put a cushion right in the middle. He couldn't have fallen off, he was so weak. We didn't have the equipment you have these days – I put a towel on the table and laid him on there. Then I did his wound. From then on, he got better in leaps and bounds.

For two or three months it was touch and go, but once he got going and he could keep his food down, he was fine. I have pictures of him when he is 1 year old and he is quite a robust child. It was getting through it on my own, which was the point.

Les joined the army in early 1940 and was in England for a year, doing his training in the Midlands. He could drive anything, lorries – even a tank. He ended up driving an ambulance. They didn't give them leave very much. Once he came home for two or three days. He came home for overseas leave for one night, and then he went overseas. Of course, we never saw him again until the war was over.

Rommel was the German commander who was doing very well in Tobruk and all around there. The next thing we knew, he was missing. I had messages from the Red Cross with information. It was just the news that he was missing, believed taken prisoner. In fact, he was with loads of others.

The first prisoner of war camp that Les went in was in Italy, in Verona. About sixteen years after the war finished, we took a holiday and drove through France and Switzerland to Italy. We had a few days at Rimini. While we were there, he said that he would like to go to Verona and see if anything remained of the camp. We drove there. It was very small then, quite a poor little village.

We stopped, and he got out of the car and there was a house very near. Somebody was watching, and suddenly a window opened and a little man looked out and shouted, 'Luigi!' – Italian for Leslie. Then he went off speaking Italian. Les picked up a bit of Italian when he was there. He said, 'He is telling me to wait.' So we waited and he came down and he was so excited. Fancy him remembering a prisoner of war! There were loads of prisoners, but he remembered Les after all that time, he still looked the same. The man took us around the village and introduced us to all his friends. He was so excited. The family took us into the house and gave us drinks and things.

Gladys Curtis still has the letter Leslie Curtis sent to the War Office, to explain his war time exploits. He was taken prisoner near Tobruk in June 1942 and sent to Southern Italy in October 1942. In May 1943 he was sent to a working camp in Verona. His guards released him in September 1943 and he hid for two months with an Italian family until he was given away and recaptured. He promptly escaped again and for two months attempted to reach the safety of Switzerland. He was caught again in February 1944 and in March was sent to Germany by train. He escaped by pulling up the carriage's floorboards and dropping on to the tracks and was again in hiding for two months. In May 1944 he was caught and this time was transferred to Germany, where he remained until the end of the war.

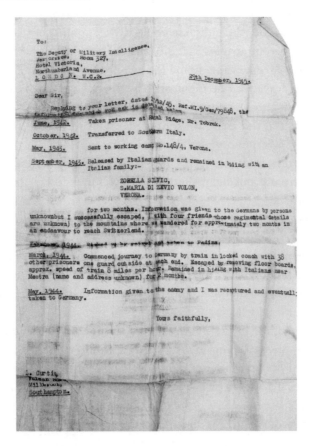

To:
The Deputy of Military Intelligence,
War Office, Room 327,
Hotel Victoria
Northumberland Avenue,
LONDON. WC2   29th December, 1945.
Dear Sir,

   Replying to your letter, dated 1*/12/45, Ref. MI.9/Gen/79848, the information for which you ask is detailed below:

June, 1942.   Taken prisoner at Regal Ridge, Nr. Tobruck.

October, 1942.   Transferred to Southern Italy.

May, 1943.   Sent to working camp No. 148/4, Verona.

September, 1943.   Released by Italian guards and remained in hiding with an Italian family:-

   ZORELLA SILVIC,
   S. MARIA DI ZEVIO VOLON,
   VERONA.

   for two months. Information was given to the Germans by persons unknown but I successfully escaped, with four friends (whose regimental details are unknown) to the mountains where we wandered for approximately two months in an endeavour to reach Switzerland.

February, 1944.   Picked up by patrol and taken to Padina.

March, 1944.   Commenced journey to Germany by train in locked coach with 38 other prisoners one guard outside at each end. Escaped by removing floor boards, approx. speed of the train 8 miles per hour. Remained in hiding with Italians near Mestra (name and address unknown) for 2 months.

May, 1944.   Information given to the enemy and I was recaptured and eventually taken to Germany.

Yours faithfully,
L. Curtis,
Vulcan House
Southampton

Rations

There was nothing to buy during the war. We had our rations. We used to have a programme on the radio, *The Kitchen Front*. Lord Woolton [Frederick Marquis, 1st Earl of Woolton, 1883–1964] was the food minister and it was Lord Wootton's recipes that we used to listen to, taking into account the rations. How to make cake without using any fat, that sort of thing.

Bananas were very thin on the ground. We were lucky because of the shop. Bananas weren't rationed but they were allocated to the shops and the shopkeepers were asked not to let anybody have them who didn't have children. My father-in-law used to get the bananas out and would have a huge queue a mile back. Before he put them out he always put some bananas to one side for John, so I didn't have to queue. John liked his bananas, but it was only perhaps once a year we'd get them.

Then I found a sandwich recipe, it must have been this Woolton. 'How to make a banana sandwich': You got some parsnips and cooked them. You must have cooked any goodness in them out as you boiled them for ages, until they were really soft and mushy. Then you mashed them like you do mashed potatoes. For some reason, I don't know where it came from, but we could get a little bottle of banana essence and honestly, when you took the lid off, the smell of bananas was really potent. You put a few drops of this banana on the parsnip and then mash it up. Then you get, I was going to say bread and butter but we didn't have butter, bread and a scraping of margarine. You spread the 'banana' on and John had it for his tea, banana sandwich. He often used to ask for it.

We used to have a thing called a Woolton pie and that was a joke in the war. [Created by Maître Chef de Cuisine at the Savoy Hotel, Francis Latry, the recipe was first published in the *Times* on 26 April 1941. Woolton pie consisted of a pound each of diced potatoes, cauliflower, swede and carrots, mixed with three or four spring onions, a teaspoon each of vegetable extract and oatmeal. This vegetarian delight was boiled together for ten minutes, allowed to cool and then turned into a pie dish. The filling was sprinkled with parsley and then topped with a potato or pastry crust. The pie was baked until the pastry was brown and then served hot with brown gravy. The recipe could be changed according to what was available. Parsnips and turnip were often included, and sometimes cheese was added to the crust.]

Corn beef hash we had a lot, because you could occasionally get tins of corned beef and potatoes were never a bother. If you had a tin of corned beef and a few potatoes you were okay. Spam came later in the war. That was wonderful! It came from the US, who started to send the country food parcels. It was like having a chicken, which was a luxury in my day. We only had chicken to eat at Christmas time. A tin of Spam was as good as chicken.

The rations were awful. That was another thing that was difficult for me because there was just the two of us. People who had a big family had a ration for everything. The meat ration was something ridiculous, a couple of pork chops and that was the ration for the whole week. You could never ever buy a joint of anything. A family say of five or six put all their rations together, it was much easier.

I think we had one egg each a week, which John had. I am not that bothered about eggs, but during the war I don't think I ever had an egg because you gave it to your children. The only thing we did well with, because of John, was milk. The milk ration was 2 pints a week but, because he was under 5, he had a pint a day, so I got 9 pints of milk a week. Cheese was, I think, 2oz a week. I love cheese now because I was so deprived. It was difficult but it didn't do us any harm.

The Bombs

On top of the rationing, we had to deal with bombs. We lived in Millbrook, Southampton. There was Millbrook Rec and there was a garage by the side of it. When the war started people said, 'We shan't have any raids. They'll never get through the barrage balloons and there will be nothing to worry about.' The very first raid on Southampton, when I was on my own with John, was on Millbrook.

The garage was razed to the ground. A house nearby had a direct hit on it. This was during the night. It really frightened you. We were in the shelter, and we weren't on our own because Mr and Mrs Wheeler, our neighbours, came in with us. The authorities supplied an air raid shelter. They came and dug it into the garden. That was all right. My neighbour the other side did not want an outdoor shelter, so she had an indoor one in her lounge, under the table.

The raid came so suddenly one night. No one was expecting it. After that, on Millbrook Rec there was a public shelter. That wasn't dug in. It was safer than ours. Wherever you were, if you got a direct hit your days had ended, so it did not matter.

The neighbours two doors away had a little boy John's age and invited us to share their shelter. We used to go there and the two kids liked it, as they were friends. I remember one night John had measles or something like that. I said to them, 'If there is a raid tonight I shan't come down, it's not fair. You don't want to get the measles. I shall be all right. I shall just sit down in the hallway.'

So, the sirens went and I got John settled and suddenly I was so frightened, I thought 'I can't stay here on my own'. I was not worried about a direct hit as it would have killed us both and we would not have known about it, but I was so frightened that we would get buried alive and nobody would find us. I got up and put John in his pram and went to another friend who lived just round the corner. I knew she would be there. Her husband was with the Merchant Navy and was always away, but she had her sister and her husband there. We went to the shelter with them. Meanwhile, the people the other way came up to see if we were OK and to offer us shelter with them. Of course, there was no answer and they were having a fit wondering where we were. We were cosy in this other shelter, and all because I didn't want their son, Ray, to get the measles.

I used to put John in his pram and walk up from Millbrook to Portswood, where my mother lived [3½ miles]. It took me a long time. One day we were walking and the air raid sirens sounded. I went to the shelter, and when I got there, the bombs had already started dropping. The air raid warden grabbed John and said, 'Come on in. Leave the pram!' It was a big raid – on Super Marine, the Spitfire factory.

When we came out, the pram was still where I had left it. These days, somebody would have nicked it. We continued on and got to my mother's. She was in a state, because rumours had spread and she had heard that Super Marine had had a direct hit and was wiped out, with all the staff. My dad worked there. She thought he was dead, and didn't know what to do.

What could you do? There was nothing. We sat and waited. Just afterwards, dad walks in all hale and hearty. He'd been in a shelter playing cards with his mates!

My father-in-law had not had a good time in the First World War and was a bit scared. He managed to get a room at Nomansland, near Salisbury. He found somebody who had a large shed, a farmer. He paid him a rent for it, about 5s a week, and offered it to my mum, John and I, and we lived there for a short spell. It was awful. I hated it.

We had just one little room. We were on rations, and all our shops were in Southampton. My mother-in-law used to take one day a week and come back into Southampton to collect all our clothes and food. Washing was difficult. We weren't there very long. I didn't like it.

Then we came back, and my mum and dad went to Reading to live. John loved going there. He was about 3 when he started going to visit. He was spoilt as he was the only grandchild. I used to go to Reading and stay, but I didn't want to live there. They wanted me to go with them. I did not want to leave my house. In wartime, goodness knows who would have squatted in there. I would often go to them for a week and leave John, and come back on my own for a week or two and then go and pick him up. Those weeks I was free! Free as a bird. I could do what I liked. I could go to the cinema, go out and dance, go out shopping.

Father Figure

My father was the father figure for John, as Les was not around. He was good financially if I needed anything. I was not very good at asking for money.

My father taught John some words. I remember when I was on the bus to Nomansland. It was always packed with people from Southampton. We were up the front, and John was interested in the other passengers, so stood up and looked over the seat at them. 'Bugger, bugger, bugger, bugger!' he said. I didn't know what to say. One of the other passengers leaned over and said, 'Just pretend you don't know him!'

The Red Cross

Hardly any letters ever got through. The Red Cross were good. You could pay, but not an awful lot, and they would take Les a food parcel, not often, just now and again. I couldn't do it when he was in Italy because he was always escaping, but once he got to Germany, we used to send him food parcels. I don't know, but perhaps once every six months.

The Red Cross were neutral. I could not have done it myself, I didn't have enough food, but the Red Cross got supplies of food and they would give it to the Red Cross in Germany and they would make sure that the prisoners got it. When we talked about it afterwards, he did get the food parcels I sent. The chaps all got them and they used to share out what they had.

I didn't have a clue what Les was up to. I don't think that the authorities knew what was going on. All these prisoners were escaping. The little chap who we saw in Verona used to open the prison gates when he saw some prisoners around and then turn his back. That was an open invitation; 'if you want to go, go'. When you read about prisoner of war escapes, like the stalags in Germany, there was nothing like that, it was just that the Italian guards didn't think that they should be prisoners. They were anti-Hitler.

All his life Les would never hear a bad word about the Italians. He thought they were all wonderful. I don't know where he went in Germany, but once he got to the German prison camp there was no question of escape. The Red Cross were good, and I had a lot of connections with them. They kept me informed.

The Royal British Legion

I remember the first Christmas. John came out of hospital in February 1940, and that was when Les went. The following Christmas, the Royal British Legion sent John 10s for a Christmas present. I have always had a lot of time for the Legion. Anybody who had a husband who was a prisoner of war and had children, they sent the children money to buy something for Christmas. It was a nice touch.

❧ MARGARET AMELIA JARRETT-KERR ❧

Sue Piper's father, Herbert Alfred Temple Jarrett-Kerr, was in the Royal Engineers (Sappers) in the Indian Army and retired as a brigadier. He married Margaret in 1936. Once again, we do not have this service spouse's words. Sue has tried to give an idea of her mother's life as a military wife during the Second World War:

I was born in York in 1940, at the beginning of the Second World War. We were there for six weeks and then moved south. My mother recounted how my father used to talk in his sleep and she happily did not understand too much what it was about, but clearly to do with the war. She remembers going to the clifftop in Christchurch and seeing a whole fleet of ships lined up. She realised afterwards that this was preparation for D-Day. My father never talked about his army experience, and especially the war. We coped with going to the air raid shelters. Later, we moved to Bristol.

In 1946, my father was posted to the Indian Staff College in Quetta. We followed later on a troop ship. I had two brothers at this stage, and my third brother was born in India. I had my 6th birthday on the ship and also suffered horrible toothache on the way out, which was eventually dealt with! We were met, I think, by my father at Bombay [now Mumbai] and travelled the long journey to Quetta.

We had a happy time there until partition happened on 14 August 1947. I can remember seeing the fires in the distance, and our Hindu Ayah [nanny] had to flee, as the country became Pakistan. It must have been such a worrying time for my parents, but we, as children, were totally unaware! Nick was born on 30 August. I never discovered if this stressful time made my mother go into labour.

Because the Indian Staff College was closed down and reopened as the Pakistani Staff College, my father (being British) had to leave. So we all travelled the long train journey to Bombay, then by ship to Liverpool and then waited in the cold on the station for the next train to take us south. My parents must have found this very trying, coping with the four of us, aged from 9 years down to my younger brother of 3 months. Later, after several different homes, we moved to Bristol. From there, my father commuted to London for thirteen years. He was still in the army. My mother found this very difficult. He weekended, and had to deal with my naughty brothers at the weekends. My mother suffered a gastric ulcer as a result of the stress and nearly died, but a wonderful Christian friend operated on her and all was well.

ROSE DAWSON

Rose Dawson, from Turn, Czechoslovakia, was born Rusena Lehrmannova in December 1919. She was a German-speaking Jew, the eldest of the three daughters of a Polish businessman. At school she learnt French, Czech and, later, English, a language that was to become invaluable to her. She practised her English, as she worked as a shorthand typist for a Jewish family firm in Prague.

'I was happy there, very contented,' said Rose, in an interview for the *This is my Home Now* project, in 2011, at the age of 90 (Rose sadly died in 2012). 'They were lovely people to work with.'

Escaping the Germans
When the Germans took over Czechoslovakia in March 1939, there was great consternation among the Jewish families in the country. Mr Krauz, Rose's employer, sold his button-making business and transferred his

family and business assets to England. He wanted Rose to come with him to England, but, not being a relative or a British subject, he was unable to sponsor her.

Speed was of the essence, as it was increasingly clear that it was not safe for Jewish people to stay in the country. When in England, Mr Krauz kept in touch with Rose by telephone and, with his assistance, Rose was able to find a British sponsor through the efforts of charitable organisations operating from Bloomsbury House in London. These worked to find sponsorship for refugees at the time. The only work available through this arrangement, though, was as a domestic servant.

'All the maids were going to munitions factories,' says Rose, 'so they were looking for people to do housework. Ladies looking for maids would put their names down at Bloomsbury House.'

Rose, whose mother urged her to go, knowing that there was no future for Jews in Czechoslovakia, was only too grateful to be given the opportunity to travel to the safety of England, and so agreed to be sponsored by a Mrs Davies from Southampton. 'She had a picture of me and lived in Bassett Avenue.'

Rose applied for a permit to enter Britain, and had to go regularly to see if her application had been granted. This took several weeks.

'I got downhearted,' says Rose. 'Then, one day, thank God, they said, "Yes, we've got your permit." There was another office, with the Gestapo, and I had to go there to show that I had a permit and my passport, and pay so much and they said I had permission to leave.'

To get permission to leave Czechoslovakia had meant queuing day after day with thousands of other Jews, all desperate to flee.

'It was awful. I had to pay so much money here and so much money there. I didn't care. I had my permit in the end. I started packing and got my ticket. I was told I could not take any jewellery or money, just clothes. My family and friends saw me off at Prague Station. It was terrible leaving. I broke down in the train. Everyone said it would be all right and I would see them again.'

Rose travelled as far as Dresden, where she had to get out of the carriage as all trains ceased travelling for the day. The railway station was full of troops.

The Gestapo

'The Gestapo were going through cases, throwing everything out. I stood there with my case, very worried. What was I going to do now?'

Two of the ordinary soldiers spoke to the stationmaster on her behalf and, for her own safety, locked her in the waiting room overnight. She was thus able to continue her journey the next day, making the perilous trip across Germany to Holland.

'I had to wait another night in Holland, as the boat wasn't going until the next morning. It was the last boat. It was full of English children coming back from a jamboree in Holland. I left three days before the war. I did not know it was so close.'

Rose and the many refugees from the boat were met in Harwich and she found herself with them on a coach bound for London. She spent her third night of travelling in a guesthouse, sharing the facilities with several other refugees.

'It was the first time I had seen a cooked breakfast. I asked if it was lunchtime yet and was told, "No, that is breakfast!" Egg and bacon – I had never seen it before!'

Rose knew Mrs Davies' address in Southampton, but not the telephone number. Mr Krauz's daughter came to see Rose at the guest house and, as her English was better than Rose's, tried to contact Rose's sponsor, only to find that the family had gone away on holiday!

Rose eventually met Mr Davies, in London on business, at Waterloo Station a few days later. She had no idea what the man looked like but he had her photograph and found her sitting on her suitcases on the busy concourse.

'He was very kind. I was very lucky. He had been gassed in the First World War and he knew what it was like to be away from home.'

Southampton

Eventually, Rose reached Southampton, a city whose parks she admired, and began work for the Davies family as their maid:

I wrote to my family that I had arrived safely but the letter came back marked 'frontier closed'. I never found out what happened to my mother and one sister but I guessed they were gassed in a concentration camp. My other sister survived a concentration camp and stayed with us for a while – I was married then. She couldn't settle here. We found out that we had friends in Israel and she wanted to go there. The climate was good for her; she was wheezing. She moved to Israel, got a little needle-work job and when she got a sum of money from the Nazis by way of compensation, bought a little flat close to our friends.

When the Southampton Blitz reduced large parts of the city to rubble, the Davies family moved to Rownhams, a few miles away from the coast, and took Rose with them. However, when they moved further afield, the authorities were adamant that Rose, an 'alien', could not go too and so she found herself out of work, with nowhere to live.

Meeting Bill

A Romanian friend came to her rescue, and found her lodgings in Basingstoke. A trip to the labour exchange produced a job growing vegetables and it was here, in the tomato hot-houses, that Rose met Bill Dawson.

'He was a very healthy-looking man, with chestnut hair. He was brought up on the land and was very sunburnt. He went to local evening classes learning English and I asked him, "Why do you go to evening classes, aren't you British?"

'"Course I am!" he replied. He didn't go to pubs and it was something to do.'

Rose went along to the classes in the hope of improving her English and Bill soon sought her out and ended up sitting next to her.

'When we had finished the class he walked with me back to my lodgings and we talked for a little bit. My English wasn't that good. I wonder whether he understood everything I said. I said, "Thank you very much," and we shook hands.'

Romance was slow to ignite, as Rose soon found that Bill was very shy:

We started going out for walks and to the pictures together, which was nice. He then took me back to my lodgings and we shook hands. It was ages before he dared to give me a little kiss – a few months! One day he kissed me on the hand and said, 'See you again,' and I realised that he liked me.

One day we saw a picture about a girl and a boy and they were different religions. Something hit me. He had never asked me. He went to church and he must like me, as he didn't go out with anyone else. I must tell him. When he took me to my front door, I started crying.

'What's the matter?'

'I have to tell you something.' I felt him stiffen up.

'What is it?'

'I am of Jewish parentage.'

'Is that all? I thought you were going to finish with me!'

'You must tell your parents. I do not want to come between you.'

He told them, and I had a lovely letter from his mother. It said, 'If my son had given you up for that, I would not have thought much of him.' I was so relieved.

My landlady said to tell Bill, 'When the weather is bad, you don't have to go out to be together. I'll make a little fire and bring up some tea. I can see he's a decent fellow. He won't get up to any hanky-panky.' So, when the weather was bad, he came up in my bedroom. She brought up tea and had a little chat.

One day, he came up and said, 'What would you say if I gave you a ring? Would you accept it?' He meant an engagement ring.

I said, 'Yes'.

He had a little box in his pocket ready. The ring was beautiful. He was very fond of blue and it had a blue stone in it. I was so excited! I went down to my landlady and said, 'Oh, look, look what Bill gave me. We are engaged.' She and her husband drank to our health, so I knew it was fine. He was so decent. Even when we got engaged, there was never any hanky-panky. We just kissed each other.

Called Up

We were not in any hurry to get married because I said I didn't want to live in someone else's home. We knew he was the man for me and I was the woman for him, but I didn't like the idea of using the same kitchen as someone else. When you have a husband there is a lot of washing to do as well and I didn't want that. So it was better to stay as we were. Then he was called up. He had to go into the infantry. He was in 'Dad's Army' training first. When he was called up, I thought it over. If he was stationed somewhere away we could never see each other unless he got leave. So, we decided it was the time to get married. I would stay in my lodgings and Bill would be in the army. Nothing changed.

Bill was 30, and Rose 23, when they were married on 25 September 1943. Bill joined the Hampshire Regiment and was sent to Lancashire for initial training, and then continued training to be a vehicle mechanic. He was posted to Brighton and joined the Royal Electrical and Mechanical Engineers (REME). After the war, he was sent to North Africa, where he was employed on war clean-up operations.

'We got married in 1943, at the registry office in Southampton. I became a British subject on my marriage and forgot my alien card.

When he had a day off I could go up on the train and see him. We continued like that until he was demobbed.'

(With thanks to Rose's daughter, Susanne Dawson, and Maianna Moreau and Jenny Cuffe at the *This is my Home Now* project.)

❧ EDITH MARSH ❧

Edith, or 'Edie' as she was known, passed away in 2012. Before she died, she spoke to her son, James, about her life during the war, when she was the wife of volunteer Army Commando William (Bill) Marsh. James has recorded her words here:

Bill

My name is Edith Ann Marsh, and for all of the six years of the Second World War I was one of millions of service wives. My husband was William James Alfred Marsh (Bill) and he was a member of 6 Troup, 6 Army Commando unit.

We met in Southampton as children, he in Duke's Road and me in nearby Empress Road. I lived there with my very Victorian grandmother because my own mother was having trouble raising our large family, who all lived in Mayfield Road, Southampton.

In 1933, William saw the way I was being treated and proposed marriage to me. It wasn't perhaps the most romantic of proposals, as he said, 'Christ Mush, let's get you out of this.' We were married that same year, on Christmas Day.

War

By the time 1939 arrived and the start of the war with Germany, we had three children, two girls and one boy, and another baby was on the way. My Bill, of course, joined up straight away, along with most of his mates, so before our next child, a boy, was born, he was already serving with his first army company. At that time I didn't know which part of the army he was in. I was too busy by then, tending my young family and trying to make ends meet financially, as well as keeping all of us safe from the bombing each night.

Bombs

There was an air raid shelter in the road outside of our house and, night after night, the lady who lodged with us helped me to get my children out and inside the relative safety of the shelter, along with all of the private papers and things my family needed, which were all kept in a black bag.

Once inside, another long and frightening night stretched in front of us. We could hear the sound of those hateful German planes overhead, then the crump of the bombs as they hit the ground. It was nerve-racking to say the least. But the one thing that got us all through those dreadful nights was the thought of hatred against all things German, and the hope that our men would very soon defeat them and put an end to this torture.

Once the all-clear did sound, though, the first thing we all had to do was get our families out of the shelter, then look to see if our house was still standing or whether it had been reduced to rubble. Fortunately, the road we lived in, Belgrave Road in Portswood, Southampton was never hit. Not one house was ever damaged.

With my children safe and being looked after by my lodger, Mrs Spender, it was time for me to think about the man in my life, Bill. He was now fighting on the front line and so many of our boys were being killed. Was my husband all right? There was one way to find the answer to that question and that was a notice board that had been put up outside our local police station.

This was situated at Portswood Junction, an old Victorian building that sat next to the Southampton Corporation Tram depot. On that board all of the British servicemen from this area who had been killed or injured in the past few days were listed, so that their relatives would know this before the dreaded telegram arrived at their homes telling them the news. So I, along with some of my neighbours, ran up to this police station on a daily basis to scrutinise the board. All of us were hoping not to see the names of our men displayed there.

It wasn't an easy thing to do, because there were so many times when we had to climb over the rubble of people's homes to get to the police station. It was heartrending to hear the cries of families who had lived in the ruined houses and who were now homeless. My worry about my wonderful Bill drove me on each morning, and the relief when, each day, his name was not on that board was one of the reasons I got through those terrible years.

I saw him only twice during the war as he hardly ever got leave. I did know he went for training in Scotland and was accepted into the army commandos and that he and the rest of his troop landed on Gold Beach on D–Day, 6 June 1944. All through that awful conflict he never received even a wound, though so many of his boyhood friends who had joined up when he did were killed.

Demobbed

After the end of the war, and when all of the celebrations had finished, I longed for the day when my husband would return home to me and our children. I had to wait for this, though, because he was billeted somewhere in France and would not be demobbed until sometime in 1946. But then I received two letters. One from my Bill telling me he was on his way home and the other from a French girl named Belle. In this, she told me that she and my husband loved each other and planned to live together for the rest of their lives!

The fury I felt when I read this made the excitement of my husband's homecoming fall flat. When he entered our home, just over a week later, and stood in our small hall in his army uniform with his rucksack over his shoulder and smiled at me, he just had time to say, 'Hello Edie, I'm home', before my right arm travelled up and connected with the right side of his face. Staggering back and holding his cheek he shouted, 'Bloody hell, what was that for?'

I then held up the letter and thrust it right up to his face before demanding, 'Who is Belle and what the bleeding hell is she talking about, you and her now going to live together?' It took him a few minutes to recover from this, before he said, 'Oh Christ Mush, that's nothing. Those French women were so pleased with the way we had liberated their country from the bloody Nazis that they were all over us. I knew this silly cow, of course, but living with her and leaving you and our kids? No, forget it.'

It was the only excuse I got, and I was so happy to have my husband home again that Belle was swiftly forgotten. Bill never spoke about the war in all the years we were together afterwards. All he ever said to me was, 'It's over Edie, so I don't want to remember anything about it ever again.'

He died in 1986.

(With thanks to James Marsh and the Marsh family for use of this material. NB: The No. 6 Army Commando unit was formed in 1940. It saw action in Norway, Algeria, Tunisia, France and Germany. The unit was disbanded in 1946.)

3

Post-war Britain

If you can't laugh, don't be a service wife.
June Stead, Military Wife 1951–1970

Immediately after the Second World War, Britain's military were either employed with mopping-up duties or involved with a plethora of 'small wars'. Military wives found themselves living in such far-flung destinations as Malaya, post-war Germany, Mauritius, Bahrain and Canada; while others found that their lot in married life was to travel around Britain.

❧ Joy Hale ☙

Earlier in this book, Joy told her mother's First World War story. Joy, too, was a military wife. She and Wilfred Montgomery Hale, known as 'Monty', were penfriends:

Monty

> I had always known of him because he used to come down on holiday to stay with my nana, Jessie, and her gentleman friend, William Hale, who was his uncle. We would go out with him as a family. I was ten years younger than he was. He was a lad of 20 and I was only 10 when we first met.
>
> He was a soldier. A warrant officer class 1, in REME. I had always known about him. I went out to India in the war with my mother and

father, which is another story. We came home in 1943, my sister and I, and we hated being home here because we had been teenagers in the days of the Raj. Nana's gentleman friend said, 'What is wrong with you? Get on and write to this lonely soldier in the 8th Army.' I wrote to him and described myself, and he wrote back.

His parents were Lincoln people. Joseph Montgomery and his wife, Safina, lived in Lincoln and kept a shop where they made umbrellas. Joseph was also a locksmith. They had a happy marriage and thirteen children. Joseph was a band leader who could play several instruments, and he insisted that all his children played instruments, some two. They were their own band and very well known in the town.

I did not marry him out of the blue, but I did write for a year, I suppose. We got quite close and knew everything about each other. He was everything that I expected when he came home from the war and, being ten years older, was very mechanically minded. I always wanted to marry an engineer and someone with a camera. We never had a camera.

When he came home, he was 30 and I was 19. I was tall, much too tall for my liking, and blondish and slim. He was very nice, very sensible, very talented – he could play the piano and the accordion and had a good voice, inherited I suppose from his background. He did well in the army. He was called up. He had done an apprenticeship in a prestige garage where they built cars like Rolls-Royce and Armstrong Sidley, an old regal sort of car. A year before the war, he started as a mechanic and he realised that the war was coming. All the mechanics joined the territorials and did their bit at the weekends. So the moment war came, they were in.

He was posted to Hilsea Barracks. I did not know that at the time. I think my nana and her partner did. He went on a course, and came out as a staff sergeant on accelerated promotion, and then quite soon he was a WO2 [warrant officer class 2] and then he went out to Africa and was promoted again. He spent the war as a WO1 [warrant officer class 1].

He landed in Africa, was in the 8th Army and was in El Alamein. At one point in the war, he was in Tobruk, and he was surrounded by the Germans and things looked a bit grim. The Coldstream Guards came up behind and they managed to cut a corridor, which they kept open for a day and they got all their technical people out – the ones that were most needed. Then the Germans advanced again, and anyone who was caught in Tobruk was a prisoner.

Monty went on to Tunisia and ended up in Algiers. He got very friendly with a girl in the embassy there called Irene Carpenter. He showed me photographs of her. Then he went up through Africa and into Italy and got as far as Trieste, almost. Then he came home and we had three weeks together. He had a week in Lincoln first, to see his mum and dad.

When the war was going well, they instituted a month's leave for those who had been out there the longest. It was a point system. He had been out there, then, just about four years and he was way up the top. Before he knew it, he was away home. They had a very elaborate system of bringing them home – they came home on Bedford lorries. It took five days to come home. The army built staging posts. They travelled all day and they came in at night and had a bed and food, and then were off again the following day. It was marvellous, the way it worked. He went home first, and then came down to me and we got engaged. Then he had to go back again by the same way. It worked very well.

The war finished in August 1945 and he was demobbed. He came home at the end of November and we were married on 1 December at Purbrook Church. We had a white wedding and a small reception. My sister was my bridesmaid and so was my best friend. We went to Bournemouth for our honeymoon for ten days. Then we came home and went up to Lincoln for Christmas.

Then he had to get a job. He was a warrant officer, which was quite a position with good pay and everything, but you didn't volunteer for anything. Nobody would volunteer to stop in the army. He went back to his old garage.

I was living with his mum and dad, and his sister and her husband, who also had a little baby, in a three-bedroomed terrace house and it really wasn't very nice. I was not happy there. Someone got us some rooms at £1 5s. The landlady said to me that she didn't want any babies. 'If you have a baby you must go,' she said. Well, of course, I fell pregnant, didn't I?

Fortuitously, there was an advert in the paper asking for senior men to go back, and I said, 'What about this then, darling?'

'No, no, no.'

'Why not?'

'I'll think about it.'

We considered it. They were offering him his rank back, so he went back into the army. He was posted first to Leicester, and I went home to mum and dad in Purbrook. I think we were both happy. However, at the end of November, when my baby was due in three weeks, he was posted to Egypt. My father was a bit of a personage in the village and had access to a local MP. He went and saw him and the posting was cancelled. He was sent down once again to Hilsea Barracks, which was heaven. It was a bit naughty knowing people in the right places.

He was home then for eighteen months until he was sent to Malaya, but by then I was quite happy to go there with him.

Malaya

I waited nine months to go out to Malaya because they thought it would all be over, but of course it wasn't.

We lived in a hiring, initially, because the army kept messing us about as to when we were going to Malaya. I was friendly with another girl who lived in Aldershot and whose husband was part of Monty's mess. We got together. She was living with her father-in-law and we decided that we would take ourselves out to Malaya by our own passage, blow them! So we went up to London, went up to P&O and booked ourselves passages. She had got one little girl and I had Roger.

We booked ourselves passages in defiance of them. We sort of got half an 'okay' from the people out in Malaya. We booked for about two months hence. It was only going to be about £136, as I remember, which I thought was just marvellous. We paid our money and then, lo and behold, the War Office acknowledged that the war was going to last. It went on and on, in actual fact. It was still on when we came home six years later! We then got passages on a troop ship.

Another odd thing was that my sister was serving in the ATS [Auxiliary Territorial Service, the wartime women's army service] and she said that she wanted to go abroad. A few weeks before I sailed she got her posting to Singapore. We went out on the same troop ship, leaving my poor mum and dad waving goodbye to the both of us on the station. We cancelled the P&O booking and got our money back.

Monty had gone out in the September and eventually, when we arrived, it was the end of June. Of course, wives subsequently followed us out, doing the right thing and waiting for the troop ships.

Dodgy

It was quite dodgy out there. They were just shooting. They didn't think. They thought they would fell the insurgents but they were shooting the rubber planters, the estate managers, and so on, even one of the district officers in Kuala Lumpur [KL] was shot and killed. We didn't go out and travel. We were in Kuala Lumpur. I thought KL was very nice, colonial. We walked about and could go on the buses.

Badminton

We lived in a boarding house to begin with, with grounds around it. It was on stilts. We managed to retrieve a badminton court. It had obviously been used by the Japanese during the war and was completely overgrown. Some of the occupants managed to clear it. We could see where it had been a proper gravel court. We managed to get all the weeds out and the jungle that had come over it, and we played.

The first day we arrived we went to the Victoria Institute, which was a big building, a school or college. The chaps we were with, Monty and his friend, said, 'We've got something today for you two darlings. It's the final of the Thomas Cup.' This still exists for badminton, and of course it was being played in the Victoria Institute, so, on the first day we were out there, we got to go along and see the final of the badminton cup. I suppose they had been following it and they all played badminton. They were great, the Malayans.

Writing on the Victoria Institute website, Chung Chee Min documents the school's long association with badminton. In 1948, he states that the school hosted the Malayan Badminton Championships. The Victoria Institute badminton hall was at the time the best in the country, and top Malayan players came to the school to compete. The used shuttlecocks were later donated to the delighted school. The Thomas Cup was played later that same year in Preston, England.

I played badminton and tennis while I was there, and hockey and rounders. We lived in a boarding house, so I did not do any cooking. I have always done a lot of sewing and I took my sewing machine out with me. In the tropics you need lots of dresses and there were lots of material shops, which was great, particularly after England and rationing. I was 12 at the beginning of the war and went right through the war with shortages and make-do-and-mend, clothing coupons and food rationing. Malaya was a land flowing with milk and honey.

However, the owner decided to pack up her boarding house and turned it into apartments, so we were sitting tenants and I was able to cook and sew to my heart's delight. My husband put on weight. He was always a little bit stocky, but he went up to 17 stone under my tender care! This stayed with him until we went back on our second tour and he started to be a bit dizzy and he was sent into hospital. It was found then that he had high blood pressure and he also got prickly heat, so they sent him off to the Cameron Highlands, which is like a holiday resort, to the hospital up there for six weeks. He was treated up there, but they told him he had to lose 5 stone. Over the years we brought him down. He cut down on beer, and he was on gin and tonic, and he came down to 12 stone and he stayed there. I was happy, because I liked cooking and there was no rationing.

We loved Malaya; the heat, having a servant – my mother had had servants, of course, in India. My grandmother, being the daughter of a warrant officer, she always used to tell us, 'Oh do this,' and 'Do this,' and my mother kept a maid. We often had a lady in to help my mother in England. She loved India. You did not have just one servant, you had one servant for this job and one for another with their caste system.

We both loved Malaya so much that my husband volunteered for another tour. In those days, because of the insurgents and the problems, it could be a little bit lively at times. I saw dead bodies brought in on the tops of Land Rovers, and things like that, but when you are young you don't think about danger, do you?

He served latterly with the Queen's Royal Lancers, a very nice, pukka regiment. We came home in 1954. We went on embarkation leave and then we went to Germany for seven years, which I loved just as much.

Germany

Germany was very different to Malaya, but hotter in summer as it was inland. It had very cold winters and it always snowed. By that time, we had adopted a son. I had had several miscarriages and our son Roger wanted a brother. I did not mind what I had.

We did a lot of camping in Germany. The Germans are great for their outdoor life. We really loved it.

My husband retired in 1961 and went to work for Rolls-Royce in Derby. We had to go somewhere because we needed a job. I had never worked. We settled in Derby and liked it. Being a mechanical man, he had the opportunity to move to the Ministry of Transport, which was his life. I was a bit lonely, because he was working quite hard and the two boys were at school activities, so something I had always wanted to do was train as a nurse. Just as a State Enrolled Nurse (SEN), but I loved it. It is still with me now. People come and knock on my door. It is nice to be needed, particularly as you are old.

MARGHERITA WOOSNAM
— AN UNUSUAL WARTIME ROMANCE

Margherita (Rita) Woosnam met her husband, Frank, when he was with the army of occupation immediately after the Second World War. Theirs was an unusual romance, as he was British and she German, working at a mining depot. Now a sprightly 90-something, Rita looks back at their meeting, which was to be the beginning of a whole new life for her:

Germany

The thing was, I had been a private secretary to a German naval captain for many years. I had my lovely office, and a big, big place it was, but towards the end of the war the captain said, 'Oh I think you had better come and sit in my office because all the things you are typing I don't want other people to see.' So I went into his office.

Then the end of the war came, and we were told to stay at home and not to come to work. After another week or so we got back to work and then, one morning, three naval officers came into the office, British naval officers, one with two stripes on his sleeve and two with one stripe. Now, I studied English at school so I had a little, and I asked what this was about. The man with two stripes said, 'I want to have a list of all the boys by tomorrow.'

They made mines in this depot. I sat up all night writing down all the names of the boys, the workers. There were loads of them – over 200 working there. So, next day came, and these three young men again and the two-stripe one said, 'What is this then?'

I said, 'This is a list of all the boys working here.'

He said, 'I can't blow up mines with those boys!'

Oh dear, oh what a start! I had confused 'boys' with 'buoys'!

I thought, I have to improve my English a little bit, and so at home I looked for a book that was called *Life in an English Girls' Boarding School*. This was all about Roedean in Brighton. So I brought it along and put it on my desk, and these three men came again. One of the one-stripe ones said, 'Oh,' looking at the picture, 'I've been there.'

I thought, 'What a liar!' I said, 'It's a girls' boarding school, how could you be there?' I didn't realise that during the war they were all evacuated and the navy had taken it over!

He was the one I could really talk to. I could understand what he was saying and he was always very friendly, and so on. Then all the German officers had to go to camps and we had a few days off, but then we all went back to work after a while.

For some reason or other, I just liked that one who had been at the girls' boarding school – Frank. So, many, many months passed and we were getting on. My English was getting better and so this is really how it started. We used to meet sometimes in the evenings, and he came round to my flat and met my parents, and so I was quite happy. Then we had to go to Hamburg. I am not quite sure why now. We drove there, Frank and me. On the way back he said, 'I have to go to a mining depot. I have to go because I may have to take them over and work there.'

I said, 'Okay.'

Now, it was just after the war, and there were craters everywhere on the road. Next moment, we were in a crater. I looked down and thought, 'my wonderful blouse!' Everything was black and red. I was bleeding [Rita remains scarred from the car accident]. I was really very, very ill. Frank was not too happy about that, and he took me to a nearby hospital. Since there was an English officer involved, we got an English doctor.

He said, 'You will be all right.'

England

It took me a while, but I was getting better. After that, Frank and I became very, very friendly. One day he asked, would I marry him? I thought, 'I don't know! I will ask my parents and see what they say.'

My mother said, 'I can't see any reason why not.'

My father said, 'No! It is so soon after the war. They won't like the Germans over there.'

But then we had made friends with an English commander called Culver, and he said to my parents, 'This man Frank will make Rita very, very happy, I can assure you.' So after he said all that, my father actually agreed, and it was in February 1948 that I got a boat from Hamburg to England.

It was wonderful. We went to Tilbury and I was walking up and down on the boat, looking for Frank on the dockside, but he was nowhere in sight. An officer came and he said, 'Who are you looking for?'

I said, 'My fiancé.'

He said, 'Well, we are not actually stopping here now, in half an hour we will be back.'

So, half an hour later, we stopped and I looked up and he was there, my darling Frank. So, I was happy! He came on board to greet me because everyone in uniform got on board.

I was asked all kinds of questions, you know. 'What was I going to do in England?'

I said, 'I am going to get married in August.'

Then, off I went and we had to go through a gate and there was an English sailor there, he was in charge. He looked at me and said, 'I know you!'

I said, 'I have only just arrived in England. How could you know me?' Do you know what, he used to be in my hometown, Bremervörde, as a guard! I thought, 'what a beginning!' He recognised Frank as well.

We drove to London first, for one night, and then Oxford. In London, we went to a very nice hotel. You know what it was called? The Goring Hotel! I said, 'Where is the umlaut then?'!

I got into bed and I thought, 'I don't know what I am going to do', because in Germany we had a different sort of bed covering. Here was just blankets. I had no idea what to do. So, the next morning, Frank asked me if I slept well. I said 'No, as I did not know how to cover myself'!

The next day, we went to Oxford because Frank's brother was there. He was working at one of the universities. So I stayed there for a week because Frank's father knew all around there and he took me around the university. It was lovely and I was so thrilled. At home in Germany, my English teacher had been studying at Oxford and she often talked about this beautiful city. So I was thrilled to bits to be there. We got married in Oxford. That was really something.

Rationing

Moving country, getting married and settling into married life had all been thrilling to young German-born Rita in 1948. Getting to grips with post-war British life and, in particular, the intricacies of rationing, was quite another thing, though:

We had to move to Gillingham, near Chatham, because Frank was working there. The house was not quite ready, so I had to stay at a hotel, which was very useful because I could go around during the day to see what was going on, and could go shopping. We used to go to the David Grieg store in Gillingham [this is still standing, but is now a Greggs bakery shop, 102–104 High Street, Gillingham]. So I did some shopping there and I had my ration card there. Things were very difficult, what with the food rationing and everything.

I did quite well at shopping, so Frank was very pleased when I came home with all I had bought. I did not realise that I had a month's shopping and I should have had a week's shopping! So, when I went back to David Grieg the week after, the staff told me that I had had my lot. The manager came, and he said, 'I am going to look after you, you come to me now. We will start from the beginning again.' So, every time I asked for some meat and it was on the scale and I asked if it was going to be too much, he replied, 'No, it is not enough!' It was absolutely wonderful.

Domestic Bliss

Rita and Frank eventually moved into a small house near Chatham. It was the start of a year of domestic bliss for the newly-weds:

That year was absolutely fantastic. While I was still working at the German place, I used to look at a beautiful German Shepherd dog – they were always going around the edge of the premises, having a look at everything. I said to Frank one day, when we were walking, that I would like to have one, so we got a little puppy. This little puppy had to come over here to England as well, but she had to come differently because she had to go in to quarantine, so we visited her several times. From that moment on, until about five years ago, we had nothing but German Shepherd dogs.

I was so happy with Frank, from the first moment.

I remember we went to Rochester Castle. Up at the top, I said to him, 'Frank, Frank, I think I'm pregnant!'

'Oh,' he said, 'well, that's that!'

Then in June of that year, 1949, my darling Tricia was born. Absolutely wonderful!

Then, two years later, we went up to Carlisle because he was posted, and the twins were born. While I was expecting the twins, Frank used to say, 'Are you having an elephant or something because you are enormous!'

I said, 'Sorry!'

In those days you had no scans or anything like that, so I went to see the doctor. The doctor wasn't there, just the nurse. She examined me and she said, 'You had better see the doctor tomorrow.'

I said, 'Well, what is it then? Can't you help me?' All she did was shrug her shoulders. So I walked out and I thought 'How am I going to do what I have to do?' – I had everything ready for one child. Two! I gave Frank a ring and I said, 'You won't believe it, but we are going to have twins.' No answer from the other side for quite some time. Then I could hear, 'Oh well, I suppose we'll manage!'

Having his children made me very, very happy.

I went into labour with a name of a girl and the name of a boy, and I thought, 'well, we will see what it is'. I had no idea! First, Gill came out. I thought, 'that is nice'. Then the boy came out, that was Peter.

Life was very happy.

RN Social Life

We had wonderful parties. For once, I had two evening dresses! The naval social life was fantastic.

Advice from Mother

Before leaving Germany, Rita's mother took her to one side and had a little chat with her daughter:

Before I left, my mother said, 'Now you are going to marry an Englishman. You shall be British. Take my advice and always do what he says. Agree.'

I said, 'Yes, I will do that.'

Then a friend of mine also came over at the same time. She married somebody in London. She was always complaining, always saying, 'We do this better in Germany.' I never said that, and I agreed with Frank all the time. My friend did not stay. She went back home, but I stayed. It was a happy, happy life. It was 1948. We had sixty-four years together.

❧ JUNE STEAD ❧

June and Ron Stead met when they were both 15 and living in Stockport. It was 1947, and Ron was a naval cadet. June recalls:

Ron's friend, Eric, was about 6ft tall and Ron is short. My girlfriend was 5ft 8in and I am short. So Ron's mate and my girlfriend thought that I should have a companion and so Ron went to meet me with his friend Eric at my grandfather's house. It was a big, double-fronted house with steps up to the porch, and I could see him through the glass door. I thought, 'Isn't he little!'

We have been together ever since, apart from Ron's first commission. That was in 1948 to Malta. He was away for two years. We married in 1951.

I was going nursing the same year that Ron joined up. He was going away from home, and I was going away from home. Ron was going to do what he wanted, and I was going to do what I wanted. His joining up did not bother me until he had gone to Malta. I did not think much of that. We kept in touch, and it so happened that I had to have my appendix out just as he was coming home and so I was on sick leave. It was as if it was meant to be, and he has kept me ever since!

Getting Married

Oh dear. It was a bit traumatic! By this time, Ron was a leading radio electrician's mate and I was nursing.

I had gone into the area where the instruments were cleaned. I took a bottle from the top shelf and someone hadn't screwed the top on it. I stretched up – being short has its disadvantages – and I pulled it down. It spilled. It was acid. I had a great big ulcer come up on my wrist. Fortunately, I had glasses on and so it didn't go into my face. It was a week before the wedding.

On the morning of our wedding I was under an anaesthetic, having the wrist seen to. The wound had grown enormous. You could have put an old penny inside it.

We had the wedding, and I still had a huge bandage on. I had to have my wedding dress cut so that I could get the sleeve on. I always say that I was married while still asleep because I was still under the anaesthetic!

I am one of those people who, when something happens, laughs. If you went outside and tripped, I would laugh and ask if it hurt! That morning I woke up and there was a red line going up my arm. It was poison. It was an emergency. I had to have it done, I had no choice. My father drove me and a friend of the family to the hospital. Father waited outside and she came in with me. She told the doctor I was getting married that morning and he didn't believe her. 'She is!' She said. He just put me under. I can't remember being put under. I suppose I had been subconsciously putting off going to get it looked at. It happened very quickly.

I can remember a lot of the wedding, but some things I can't remember even now. I suppose it was the anaesthetic. I remember actually getting married, though, although Ron couldn't get the ring on my finger. The vicar was saying, 'You have got to do it, you have got to do it!' Eventually it went on, but not full on. It was very tight.

We had the reception at home. Remember, we were still in wartime conditions. Everybody gave their sugar ration to be made into icing sugar, so we could have icing on the cake.

We went to Llandudno for our honeymoon for a week. Ron had just been promoted, and his promotion was backdated to when he came home from Malta. His £30 back-pay paid for our honeymoon. I had to go to hospital while we were away and that was when Ron saw the wound on my wrist. The bandages came off while I was waiting to be seen.

We were coming home on the train and we had been very careful because they had stacked confetti in the case. Ron put the case on the overhead rack and all the confetti came out! It went everywhere.

The other thing about our wedding date was that it was due to be in August, when Ron had leave, but I couldn't get the time off. The wedding was brought forward to the April when both of us could get leave at Easter. You can imagine, the tongues were all wagging that we had brought the date forward! We had the last laugh because we had a son, born on our first wedding anniversary! That shut them up.

I think that when you marry into a service, whatever it is, you have got to be jack of all trades, because your husband goes away and you have to deal with emergencies like water coming out of a pipe which shouldn't, and broken bathroom windows because boys will kick footballs through it! The day the ship sails something always happens.

DIY

When Ron was leaving on deployment on HMS *Carysfort* [commissioned in 1945, broken up for scrap in 1970], the sailing was delayed several times. It was sailing today, then it was not sailing today, so the men went home again. This happened a couple of times, and I was getting a bit fed up.

'Are you going, or not?' I asked him.

He was going this day, fine. I had the two boys downstairs and I said to them, 'Please do not come upstairs, I have a blowlamp.' I went upstairs, got the blowlamp and was busy burning off this horrible paint when the bedroom door opened. 'I asked you not to come upstairs because I have a blowlamp.' I turned around and Ron was there.

He said, 'What the hell do you think you're doing?' It was a bit of a shock for Ron to see his little wife doing what he normally would have done!

I can't do the, 'Oh dear, what am I going to do now he is not at home.' I can't do that at all.

I wanted a shelf put up. I got the spirit level and I did it proper. He comes home and he says, 'What's that?'

'It's my shelf.'

He leaned on it and it came down. I said, 'I worked hard on that shelf to get it straight!' I got my shelf in the end. I can laugh at things like that.

I remember the window pane I was putting back in that was an inch too short. There was all this rubber felt, draught excluder, which went across the top of it. I had to do something. This was after the football incident.

I used to love to strip wallpaper. I didn't like rubbing the paintwork down, but I did like to strip the paper. I used to decorate every room while he was away, even ceiling paper. You know the cartoon, you are one end of the room putting it up and it is coming down at the other? The broom head came in very useful. I had a good DIY book – my bible. DIY was my outlet and kept me busy.

I enjoyed my life as a military wife. It had its ups and downs, obviously, but you have to put them behind you and laugh at them. If you can't laugh, don't be a service wife. You have got to be able to do things on your own. Things happen, and you have got to be able to cope with them. For example, the polio vaccine came out while Ron was away. It was iffy. What do I do? Do I, or don't I, with the boys? The doctor said, 'You'd better wait until Ron comes home.'

I said, 'I can't wait until he comes home!'

The first lot of the vaccine was not very good. Fortunately, the second lot was fine, so I had them vaccinated with the second lot. No problems, but I had that decision to make. It was about 1955 or 1956, and they were small. Some decisions just can't wait.

I never ever said to the boys, if they were naughty, 'When your father comes home, I'll tell him', because it was all done and dusted before he came home. You had to be self-reliant. This is in the days when we couldn't communicate – there were no emails, mobile phones, nothing. You didn't have a phone in the house where you lived. You could share, but that wasn't very good. We didn't have one. At the end of the road there was a phone box but if there was someone else waiting to go into the phone box, you had to be brief, 'Hello' and 'Goodbye'!

Mauritius

Ron was, generally speaking, away nine months at a time. He was ashore at HMS *Collingwood* once for eighteen months. Otherwise, he was always on ships. In all those years of serving in the navy we only ever had one foreign accompanied draft. To Mauritius at the end of his career. We had two years there and it was the longest we had together as a family. All four of us went.

Wives couldn't work. Even if you wanted to you weren't allowed. You had to have a maid. It is very nice to have someone come in to do your work every day except Sundays, and she left about one or two in the afternoon. She had lunch exactly the same as us but she ate it in the kitchen. Then she would clear up and go. Sometimes I got that I would like the place to myself, though, but she was a lovely girl.

When we first got there we could not get into a married quarter. This was in 1965–1967. We were put into an apartment. Ron was a chief petty officer by then, and we had a do in the mess. Ron and I went out and our maid came in as a babysitter. The following morning, Alan [their son] said, 'You will not do that to us again. We do not need a baby sitter!' – and we didn't. There was a phone in the flat and they knew the numbers if there was something wrong.

Alan was the only one of his age going to the school. He couldn't take his O levels. He had to do Royal Society of Arts exams instead. The O level board wouldn't allow the exams to be taken abroad because of cheating. There was a Royal Naval headmaster and it was a Royal Naval school. Part of the library was boarded up for Alan, and that became his study. He had private tutors, the wives of the serving men. One wife was a maths teacher teaching 16–17-year-olds. She was very good, and of course he was taught maths to quite a high level for his age. The Ministry of Public Works & Buildings was there and they had a drawing office. That is where Alan went to do mechanical drawing. That is now his career, he is a design draftsman. The only thing he couldn't do in Mauritius was study art because there were no studios, not even a gallery he could go to. Everything was done through books.

The wives were talking, and they said that I was fortunate for not having to have a babysitter and being able to go out to the mess every night because I didn't have babies. I turned around and said to them, 'Well, they weren't born this age. We had to go through the baby stage.' Our family was the oldest there and Ron was probably the oldest serviceman there.

Ron was the treasurer of the mess, and also the treasurer and secretary of the badminton club. I was the secretary of the Naval Wives and the treasurer. One year we had a collection for the church and all over the floor were rupees! We were counting rupees for the collection.

No Regrets
Looking back over my life, I have no regrets.

❧ PHYLLIS HOLROYD ❧

Phyllis was in the Women's Royal Naval Service (WRNS), working as a radio mechanic when she met Granville Holroyd, universally known as 'Rod' within the service, also a radio mechanic in the Royal Navy, at HMS *Ariel* in Warrington in 1949. Rod was later commissioned as an engineering officer:

Meeting Rod
He was an acting petty officer [PO] when I met him. Both he and I were in a trade where you got automatic promotion. One year after you passed out as leading hand you got PO, except the men had to do a year as acting PO, so in actual fact I pipped him to the post just before I came out to get married.

Leaving the Service
I wanted to come out. I would have stayed in if I had not met him. One or two women stayed in when married, but not many in those days.

Nowadays, you would go to university, wouldn't you? I left school and went into the Civil Service, in the tax office as a tax officer. I knew it wasn't for me. The first thing I had to do was put a pile of papers into alphabetical order. I ask you! So, I joined up.

Married Quarters
Our first married quarter was at Rowner, Portsmouth, between 1957 and 1959. Up until that time, we had lived in a caravan. I was friendly with my neighbours. They had children of the same age. The quarter was furnished. It was adequate and functional.

I spent a lot of time polishing floors. We had carpet in the middle of the room and there was a thick lino, brown, that looked awful if it wasn't polished. Then we had Marley tiles. The kitchen was a bit basic, but then kitchens were in those days. There was a gas boiler that we never used, but there was running water. There were three bedrooms. It was all right. There were coal fires, of course.

After that we went to Lossiemouth. That was great. The people were lovely. I was in digs to start with. It was a flat with a doorway up high in the wall and I think that is where they used to dry the nets for fishing. I had a lovely landlady. There were only two rooms and a kitchen. We shared the lavatory, which was in the garden. It had two doors. You had to remember to lock their one when you went in and unlock it when you came out so that they could get in and out of it. I had my first washing machine, so that was all right. It didn't have a roller, it just washed. You had to put the washing through a mangle, out in the garden.

The worst thing about Lossiemouth was that it was Rod's first seagoing draft, on HMS *Ark Royal*. I was barely pregnant, and one day he went out the door and was away for six months. One day, we were just near the end of the six months, we were on the sea front and the buzz went around that the *Ark Royal* was in the bay. We all dashed down and some people came ashore, and we asked when the rest were coming ashore. They said, 'Oh no, there is only us going ashore.'

It was so cruel – six months. I was so pregnant and so sorry for myself. I had not told him that, once again, I had been violently sick all the time. The people they put ashore were going to Culdrose, Cornwall, and the reason the rest did not come ashore was to do with school fees. You had to be out of the country six months for them to be paid by the navy. So they couldn't come ashore until that six months were up. So, they sailed away again. They went into Liverpool but I did not go because of my state. They then came home.

I had Christine in Aberdeen, which was 80 miles away, because of the difficult births. That was fun as well! That was absolutely great, one of the best fortnights I have ever spent! The people there, they were such fun. Granville used to come in often, more or less every day. But if he wasn't coming in there was a dishy doctor there and everyone used to get ready to see him! I was in a room on my own.

The sad thing about it was that, in those days, they did not let children in, so Steven used to come with Granville but used to have to stay downstairs. Granville delayed the leave he had from being abroad so he could look after Steven.

That was the first time he went abroad. You always knew it was coming. The thing is, it was awful. I remember standing at the door as he was going out and knowing that at lunch and teatime all the other husbands would be coming home. I didn't know how long they had gone for. I knew it was to be a long time. He was lucky – he was on the first relief, otherwise it could have been a very long time.

The day they came back, that day was indescribable. I would not say it was worth it, but I think people who had always had their husbands home did not know what it was like to meet their husbands coming back. I went out to the airport.

Borneo

Granville went to Borneo for the Malayan Crisis in 1964. He was in the jungle there. I was very worried when he said he was going to a war zone. It just came out of the blue. We did not have a lot of people out there, so it was not really talked about. The Royal Navy were flying helicopters.

I had to go home because we were in Dorchester and there was nowhere for me to go because he was joining the ship. The navy said I had to go home. I was in a hiring and I was so isolated there. I was in Winterbourne Monkton, a couple of miles from Dorchester, and there were only three houses there, a little hamlet. Felicity, our youngest, was 4 years old.

The sad thing was that I went home and I met people I knew. I said my husband was in Borneo and they said, 'Didn't you fancy going?'! They just did not know there was a war on at that time. I used to search the newspapers looking for a little snippet to say what was happening. I am not saying that Borneo was anything like as dangerous as other wars but it *was* a little war. He was lucky again, he was on first release, so he had six months away. That was wonderful, a complete surprise. I got a letter to say he was coming home. By now, he was a commissioned officer.

Being the Wife of a Commissioned Officer

I knew he wanted it. I was a bit apprehensive. We had a better married quarter and more money. He was happy.

What happened was that he was a good radio mechanic and he loved wandering around and seeing what the men were up to. The navy shoved him into an office and he just said, 'If they are going to shove me

Margaret Winter.

William, Margaret and Emily just before
William went off to France in early 1917.

Margaret and Stephen Middleton-West
later became missionaries in Burma.

Jessie Maud White in 1904, with her 6-year-old daughter, Doris Jessie, and 2-year-old son, Gibeon Henry William. Doris was Joy Hale's mother.

Jessie Maud White's husband, CPO Shipwright William White (centre back), aged about 42 years.

Lily Hannah Payne's husband, Ernest, in India during the First World War.

Lily Hannah wearing the wedding dress made of Indian lace that Ernest brought back for her, 1919.

Anstey Church, where Lily Hannah and Ernest were married. (Photograph by, and courtesy of, Peter Smith)

1946 – a happy scene in Quetta, India. Sue (centre) and her brothers with domestic staff. The ayah (centre back) was Hindu and had to flee the country at partition in 1947, when Muslim Pakistan came into being.

Rose Dawson, born Rusena
Lehrmannova in Czechoslovakia,
1919.

Rose and Bill Dawson on their
wedding day, 1943.

Rose kept her Alien Card, without which she could not go anywhere until she married Bill Dawson and became a British citizen. (Photograph courtesy of Maianna Moreau and Jenny Cuffe of the *This is my Home Now* project.)

Joy and Monty Hale on their wedding day, December 1945.

A young Rita Woosnam, at home in Germany just before the outbreak of the Second World War.

A dashing Royal Naval hero – Frank Woosnam, who swept Rita off her feet and brought her to Britain.

Rita and Frank Woosnam on their wedding day. They had sixty-four happy years together.

Phyllis and Granville 'Rod' Holroyd (left). Phyllis was a bit apprehensive when Rod was promoted to become an officer but appreciated the better accommodation and higher salary that went with the change.

Jean Weeks and her family, about to set off to see their family in Kent.

The dashing Thomas Marsh Hill in the mid-1950s.

Barbara Hill. She and Thomas met when he was 15 and she was 16.

in an office, they may as well pay me for being in an office.' So, he went for the commission. He had exams to pass after being recommended.

Naval Life with Children

We went into a temporary house in Catherington. We moved at the end of 1965, during the children's Christmas holidays. We knew the married quarters would not be long, just a few weeks. But then school term started.

Felicity used to react so badly to changes. It really used to upset her. I kept her home for three weeks, then we moved into married quarters and she started school. I would not have got away with it now, but it was the right thing to do. To have given her two quick moves like that, would have been so bad.

From Catherington, Steven had to catch a bus into Portsmouth and then another to Fareham. Granville used to take him most days, but when he was on duty he had to take the buses to Price's Grammar School in Fareham [opened in 1721, closed in 1989]. When we were interviewed by the headmaster, I explained this, and I said he may be unavoidably late when my husband is not able to bring him. 'Oh no, you must get him here on time,' I was told. They had no idea of our problems! There was no way of getting him there sooner. I don't know if he was late, in the event, but sometimes they weren't co-operative, although on the whole they were. We weren't very long before we moved into our quarter at Hill Head, luckily.

❧ JEAN WEEKS ☙

Jean and Anthony (Tony) Weeks BEM (British Empire Medal), were married in 1953. Career girl Jean spotted him while she was a Wren, a member of the WRNS as a Wren air mechanic, posted to the Royal Naval Air Station Yeovilton, in Somerset:

The Deal

I had three years as a Wren and then came outside. Then I re-entered and did another two years. I went down to Yeovilton to do my leading Wren's course and that is where I met Tony.

I was a WRNS air mechanic down at Yeovilton. I can't remember if we met playing hockey or down the pub – the pub probably. Once a fortnight, you could afford to go. He was the love of my life, a lovely, lovely man.

Tony was part of the Royal Navy's Fleet Air Arm, and was an aircraft artificer:

> I was married a year or two before he went away the first time. We had had our daughter Shelley, and he went on HMS *Centaur*. I accepted the separation. It was part of the deal. You marry into the services. You have to accept these things. I did not get upset about it. I took it in my stride. There were other people in the same position. Probably there were other people whose husbands were gone longer than Tony was.
>
> He hopped around – Aden, Lossiemouth, Arbroath. Tony was a chief, and did twenty-two years. He got his British Empire Medal at HMS *Daedalus*.

Jean and Tony bought a small house in Lee-on-the-Solent when they married. It is still the family home, although, sadly, Tony died sixteen years ago:

> He was away on HMS *Centaur* for the best part of a year in the early 1960s. I was left with four small children in this little house. The boys upstairs in the room I have now, in bunk beds and a single bed, and Shelley in another bedroom.
>
> One thing that I was proud of was taking all four children, Shelley, Andrew, Peter and Simon, up to my mother-in-law's when he was away. We went up there for Christmas. My youngest, Simon, was still a babe in arms.
>
> I had to get the bus from Lee-on-the-Solent, cross on the Gosport ferry and then get the train from Portsmouth Harbour to London. I don't think I took them on the underground, I probably took them on a bus and then we had to walk from the bus stop to their grandparents' house in Sydenham, Kent. Things were quieter then. There were not so many people travelling. Life was a lot easier. In a lot of ways, life was a lot better. When your husband was away, you carried life on for the kids. You had to. I am not one for sitting around.
>
> We went to Lossiemouth in Scotland with Tony. It was nice up there. We were there for a year or so. The quarters were great, but I had to polish the lino floors. When we were there we did not have a car but there were families with cars. We got very friendly with three families: next door, across the road and around the corner. We all ended up in this area of Hampshire, and for forty years we have been giving each other lunch every three months.

Tony went to the Falkland Islands in the late sixties. He was then away for thirteen months. That was a long time, thirteen months. The only correspondence was sending airmails. But, on Christmas Day, the governor, who was the only one on the island with a phone, allowed Tony to call us. My neighbour had a phone, so we did speak to him at Christmas. They had to build their own quarters in the Falklands. He got the BEM for that.

Off to the Pub!

Tony was put on the Joint Services Hovercraft Unit at HMS *Daedalus*. He was there for years. He ran a local Scout troop for ten years. I helped with the cub scouts.

We could not afford holidays. We only had his money. We had the beach near our home and Scout camp was our holiday, at Tollard Royal, down near Shaftesbury. That was great. We all went, except Shelley, who went to Guide camp and stayed with a friend while we were away.

There were about thirty children plus Tony and two assistant Scout leaders. We used to get a lorry to take all the equipment, and then I think we hired a coach to take us there and back. We had to take it all with us. We got milk from the little village next door and we did well.

We had a wood fire and a huge great dustbin to dish out water for the boys to wash in. Once a week I would make a spotted dick and wrap it in a towel and drop it in the old dustbin and it would cook away for about three hours. The boys thought it was great! Can you imagine it now?

They were inspected every morning. 'Hold your hands out!'

They weren't allowed to wear socks – ever – because my husband's theory was that they got wet and smelly. If you have just got plimsolls on your feet it was easier to wash and we did not have smelly socks about the place.

They built bridges, slung things between trees, had raft races; it was great. They loved to help the shepherd of course, rounding up the sheep. He was a lovely man.

We used to send the boys out on a hike on the Wednesday and we would adjourn to the pub at lunchtime! They were gone all day. It was great! I had a little bell tent. We had our own loos with the help of the shepherd, who looked after the site, dug out and kept an eye on us if need be. He was a lovely man named Bob Meon, a Scotsman.

Part of my duty was, after lunch, to open up the tuck-shop tent. The boys had a certain amount of money that they could spend. I used to threaten the boys – 'If I hear any of you swearing in front of me, you will get the soap bottle in your mouth!' They knew I meant it. I never had any trouble with them.

When Tony died, the letters I got from ex-Scouts … they are in the loft.

A Housewife …

I was a housewife, after leaving the WRNS. I did a little part-time work when Shelley wanted to go to teacher training college. I helped someone who was a picture restorer and photographer, putting pictures in frames. It was interesting. People did not go out to work so much then. People have more possessions now. You had one lot of clothes for the week and then your Sunday best.

Ӿ БARBARA HILL ᴔ

Barbara married her Royal Artillery parachutist husband, Thomas Marsh Hill, in 1956, when she was 24. Thomas served until 1975, when he retired, and the pair then bought a fish and chip shop:

Meeting Up

I knew my husband when he was just 15. I was 16, going on 17. He was far more intelligent than me! I come from Lancashire, but we moved to Liverpool. I was working and had lots of boyfriends, as you do at that age, and we met when he visited my mother's house. He said to me later, 'I saw you and I said to myself, "That is the girl I'm going to marry."'

Seventh Royal Horse Artillery

He belonged to the 33rd, as it was known in those days. It was amalgamated and became the 7th Royal Horse Artillery.

First Married Quarter

I remember my first quarter was 62 Somerset Square, Aldershot. The quarters there have been demolished now.

I loved it. It was my first home and I was a new wife. My husband could walk home to lunch or even, if he had time, pop home in his NAAFI break. You went into a main entrance and there were two apartments on the ground floor and two upstairs. Mine was upstairs, and they were all one bedroom in that block – we called them blocks. Ours was one bedroom but it was huge, massive. They were big quarters.

You had one bedroom, bathroom and separate toilet, a coal fire – we didn't have central heating in those days – and all the furniture was supplied. In fact, everything was supplied apart from our own personal pictures and things, right down to the last tea and mustard spoon and the bed linen. You signed for it all. You kept an inventory of it and you ticked it off. When you broke a cup and saucer, you would go and have it replaced but you had to take the broken one in to get a new one. We replaced their china with our own china, which were wedding presents. The flat was regularly decorated. It was usually cream and green; we had no choice in colour.

We had a little garden, and one time the army started to tarmac at the back. The block had a back entrance and a front entrance. The coalman delivered the coal for the fire round the back. They wanted to tarmac over the little gardens that we had and I was quite upset about this, as I liked my garden. I didn't think of pots in those days! I asked them if they could leave a strip of land, which they did.

It was rather nice when we had our first child, Gregory, because my husband made this lovely crossover fence, so that it was sectioned off and he was safe. Some of the residents did not keep their gardens very nice and they were probably looking scruffy. It was the army, so everything had to be whitewashed and brushed, sown and clean, so the powers that be said, 'We'll tarmac all of these back entrances'. Fair enough, but I just wanted it to be a strip for some flowers.

The NAAFI

In those days my husband smoked and I didn't. The NAAFI was just across the road so he would come home expecting me to have got a packet of cigarettes, which, more often than not, I completely forgot about! I wasn't very popular then!

A New Military Hospital

Gregory was born in August, and I was 27 in October, 1959. I was rushed off to this wonderful hospital, called the Louise Margaret Maternity Hospital. [This was built on the same site as the Cambridge Military Hospital, Aldershot, which opened in 1898. The maternity hospital opened in 1958. Both were closed in 1995. The hospital would have been new when Barbara first went there.] It was for military personnel. I had never been into a military hospital before. It was wonderful. You were treated well. It was my first child and I could not have wished for better care. I could not fault it. There were QARANCs [Queen Alexandra's Royal Army Nursing Corps] – proper, fully trained nursing staff.

My children have done well. They were brought up in a happy, loving home. They were children that were wanted. I was very lucky, as I had boy, girl, boy, girl. All were born in the same hospital.

When Suzie was born, my youngest daughter, Tom had a posting in Woolwich. I came back to Louise Margaret's to have her. Very often military children are born all over the world, but I wanted to come back to Aldershot. The army said I could come back provided I stayed there for three weeks before the baby was born. My sister-in-law was still stationed in Aldershot and I stayed with her. That was useful. I wanted continuity in the family and they were christened in the All Saints Church in Aldershot, which was the army church in the Avenue.

Going Up in the World

Tom was 'other ranks', known as OR. He was a bombardier with two stripes when we got married. Not long afterwards, he was made a sergeant, which meant then that we could go to the Sergeants' Mess. This was a real step up. When he had two stripes we were with the other ranks, the privates and the lance corporals or lance bombardiers, but once he became a sergeant then they had their own specific mess, which went up to RSM – Regimental Sergeant Major.

After that, of course, you would become an officer if you applied or you came in as an officer. My eldest daughter went to Sandhurst and my youngest son went to RAF Cranwell, for officer training.

There was great excitement when Tom went from a bombardier to a sergeant – there was a pay increase! You got 7s a week extra if you were airborne, too, which was a huge amount of money in those days.

Being Airborne

Tom explained being airborne. You go up in an aeroplane with a parachute strapped on your back and you release the cords and out you jump. It is an automatic release, I think, but you do have a safety device, I believe, where you can pull a second chute if the main one should fail. I have never jumped out of a plane in my life! I never thought about it. It was his job.

They were a small band, not like a huge regiment. You all more or less knew each other. Our soldiers are ready to go anywhere in the world at any time. You can be asleep, and there is a knock on the door: 'Come on! We're off!' Suez in 1956, Cyprus in 1974 – wherever there was trouble in the world. And you, as a wife, just coped. They always left behind a families' officer just in case you needed anything.

Tom went to Suez and Palestine and then there was Cyprus. You missed him, of course you did, but I am a down-to-earth, practical person. When he was in Suez I had no children then. I drove, and I went to work and saved up quite a bit of money.

News Trickled Through

The families' officer was left behind. If anything happened to any of the men, you would have known immediately. We were military wives, and it would come through to the families' officer that Mrs So-and-So's husband has been shot, or someone has broken a leg, or whatever. It was community news. If it was really serious, an officer would come around to visit you. The padre used to come around and make sure you were OK, which was rather nice. I felt very much looked after. I never felt abandoned in any way whatsoever.

There was a Wives' Club, too. We just chatted, had coffee mornings, get-togethers, those sort of things. It was held in the Sergeants' Mess, which was for the men really, but when they were away, it was used for the wives.

Social Life

We always had a Sergeants' Mess on a Saturday night. There was always something going on there, so that was good. If you could, you went. We had balls etc. The thing was, there were lots of messes, because you had the 33rd Airborne Division, the 1st and 2nd Parachute Division and they would all have their own messes and so you would be invited to all these different functions as well. It was a very good social life. We could always take guests too, when family came to visit.

Germany

I did not do a lot of moves, just Aldershot to Woolwich, and to Germany.

In Woolwich, Tom was in charge of the Parachute Regiment TA Centre in East Ham, which was interesting.

Then we were posted to Germany, to Fallingbostel. Tom had come out of the airborne by that stage. He was the GSM, the senior sergeant major at that time. It was my first time in Germany.

I quite enjoyed Germany. Packing up and getting there was just boxes – no problem! Boxes and boxes and boxes!

I don't ski, but all my children learnt to ski because we had a caravan and we used to drive up to the Harz Mountains in Germany. Of course, they had skis and snowboards and what have you. I just used to be a mother.

❧ DR JEAN POWELL ❧

Jean was a navy wife, having married senior artificer, Ray, in 1958. He left the service in 1972. Unusually for the time, Jean also had her own career. This was something that she was able to turn to her advantage throughout the many moves around the country that marriage to a service man entailed:

It all Slotted into Place

We had two children. We did not accompany when he was foreign because he was Fleet Air Arm. He was on carriers and then he got involved with the hovercraft. He was out in Borneo, too, and it wasn't convenient to go along there. So we moved about in this country.

We went up to Paisley in Scotland, back to Weymouth, up to Somerset and then, when he was going to Borneo, I went up to Lancashire, where I come from, and took both the children with me. I had a chat with my brother first, and said, 'What do you think about me coming back to live with mum and dad?'

I'm a qualified nurse and I was a district nurse in Somerset. I wanted a midwifery qualification, so I went back to Lancashire. My brother said that coming back to stay would be brilliant because dad had retired and it would give him something to do, helping with the children. It was great fun, and it was wonderful for the children because they got to know their grandparents a lot better. We were there for eighteen months.

I got a midwifery qualification and Ray then came back to Britain. We came down here to Lee-on-the-Solent and eventually we moved to another house, in Stubbington. By then I had practiced as a midwife and a district nurse. Later, I went to university, came back as a health visitor, and I was health visitor in the village as I had been district nurse in the village. It all slotted into place. The children were 9 and 10 by then.

You got your Chances ...

After we married in 1958, we lived in Scotland, but Ray was just away for three or four nights as he was on a mobile repair unit. Then we went to Weymouth, where his parents lived, in 1959, which was nice. I was a staff nurse then, which was okay, and Ray had a nine to five job, more or less, which was good.

I was pregnant with Catherine and he moved up to Somerset in 1960. When she was 6 weeks old, we joined him. We lived in a hiring, and he was going foreign and on a carrier at that time. He more or less settled me in and off he went. They were working locally, but they were out and about in the country.

He came home in October and I was pregnant when he left, and from then on until July I didn't see him. I was pregnant the total time he was away. Catherine was about 9 months when I was pregnant for the second time. This was great, because I did want the children close together. You got your chances, you either took them or you waited another nine months, or a year, until he came back again! It all worked out.

I was well established in the village by then. It was a small place called Pitney Lortie and it was surrounded by hills. We lived in a little valley. I don't know what the population was, but not very big. It was nearly all farms and a few cottages on the hill. I had Catherine there, and every afternoon we used to go out and meet up with a lot of people and I got chatting to some of the youngsters.

I got friendly with a farmer, Frank, and his wife, their daughter-in-law, Ruth, (their son was in the army and away) and their granddaughter, who was Catherine's age. 'Come in for a coffee tomorrow,' they said, and our relationship developed then. They were brilliant people. I also met another girl who I had met in Scotland. This is a good thing about being in the navy, you are always meeting up with people you have met somewhere else. She was a good mate. I had looked after her while she was having her second child. She had four under about 6, one after the other! Her husband was full of himself, but she was a star. I used to see Diane every two or three weeks and we both had cars – I had a little bubble car at this stage, which was fun, and we used to go backwards and forwards.

However, I nearly miscarried. I had done a daft thing. I had made some stools with my brother's help. I had gone up north, with Catherine in a pram. My brother was a timber merchant. I had done a woodworking class with the Women's Institute while I was in Pitney. We used to go out every Monday night, and I would take Catherine in her carry cot to stay with Frank, who was looking after the two babies, mine and Ruth's. We used to go to a woodwork class in Langport, which was about 3 miles away from Pitney.

By this time, I had made a bookcase for Catherine's room, a medicine cabinet and a tea trolley. I went to my brother and I asked if I could make three stools while I was staying up there, a big one, a middle-sized one and a little one for Catherine. He agreed, so we worked together and he showed me what to do. I had a big pram and the stools were all roped together and put on top of the pram and I brought them home with me.

Diane and I were in the kitchen because the babies were outside and we were keeping an eye, and I had made us a drink. She sat on the tall stool and she asked where I would sit. I sat on the middle one and she said that I looked too low. I said that I'd put the other one on top. So I sat on these two stools and, of course, as I twisted they both fell apart and I landed on the floor. I jolted the placenta obviously and I bled a bit, and the doctor said that I needed bed rest for a week.

The farmer's wife used to come in at nine every morning, collect Catherine, take her away all day and then bring her back at six o'clock ready for bed. Isn't that wonderful? Without them, we would never have had Geoffrey. This shows how kind and good people are, doesn't it?'

Mrs Productivity

It was wonderful really, because we had about half an acre of garden with this hiring. So, Ray had left me with all this – pregnant, a small baby, half an acre and a bubble car for transport. Frank and his son, Brian, took me under their wing and taught me gardening, as I came from a terrace house so we did not have a garden. This was brilliant because I could learn all about it. I got the books out of the library and then, with all the produce, I could make chutney and I could do jam.

When I left Weymouth, the casualty officer had bought me a wine-making kit and two demijohns and had patted me on the head and said, 'Away you go'. The kit came with a book telling me what to do, and so I was Mrs Productivity! It was like *Homes and Gardens* every day. Ray came back and I had all these jars glooping away and a larder full of jams and chutneys and marmalade, and you name it and I would make it. I used to sew as well. Evenings weren't boring. The children would go to bed and that was fine.

Violated

I came back from woodwork one night and opened the back door. I had strung some washing up in the kitchen on the line and my washing was all scattered about and the drawers were all pulled open. Someone had been in and done the house over while I was out. We were right on the edge of the village.

I thought, 'He's not getting my baby, whoever he is!' So I took the baby under my arm and I had a carving knife out of the drawer. I put the lights on and checked downstairs, there was nobody there. So, with baby under my arm, upstairs we went. There was nobody there, but then I thought that I would bring the cot in my room and put a chair behind the door because it was the old latchy doors, like in a cottage, and I thought that at least nobody would get in if they came back. We'd be alright tonight and I'd ring the police in the morning.

I didn't ring them there and then. It was about half ten, because we used to come back to Frank, who would get bread and cheese ready, and we would sit watching *Come Dancing* and then I would go home with the baby. She was asleep. Anyway, the police came the next day and asked why I didn't call them at the time. I said, 'Well, I did not want to inconvenience anybody and he wasn't still here.' The police looked at me as if asking, 'Who is this strange lady?'

Anyway, it was a lad. We had a Borstal fairly near. He was a local lad who had been walking home. I had left a top window open and he had gone in through there and had taken some money and some little miniatures that my dad had left. But it was the fact that when you are broken into, you are violated, aren't you? It did not make any difference though. I just got on.

Skittering

I was into reading Dennis Wheatley at that stage. A horrid read, those Dennis Wheatley novels! I was in bed, reading. Catherine was in the room next door and she was just over a year old by then. She had been with me at first, then she went in the room next door. I heard this scratching overhead. I was reading this horrid, frightening book and my hair was nearly standing up on end! Aah! It wasn't a ghost though. I stood on the bed and hit the roof and it kind of skittered and I thought, 'It's probably rats'.

The New House

Our time in Pitney Lortie was lovely because I was involved with the Women's Institute, so I knew everyone in the village. Then Ray came back. I had been saving up while he was away and it was a case of, do we buy a new car or a new house? We might as well buy a house.

You didn't need a lot then. So, we had enough for a deposit and we bought a house about 5 miles away. Then we had lots of new skills to learn as, again, the people before us had not done anything much. So, it was a case of stripping it all and decorating it. Doing whatever needed doing. It was good. There was about half an acre of garden there as well. We have always had these big gardens. We had been left with nettles 5ft high, so we got some chickens from the people next door. He was the blacksmith in the village. They were lovely people, and they were kind to us.

We got snowed in. It was the bad winter of 1963. Geoffrey was a toddler and we were snowed in for about three weeks because we lived outside the village then, on top of the hill. We did all right. We were used to having food in and I learnt how to do bottling there, in my washing machine. It was a twin-tub and you could raise the temperature in it to boiling so you could wash nappies and things. The nappies were always beautiful because they were always boiled. Anyway, I read about bottling and I thought I could do it because we had all sorts of trees: gooseberries, currants, apples, pears. I got hold of Kilner jars and had a go.

I started going to auctions too, then, which was great fun because you can get stuff for next to nothing in an auction. I came home with all these treasures and you could see my husband thinking, 'oh my God, what is she going to do with those?' – 200 coat hangers, and that sort of thing. He would be cringing when I came in! But he was all right when we got that house of our own because I had free rein there.

I took my dad with me and borrowed Frank's van when we went to the auctions. I used to take Catherine with me in the bubble car when she was little. It was left-hand drive and the pushchair was a lie-down one. You could just jam it in, so she was safe and she was always strapped in. The engine was at the back and there was a platform, so when Geoffrey came along the carrycot would fit on there. I have had as many as about six of us in that little bubble car, another mum and two or three kids! It used to be good fun.

Filling the House

I took dad to Taunton to the auction. He thought this was absolutely fantastic. We had nothing in that house hardly. He and mum came down from Lancashire and brought a couple of armchairs, odds and ends and all sorts of things and it was a case of living with what we had got. They brought beds down for us, too.

My uncle did deliveries for furniture people and so we bought a couple of beds and they kitted us up with basics, anyway. One of the lots at auction was a big Axminster carpet. Dad said, 'I'll buy you that.' He had to pay all of 1s 6d for this big Axminster carpet, which was massive. It fitted all over our 30ft-long room. The day after, he said, 'Aren't you going to clean it?' So I got the broom out and some shampoo and kind of washed it and then sprayed it all. Then we rolled it up and we walked it down the garden. My dad was quite tall and all this water was running down. Then we put a double washing line up and we hung it up there. Talk about do it yourself!

I got four chairs for 5s at the auction, two dining room and two bed-room chairs. We are still using the wheel back ones. It was amazing what you could get in those days – big oak sideboards that did us good for all the wine I made then.

District Nurse

I used to go down to the local clinic because the children were small. Then I was asked if I would like to help out there. They had things for the children to play with, so I helped by weighing the babies. One day, two of the district nurses came around and asked if I would help them out because one of them had gone sick. Would I become a district nurse? I said, 'I'm not a trained district nurse, I just have an SRN qualifi-cation.' 'That's all right,' they said, 'you can come out with us for a week. Then you can be interviewed and away you go.'

IRENE NOYCE

Irene and Colin Noyce were boyfriend and girlfriend from school days:

Colin was 15 when he joined the Royal Navy. I went with him and his dad to the central recruiting office at Charing Cross on the day he joined, 24 November 1960. We left him there to travel with the rest of the recruits to Portsmouth and join HMS *St Vincent*. Colin's mum and dad and I made the journey to Gosport a few times during his time under training to see him as the Bugle Band drum major, and for his promotions to petty officer junior and junior instructor. He did his part two training at HMS *Collingwood*, and then went off to sea in HMS *Pellew*, running out of Portland.

We planned to marry in the summer of 1964, but Colin was given a draft to HMS *Anzio* in the Gulf to join in June, so we brought the wedding forward to May 1964 and he promptly left me for eleven months. I was still living at home with my parents in Essex and working in Dovercourt, so life carried on pretty much as usual, except for missing him greatly.

When he returned in 1965 we were still too young to have a naval quarter so we lived in various flats in Fareham and Gosport while Colin did his leading electrical mechanic's (LEM) course in Collingwood. I fell pregnant with our first child and Colin was drafted to HMS *Maidstone* in Scotland. I joined him after a few weeks and we lodged with friends in their quarter, but May, the wife, was also pregnant and about to deliver at the same time as me.

This was quite a pressured time, especially when the men were away at sea. However, we were promised a new quarter before my baby was due so all would be well. The quarter didn't materialise, so I moved back down south to live with my in-laws who had room for me and a baby. Our daughter was born, and eventually I moved back up to a new quarter in Helensborough.

Colin's next move was to a mechanician's course, so we moved again to Fareham.

After the two year course, Colin was the only one of twelve in his class to be given a married accompanied draft, which was to HMS *Jufair* in Bahrain. Having not long had our second child, I was left for three weeks after Colin flew out and then had to travel with the two children, then 2½ and 6 months old via Brize Norton to Bahrain.

Both our families were very anxious for us, as this was the first long-distance flight I had undertaken. Our daughter was unwell with an ear infection and I was terrified this would mean the cancellation of my flight. However, a kind RAF family befriended me and looked after the baby while I took our daughter to the medics, and we were allowed to fly. It was not a pleasant flight, with the baby in a sky-cot (on the VC10) and our daughter strapped on my lap and crying for most of the time.

Sadly, we never did meet that couple on the island of Bahrain again, but I owe them a great debt of thanks.

That flight carried entertainers for the troops, and Tom Jones also had a word of encouragement for me.

My impressions on arrival at Muharraq Airport were of intense heat and particular smells that were to equip me for later life in other such places in the Middle East. Colin had prepared our apartment and even obtained a puppy for the children, so we soon settled in.

Life in Bahrain was good with regular bus trips every week to the Sheik's beach for the families, Sunday dhow trips to the sand bar to picnic and swim, and a mess social life to be envied by anyone. The low times were when Colin suffered back injuries and ended up in hospital, and when our son, while visiting a friend at his garage, drank from a Pepsi bottle that contained petrol. This meant he was rushed to hospital and we thought we might lose him. Thankfully, he recovered and suffered no lasting damage.

It was a time of sadness when it was announced that *Jufair* would close. We extended our tour by six months, and were among the last to leave after two and a half years there.

It was during our time in Bahrain that Colin felt a calling to the ordained ministry of the Church, which was followed up and, after another ship (HMS *Norfolk* with HRH Sub Lt the Prince of Wales), he left to train for the ministry. After training and a curacy he was asked to return to the Royal Navy as a chaplain, and so it all began again.

This time, during his four year commission, I spent a great deal of time alone as the children were at boarding school and Colin was chaplain to the Type 42s, and going from ship to ship. Before, I had been a stay-at-home wife and mother, but now, for a while, I decided to take a little job.

Having spent a total of twelve and a half years as a navy wife, I think I coped quite well and wives always supported one another when husbands were away. Since those days we have travelled together for many jobs abroad and are now settled back into semi-retirement in Portsmouth and a ministry with the Royal Navy, once again at St Ann's Church in the dockyard.

❧ KAY WYLIE ❧ RAF WIFE

Kathleen, known far and wide as 'Kay', met RAF caterer, Alex, at a dance a few months after he returned from a stint in Aden in the late 1950s. Alex had been to Turkey on a hush-hush mission in 1956 and then spent two years on the Aden posting, one of which was spent on an island in the Persian Gulf. Here, among many things, he organised water drops from the only fresh water hole on the island to the local villages, and ran the camp cinema. He must have seemed very exotic to secretary, Kay:

RAF Uxbridge used to hold dances every week. Alex came from the base at Ruislip on the train. The venue was called the Battle of Britain Dance Hall. The music was supplied by 'Fritz and his music'. He played an accordion. All of us locals used to go to the dance. It was quite popular. That is where I met Alex.

He asked me to dance and the first thing he said to me was, 'Do you like Sammy Davis Jnr?'

I said, 'Who?'

He was most disgusted because I didn't know who Sammy Davis Jnr was! Anyway, we got over that and we went out for seven months. Then he heard he was getting posted to RAF Odiham. We got engaged. Then, the following year, we got married – 1961. We were both 23, our birthdays were quite close together. In them days, if you weren't married by the time you were 25 you were classed as an old maid, on the shelf. Not like today when brides are often well in their thirties.

Our Wedding

We got married in St Peter's Church, Iver, Buckinghamshire, my home village. A month to the day earlier, the Duke and Duchess of Kent got married, so all the flags were up in the fields. They came back from their honeymoon the day we got married. Alex was the first Scotsman to be married in that church.

I had gone to London and got the bridesmaid's dresses, which were mauve and pink. I brought my French lace gown from my local town. I saw it in a shop window. It was a short one. Short wedding dresses were in then. I got it made to fit. There were all these sticky-out ones, which made me look as fat as hell! I tried a lot on in London but that local one just hung right. Alex had trouble when he helped me to get into the car later –there was so much of it. The reception was only up the road, but you don't walk, do you?

I was annoyed with Alex as I wanted him to get married in uniform and he wouldn't. It was his mother's fault. He had gone home to Scotland on leave just before we got married and his mother had insisted on buying him his wedding suit and a matching one for his brother. It annoyed me, but I suppose she thought that she was doing the right thing.

The reception afterwards was in the village hall up the road. Quite a few of the lads couldn't come to the wedding. Alex asked them if they'd like to come along in the evening for a drink and the band. They turned up – a whole coachload! It came bowling up and my dad had to go out and buy more crates of beer!

My sister worked in a shop and knew a lot of people. She got us the band. She knew a lady who used to make wedding cakes and she made it.

We went up to Loch Lomond for a week for our honeymoon. The train journey was overnight and we did not have a sleeper. We had our first night of marriage stuck on a train! That was a mistake. These days you just wouldn't do that. You would just go to a hotel automatically.

Accommodation

We came down to Hampshire and I was not really looking forward to it. At that time, Odiham did not have very many married quarters so we had to go into hirings, which people let. It was a bit difficult. In November he went down to Odiham and I stayed in our first home, in Acton, North London. I had to stay there until he found somewhere for me to move down to.

My family helped us move down. We did not have much furniture. We had a nice little rented flat in London although it was right up the top of those tall Victorian houses, but it was a nice flat. Then we went there. Men don't see all the things you would see in a place. Alex thought that it would be good, not too far, and he had a put-put to go to work because we did not have a car.

I don't think it was a place I would have chosen. It was a farmhouse in Hook, Hook House Farm. It was a really old farmhouse. It was quite a way to Odiham but if you wanted to go shopping you could go up to Hook village.

The owners played at farming. They never had anything. The pigs were always getting out. They had a huge bull. The husband used to take it up the road and walk it along the main road, like a dog. It was a busy road, that Hook Road. I can see it now because there was sort of a long path, driveway, to the farm and it sort of went up a bit and there was the road and you could see him with his great big bull.

The wife was horrible, and the son was a lazy so-and-so. He was supposed to help them on the farm but he never used to get up in the morning. The wife was a thrifty woman, in as much as she used to like the old cash. There were three or four of us in the house. We had a living room, a bedroom above and we shared a kitchen, an old, old kitchen. Never go out there at night! This was because you used to have these slugs walking across it! They were horrible, big, yellow ones and I hate slugs.

Several other people also lived in that farmhouse. We shared a bathroom. There was hardly any water. It was freezing in there. The owners lived in half of the house. I used to buy eggs from the wife. They had chickens and a horrible dog, a big Alsatian that was always tied up and it barked like hell when you walked by. God knows what it would have been like if it had been let go. I dread to think.

I don't know how the air force passed it as living accommodation. I think before we went there other RAF people had lived there. We had the bedroom upstairs and it was a nice sized room. There were three mattresses on the bed, each about an inch and a half thick. God knows where she got the mattresses from. They were ever so thin. The floor sloped down, too! The driveway was all mud in the winter and when it rained it was all great puddles. It was not tarmacked. We had a bit of garden and we could hang out our washing if we wanted. The back was not so bad. The wife let out the caravans and it was all service people. She rented out so many rooms and the caravans if they were desperate.

You manage, don't you? You have to. You couldn't say no. It was not like today when people won't put up with these things. There was no other accommodation. You had to wait until something came up. I think Alex went wherever you go to find out about accommodation at the RAF and told them it was not a very nice place. They said they were sorry but, 'You have to wait for people to let out their places to you.'

We were there a year. We kept saying we had got to get out of there. The Christmas of 1963 we went to my mum's. That was when we had that dreadful winter. When we came back we could not get in, the snow was so high! The owners never cleared it and they knew we were away. They never made a path up to the front door. So Alex had to go around and ask for a spade so we could get to the front door!

Is this Air Force Life?

The owner had two caravans in the garden. An air force girl with a young baby lived in one. The caravans were not like they are today. That cold winter she was absolutely frozen and she used to have to do her washing outside. We had boilers in those days and we had to cook by Calor gas. We had to have a bath to do our washing in and we had a coal fire.

The owner must have bought all her furniture from an auction, because we had the most horrendous table in one room, which was quite unnecessary. It filled up half the room when you could have done with the space. The poor girl from the caravan used to come around just to get warm and have cups of tea. She had a really young baby. I thought, 'Oh my God, is this air force life?'

We moved there in the November, and Janice was born at Alton Hospital in the April of the following year, 1962. We had her christened at Hook. The next year we went to see another place, but that was sharing with another family and I did not fancy that. Then a house in Upton Grey, a hamlet near Basingstoke, which was ever such a lovely place, came up. We have been back several times over the years to see if it has changed. The hamlet had a duck pond and a manor house. Mind you, there were three buses a week to Basingstoke and that was your lot. Then there was a village shop come post office and it sold everything.

It was a nice place and we moved there in that cold winter of 1963. I know the snow laid on the ground there until March. Next door but one there was a nice couple we got friendly with. On the other side was a nice lady called Mrs Sutton. Her husband used to be a pilot for Dan Air. She had a little child, although she was older when she had her. She often used to ask us if Jack and Janice could play together.

Fun?

We didn't have any fun! It never kind of bothered me that much. I had my children. I was quite happy. We used to go for walks.

The First Car

When we were at Upton Grey our first car was a three-wheeler. This was in 1963. It belonged to a friend. He was getting another one. They had a posher car. We thought it was great for Alex, particularly, to go to work. I didn't drive it. Mind you, it was a bit of a death trap, to be honest! We drove up to me mum's and Janice was only a baby. The fumes used to come up through the floor! It wasn't so bad if you just went a short distance, but if you went a long way … It shouldn't have been on the road! It was called a Bond. There was no motorway up to London then, and we had to go all around Aldershot and Farnborough. It used to take about two hours to get to my mum's. Having a car was a luxury to us though.

Unfortunately, after we were at Upton Grey a year, we got a letter from the owner to say that she wanted the house for her mother. So we had to get out. It was a shame. That is when we had another move. We moved four times in three years.

Isolation

I did not really meet any other military wives. We did not have any transport apart from Alex's put-put, so if we wanted to go anywhere we couldn't because we hadn't got a car for the first few years. I think Odiham was 3 miles or so, maybe more than that, from Hook. Upton Grey was right out in the sticks.

We did not really mix. Because we weren't living on the camp it made a big difference. We never got invited to anything. I met no other military wives, apart from the girl who lived in the caravan and another lady, who was a lovely woman, who I shared a kitchen with at the farmhouse. Her husband was a sergeant, and I think she had come from a well-to-do home. She had a little girl. She was older than me. I was only in my twenties. She was a very nice person.

Then another couple came. They seemed to spend all day in bed! We never used to see them. In the kitchen, we had our designated places where we hung our tea towels up. She always had the same one. She never washed it. She only seemed to have the one! Every time I went in, I would think, 'blimey, it is still there!' I don't think she was much of a housewife.

When we wanted to move out of Hook House Farm, we were told that there wasn't anything and we'd have to wait. For us to move to Upton Grey, we got one of the military police section to help, and loaded everything up. Sitting right on the top was my pram! In catering, everyone was your mate. Alex had said, 'Is there any chance of getting some transport?' Three lads came with it. I probably knew them more than the women as they sometimes came up to the house.

Alton

We went to Alton and got a house there. That was a hiring, the same as the last. Mostly officers and higher ranks got the available accommodation. There was no hope of us getting anywhere on the camp, and that is miles from anywhere, anyway. So we came to Alton and this time I went to see the house! By then I was expecting Carol, born the following year. We could walk to the town.

Young Wives' Club

We were opposite a church, which was nice because I could join the local young wives. They were affiliated to the Mothers' Union. Somebody knew I was new to the area and knocked on my door and asked if I would like to come to one of their meetings. They used to bring all the kids because it was in the afternoon. One of the hardest things I have done is to go somewhere where I didn't know a soul. Having to just walk in was difficult. It was one of the best things I did, though.

It was a bit churchy, and we used to do jumble sales. I enjoyed the young wives' group and I liked Alton. I must admit, I did not want to leave there.

Job Opportunities

I did washing for a very posh woman who lived two or three doors down. Her husband was a steward at the race courses, and she had this little boy and she was 40. I used to have a high washing line then and we had terry nappies. She used to see them all flying in the breeze. She came around and asked if I would do the baby's washing. 'Your washing is always lovely and white,' she said. I said I would do it. She used to put it in a bag by the front door.

I said that the only thing I would like her to buy was the washing powder. Even then washing powder was dear. It would not have been worth my doing it if I had to provide that. I never had to dry it. I just washed it and took it back around to her and put it in her porch. I did hand washing and I had a Burco boiler for the nappies. I did that for eighteen months and then I was expecting Paula so I said I would have to finish doing it. I don't know what she did then after me!

I used to go and clean a jewellers in the evenings after I had Paula. I went twice a week down in the town. It was easy because Alex was home and he could look after the children. The owner was a friend in the young wives'. Her mother and father had their own jewellers and they wanted someone to come and clean in the evening. I only did about an hour and a half. It was fascinating, because he used to repair clocks and watches. Clocks particularly. She used to say, 'I would like you to do the floor in the work room. Don't touch anything on the benches. That is all you need to do.'

They used to have lovely clocks in there. When you went in, they were all ticking away! They sold nice stuff. I know one night I knocked a vase over. I was mopping the floor and I don't know what happened but I must have caught it and I broke it. Oh my God! I didn't know how much it was. Some of it was very expensive. So I put it in the kitchen. I wrote a note to say take it out of my wages, but she was very nice. She said, 'Accidents happen'. That was a nice little job and she used to provide the Flash. I did that job until I moved to Southampton.

Leaving the RAF

We had to decide whether to come out of the forces. His twelve years were up. He would have liked to have gone abroad again. Germany was quite a big posting, and they had stopped sending people there and to Christmas Island, so you didn't really get any postings by then. So we made the decision to come out.

Just joking, I said, 'I wonder if the owner would sell us this house?' Alex went to see her and, much to our surprise, she said, 'Yes, £2,500 as it stands with all the furniture'. That was all secondhand. It was a cottage and really nice. We had two children and no home. 'You can't bargain with me,' she said. 'That is what it is.' She had a lot of property all over Alton.

We thought, 'Oh my God! How are we going to afford it?' At that time to have a council mortgage was a lot cheaper. It was six and three eighths per cent, but it was cheaper than the building society. We paid £10 13s 1d and they took the penny. It always got me, that did. I used to have to go to the council offices to pay it and they always took that penny.

We were there nine years, and then the house got too small. We had two more kids by then. I did like it there. Alex's first job after the army was with the Leonard Cheshire Home and then they were starting to build Southampton Hospital, and so they wanted a catering manager. He applied and he got the job, so we had to move. We have been here in Southampton forty-two years now.

Sadly, since recording this interview, Alex Wylie has passed away. Ever the caterer, and working long past the point when most would have hung up their apron, Alex was working part-time at a respite care home and at a local pub almost to the last. Ill health came swiftly, but did not stop him going to his beloved Weston Shore, in Southampton, to watch the ships in the Solent. Sincere condolences are sent to Kay and all the family.

❧ ANTHEA FILLINGHAM ❧

Anthea paints a vivid portrait of life as an army spouse in the 1960s, when she was a very young wife, trying to take in her stride what military life was to throw at her:

Mark and I were married in 1962. I was 17 at the time.

We had a very disturbed six months to begin with, because Mark was still doing his civilian engineering attachment with Roots Group. We lived in lots of different places for six months and then we had six weeks in a caravan for a course that he did in Arborfield. He was in REME, and Arborfield is their HQ. Then we went up to Edinburgh for three months because Mark was attached to the 4th Royal Tank Regiment. We were very fortunate as lots of Mark's friends in REME were attached to rather snooty regiments and they were made to feel very much outsiders. The 4th Tanks were lovely and made us feel very welcome. We really felt one of them. It is quite a family feeling when you are part of a regiment. That was nice.

Aden

Sometime during that first year of marriage we learnt that Mark was going to be sent abroad after only eleven months of marriage – one year unaccompanied, to Aden. I was devastated. I had no idea it was possible. If I had married a naval officer, I would have understood that that might have been on the cards, but it had not occurred to me that it was possible. I was devastated. I am ashamed to say that I gave Mark a very hard time about it.

I was 18. It was hard. However, the Lord was very kind to us. During that year we were apart we were able to get together three times. Mark went out in August, so that was one month before our first anniversary, but at Christmas he was allowed to fly home for two weeks' leave. An RAF sergeant, who was stationed out in Aden, organised a flight for a whole lot of them to come back. So that was brilliant.

Then, in the spring, Mark was sent on a course to the UK, learning how to repair aircraft. REME had never done that before, but they were about to go out to Malaya and there were going to be Beavers – very old and small aircraft – and we had a very small air strip out there. Although the course was only one week, because the flights did not fit in perfectly he was actually in the UK for two weeks, so we got together again then.

Finally, out in Aden at the same time as the 4th Tanks, there was another outfit, I have no idea quite what, but Mark got to know another REME officer. He was accompanied and had a quarter. Although he barely knew Mark, he kindly invited Mark and I to go and stay in his quarter with his wife and family. So Mark spoke to his CO and asked if it would be possible. His CO said it would, provided that I only stayed for one month. So, these almost-strangers welcomed us into their home. They had two small children and they had us to stay for a month. Mark was able to live in the house with me, and it was absolutely wonderful. We are still in touch with them now.

In fact, that one year in Aden turned into fourteen months as the flights were delayed and there were lots of hold-ups. They sent them in three different blocks from Aden to Malaya, which was the next destination the 4th Tanks were going on to. They had to go in batches. It worked out that Mark was actually away for fourteen months, despite the fact that we had those three times together. It was wonderfully broken into about four-month patches of being apart, so it wasn't too bad.

Malaya

We then went to Malaya. There was no quarter available to us and we lived in a hiring. It was run by local people and there was one New Zealand couple living opposite us. By this time, I was all of 19.

It was a little bit scary, in a way. The garden had a high fence and a padlocked gate, the criss-cross ones you had on shops, the concertina type. All the windows had bars on them. It was quite scary to feel that I had been dumped down into the middle of nowhere with only one other white couple anywhere near. She was very sweet, the New Zealand lady. I got to know her quite well.

We were in Serembang. Personally, I love England and hated being abroad. Most of Malaya was really thick jungle. It didn't appeal to me in the least. There were lots of leeches and snakes – I couldn't see the attraction of the jungle at all. Serembang was the largest town and it was very smelly. There were large open sewers and it did have quite a pong to it.

I can remember when I first went into the shops I thought they were all speaking Malay or something, but in fact it was English with a very strong accent. It took quite a while to get attuned to the fact that the people were speaking English. I found it quite scary to start with, shopping in the market. You could get good value there. It was quite a good idea to go the market and get local fruit and vegetables. We actually had a papaya tree in the garden, though, which was nice.

The one highlight was the Sungei Ugong Club that was a sort of country club. It had an outdoor swimming pool and all around it were tables and umbrellas; that was really lovely. I think that was one of the few things that kept me sane. Our favourite thing was to go there in the evening and have a lime juice, freshly squeezed, nearly a pint because you lost a lot of fluid in that heat, and a steak sandwich, that was just delicious.

It was very, very hot weather and very humid. Now I am always interested when the Formula One crowd go to Malaysia and they talk about it being the hottest of all of the Grand Prix. The heat really was very draining. If you did not mind going past a chap with a rifle and a turban, going into the bank was one of the few places that had air conditioning. We were there for two years, and I can remember when we came back to the UK, after about six weeks I suddenly thought, 'Gosh, I feel so different,' and I realised how draining that heat had been.

It was so humid that Mark had to come back every day at lunchtime to change out of his damp clothes into a fresh set. He also worked quite a long day. In the old days, so I gather, if you were working in a hot country, you would start early in the morning and work until lunchtime and then you would have the afternoon off. Actually, they started early, I think it was seven in the morning, and he came home for lunch but then went back again and didn't get home again until about five in the evening. It was quite a long day in the heat.

There was a lot of social life as the 4th Tanks were so friendly, and it was nice to get to know people and make friends. When you are abroad it is so important, your little clique of British people. It was nice to get to know them. It was quite an exhausting regime, really, and I think we both got very, very tired.

Vulnerable

The Malays we liked very much, but they were almost in a minority. There were masses of Chinese; very clean and very industrious and did very well in business. There were a lot of Indians. We had an Indian gardener.

One of the really scary things, when we were there, was that we were burgled. We came home one night to find that somebody had forced open the guard across the front door. The garden gates were open. We drove up thinking, 'Oi, what's going on?' The grill across the front door was open. The front door had been kicked in. Mark picked up the chain and padlock and just sort of swirled it around in a circle – that was all he could think of as a weapon to defend himself. He walked around the house and we clearly had disturbed them. I think they were there when we arrived, but they had managed to scarper, which I was very relieved about.

I felt physically sick for about forty-eight hours, and that was really upsetting. We were so fortunate to have got to know some Australian missionaries in the town. They very sweetly let me go to their house for a few days, while Mark was out at work. I just did not like being in the house on my own. The really scary thing was that, somehow, we discovered that word got out that probably our Indian gardener was involved, but the police were not prepared to do anything about it. This made us feel as if we were not protected. Apart from the army and the MPs, who have limited powers, it was not as if we were in a camp with barbed wire around it, you did feel quite vulnerable.

We had had an *armah* [housekeeper] originally, as everyone had one, and then I had decided that as there were only two of us and, although they weren't expensive, it was money we could save towards kitting up a house when we went back to the UK, so I did without one. After the burglary, we were advised to have an *armah* in the house. We then understood that, a) the locals rather resent you being in their country and not giving employment to a local person, and b) it was a security thing: if you have an *armah* living in, you are much less likely to get burgled.

From time to time, Mark had to go away for two to three weeks to Borneo and other parts of Malaya, where some of his men were deployed. Again, the Lord took great care of me by providing some old friends who were posted to Terandak Camp, and so whenever Mark had to go away I would go and stay with them. I think there was one occasion when he had to go to a dinner and he was out most of the night. I remember I was too scared to go to sleep and just stayed up all night reading till he came in.

I was rather pleased the other day, I won't say who, but I was talking to another army wife. Funnily enough, she was actually an army officer herself. She said she is still very creepy when her husband is away. I felt rather encouraged to know I wasn't the only one!

Well, there I was, aged 19 in Malaya, with very little experience of being an army wife. Mark had fifty men in his LAD – this is a REME expression. It is a workshop that supports the regiment and is there to repair all the trucks and aircraft. Mark was a captain in charge of a LAD. He had fifty soldiers, most of whom had wives, and I was supposed to go and visit them and ask them all if they were all right. I don't know what I was supposed to do if they said they weren't! They were mostly old enough to be my mother, so it was a bit farcical, but that was what was expected of me.

Creepy Crawlies!

I hated any form of creepy crawly or wildlife, and we had plenty of those. There were little lizards that ran up the walls and along the ceilings. They had little sucker feet. We also had a rat that made a regular little trip each evening from one end of the bungalow, past the sitting room, which was open plan, to the other end. With open drains, there was no way we could stop this happening. He appeared regularly each evening as we were sitting there. We were given some boards with thick black glue on it to try to catch him. We did catch one mouse under our bed this way. For ages we caught nothing, so we stopped checking and then began to notice an awful smell in our bedroom. We finally thought to look under the bed and found a rotting mouse!

Another horror for me were tree frogs. They jump up quite high and have sucker feet. They stick onto things. One of them landed on my hand once and I nearly became hysterical until it jumped off again! We had the sort of drains that were just gullies so there was no way of stopping things coming into the house. They were open, these gullies, and anything the size of a tree frog or a rat could easily get into the house.

The other thing I was worried about was snakes. Everyone said, 'Oh, don't worry about snakes. You will spend two years and you'll never see a single snake.' Within a week we discovered a cobra in our garden! I was really worried that if we didn't kill it, we would never know where it was. I suppose that there were plenty more, but that one really bugged me. So I persuaded Mark to get a garden hoe and he very skillfully killed it. With just one blow he caught it behind its head and just managed to stamp on the hoe strongly enough to kill it. We discovered afterwards that the cobra could easily have spat in his eyes and blinded him. They are really vicious creatures.

You can imagine this, just one week into this two year posting in Malaya, that episode was really reassuring! We wrote to London Zoo, asking for advice, thinking that they might be able to tell us how to discourage them from coming into the garden. All they did was write back with great enthusiasm telling us, 'Oh, if you ever see another one, do catch it and send it to us'. They gave us careful details of what size the box should be! That was not quite what we had in mind!

Home Again

After Malaya, we were posted to beautiful Woolwich. Here, our first child was born. However, because there was no quarter available we were again living in a hiring. Two weeks after Paul was born we had to move to another house as the owners suddenly wanted their house back. My GP was absolutely furious. He said that he liked his mums to have a nice stable start to motherhood!

Canada

When Paul was about 18 months old, Mark had an exchange posting to Canada and we lived in the truly beautiful city of Ottawa.

We got to know a Canadian military couple while they were living in the UK and they were brilliant in helping us to find a house. It was left to us to find a house to rent, and it was almost impossible to get one with furniture, so they advised us to rent an unfurnished one and buy repossessed furniture, so we bought a fairly motley lot of cheap furniture.

We had been met by a Canadian officer on our arrival, and he took us to a little apartment for a week or two while we were looking for accommodation. It was incredible that the army effectively just picked us up, dumped us down and said just get on with it. Had we not known these friends, we would not have known where to begin. They were wonderful. They got us the newspaper and told us to 'look for the ads in that', 'do this', 'do that', I think they helped us get a car, too. When you are in a new country, let alone a new place, you just don't know the form, do you?

We had cardboard boxes as bedside tables. We slept on a mattress, Paul had a camping bed. We did have proper furniture in the living room, and the kitchen was well equipped. That was lovely. We had a really big American fridge and that was unheard of in the UK. We enjoyed owning an enormous American car – it was almost as long as our present house! That was fun.

Wednesday afternoons, Mark had off, for either skiing or sailing. We both enjoyed sailing. There was a lake where we sailed. The army provided boats, but not accommodation.

It was a most peculiar climate in Ottawa because it was snow for at least four months of the year, and when I say snow, I mean really deep snow. If he went off the pavement, Paul would disappear out of sight.

It was fun dressing Paul. They had wonderful clothes. The Canadians were far more advanced than we were at the time. He had a wonderful all-in-one snow suit that kept him snug and warm, but it took forever getting this little toddler into it. I will never forget one day finally getting everything in and gloves on – you know what it is like getting gloves on a tiny tot's hands – and he said, 'Mummy, I want a wee!' We had to take it all off!

We took our dog with us. Mark had a girlfriend who was an air hostess, and she very sweetly arranged for our dog to go with her as cargo on a commercial flight. What was absolutely awful, and was probably one of our worst moments, was when we went to meet her at the airport and she did not come in on the flight. In those days, not many, if any, flights were direct to Ottawa. We went to meet her, all excited, but she wasn't on the plane. Nobody knew why, or where she was.

She was quite a nervous dog. She had been put in a crate hours and hours earlier with limited amounts of water and food, and that was just horrible. We subsequently learnt that the crate was too big to go on the particular flight that we had booked her on, so they put her on the next one. She arrived about two hours later. It was a very long two hours.

I used to walk the dog and Paul. That was really funny. Canadians just did not walk, particularly in the winter. Some people driving would almost drive into the kerb because they could not believe that there was this mad woman walking a dog and a toddler! Why not use wheels?!

❧ SUE PIPER ☙

Sue's engineer husband, Michael, was a commander in the Royal Navy. They married in 1967 and had three children. He left the Royal Navy in 1989 and was awarded the OBE. Sue was a midwife, but gave up practice soon after having her children. Now a grandmother to five and a step-grandmother to two, Sue is still very active in the community, as she works as a Citizen's Advice volunteer adviser. She also leads Sunday Suppers every week – an outreach to the homeless and vulnerable.

1960s

Our first quarter after marriage was a bedsit, as there were no available quarters in the Bath area. We lasted there for six months until we were able to move into the house, comprising two attached cottages, about 300 years old, owned by the local squire, which Michael bought at an auction in the pub for £1,325!

It had no water, with outside loos – one near the house, the other two at the bottom of the garden! We took out a small mortgage (it seemed a lot to us in those days) and revamped the place. We kept this for twenty-five years and lived in it about five times, when Michael was working locally or when he was at sea. When we were posted to other places, we found that God looked after us and we were always able to let it for a low rent, often to missionaries or adult students at the uni. We never had to use an agent.

Burst Pipes

On one of Michael's trips away, the children and myself came home to find the pipes had frozen and there was no water coming out of the taps. I was pretty helpless, but managed to contact Michael by phone. He advised me to warm up the loft with a blow heater, which then revealed numerous leaks so there was water everywhere! Andy, aged about 8, was brilliant and put bags on doors to catch the water! Michael then told me to shut off the water and get in a plumber!

4

THE END OF THE TWENTIETH CENTURY

Three months is not so bad. By the time you adjust to them going, they're on the way back.
Lorraine Matthews, navy wife.

The last thirty years of the twentieth century were marked with more discord, as the Falklands Conflict, war in the Balkans and the Gulf Wars all kept the military busy – and away from home. This time, though, technology played its part as never before, with often in-depth coverage of world events. For the women married to servicemen, this was a mixed blessing, bringing, as it did, better communication with their men, but also the real possibility of learning of tragic events by switching on the evening news.

❧ DR JEAN POWELL ❧

By the 1970s, Jean was now a health visitor and moving along in her career:

Our House
So, I was a bright, shiny, new health visitor with high ideals. Up north it was a very gregarious family situation with my grandma and granddad and lots of aunties and uncles. Twenty-odd cousins all lived in a terraced street. It was very different being in a nuclear family down in Hampshire and seeing people on their own, nobody caring. My dad died and we

were in a three-bedroomed property and I said that we needed a bigger property so mum and Ray's parents could live with us. We went for a four-bedroomed property.

This was in the early 1970s. People were gazumping then. We had looked at three properties and been gazumped on all of them. Then the vicar mentioned that this house was for sale. I did not know where he meant first of all. I came down the lane and thought, does anyone really live down here? I came and looked and it was in a bit of a mess, really, because the lad who lived here, he and his wife had two little ones at that stage, had started projects in every room and never completed any of them. We had 100 broken window panes in the whole property. No room was comfortable, and the whole place was painted in white gloss throughout – even the walls. The dining room was like an operating theatre!

There was a lot to do, and we were both working full-time then. We prayed about it. God had led us here, so here we came. My mum moved in with us. She came in and said 'Not sure about this!' She went upstairs, and on the landing she looked one way and then she looked the other way, and she said, 'Oh, it's a great wasty house, this one!'

I said, 'It will be all right when we get settled, Mum.'

Then, Ray's dad died and his mum came to live with us for her terminal care. The house has done the job and we have had teenagers living with us and all sorts of things.

❧ PHYLLIS HOLROYD ☙

For Phyllis, political events in the Mediterranean were reflected in post home:

Correspondence
One thing that struck me as strange was that my husband was very good at corresponding. He used to write every day. I didn't get them every day, though. It depended on when they were picked up. I used to get them in a batch.

One day, I got this letter and it was obvious that he had been called away. The thing is, I knew what had happened because I had heard it on the radio. He was on the *Ark* [HMS *Ark Royal*]. A Russian ship that was shadowing them hit them. It was more damaged than the *Ark*. I had

heard this on the radio, so it was really strange to have this time shift.
I knew what had happened. They were all right.

[A dip into the Hansard record of the Commons sitting for 11 November
1970 reveals that Lord Balneil, the Secretary of State for Defence, was
asked for a statement about this collision. In his statement, he said that
the aircraft carrier had been taking part in a night flying exercise with
the Royal Air Force in open waters between Malta and Crete. As she was
launching her first aircraft, a Soviet Kotlin-class destroyer set a collision
course and, despite avoiding action by the *Ark Royal*, the Soviet ship's port
quarter hit the carrier's port bow. Two of the Soviet craft's company died
in the incident, which, as Phyllis says, was reported in England, but no one
was hurt from the *Ark Royal*.]

❧ ANTHEA FILLINGHAM ☙

Anthea was in Canada at the beginning of the 1970s and about to have a
new addition to the family:

Nessa

Vanessa, our daughter, known as Nessa, was born in April 1970. She was
born with a harelip and a cleft palate. We were advised to return to the
UK because she needed to have surgery at 3 months old and it was
deemed better to have it all done in the UK rather than have some done
in Canada and some in the UK. The army was very good in that they
posted Mark straight back to Woolwich, close to Great Ormond Street,
which was perfect. She couldn't have been in better hands.

Unfortunately, the hospital she was born at in Canada told me
they had had no experience of harelips and, considering one in 1,000
babies are born with a harelip, it seemed most peculiar. They were
useless about giving me advice about feeding her. Poor little mite, she
just screamed the whole time, as she was either hungry or had terrible wind. Of course, with a hole through the roof of her mouth to
her nose, milk went up her nose and she choked and spluttered. It
was awful.

With a very unhappy baby and a toddler, I began packing all our
belongings into an MFO box. In those days you didn't have removal
men. You were issued with boxes made of thin ply and they were prob-

ably about 3ft by 4ft by 3ft and you just had to put all your belongings into them. The difficulty was, you had to pack it really carefully and you had to get the top of the box absolutely tight, because if you had any gaps and they were thrown by some lovely soldier onto the ground out of a Bedford 3-tonner, they had to be able to bounce with all your crockery and ornaments and precious belongings inside. I was putting all our belongings into those, so that was quite a performance with a screaming baby and a little toddler. Fortunately, my mother very sweetly came out and helped me for a couple of weeks.

As soon as we got back to Great Ormond Street they gave me a specially shaped spoon and I spooned milk into Vanessa. It made a world of difference.

Married Quarter

We had our first married quarter after eight years of married life! It was in Aldershot. Three years later, Mark retired.

I didn't enjoy being an army wife. I was thrilled when Mark left, although funnily enough he went to work for an organisation that is involved with military people and, still to this day, I am involved with the military and have a real heart for it. But how people survived military life if they don't believe God's in control of their lives, I just don't know. I could not have begun to cope with it. I found it very difficult really. The dangers, the uncertainty of where you were going to go next, all that sort of thing. Both Aden and Malaya were danger zones, too. The Lord did take great care of both Mark and the regiment. One of their vehicles was blown up by a bomb in Aden as it was driven down a wadi [river] track. Again, in Malaya there was live firing but wonderfully they were all kept safe.

Had we stayed in longer, our children were 6 and 3 when Mark retired, we would have had the issue of boarding school and I think that is really hard. We were fortunate to be spared all of that.

❧ SUE PIPER ☙

In the 1970s, Sue's husband, Michael, was busy travelling the world with the Royal Navy. Sue and the growing family found ways to follow:

Fiddling …

When Michael was on HMS *Penelope*, the boys (approximately 3 and 18 months) and I managed to get an indulgence flight to Gibraltar. We stayed in a friend's flat while they were away. On the Sunday, another engineering friend, whose ship was also docked in Gibraltar, came to lunch. We put the boys in the bedroom for a rest, and later found that Andrew, who loved fiddling, had locked them in. What to do? The flat was high up with a well on the side of their bedroom and we had no idea where there were any tools, but somehow the men managed to take the door handle off and rescue the boys!

£9 a Head

We had a few happy days together, and then had to bid farewell to Michael. On our flight back we were diverted to Glasgow, because of fog at Brize Norton. We landed in the middle of the night in our noisy plane, were taken to a hotel, where the boys and I had about two hours sleep before having to return to the airport in the early hours. It was the one occasion where it was every man/woman for himself, and no one helped me with my baggage, pushchair and two little boys! Michael was furious that the navy did not help, but then the rules of indulgence flights were that you came if there was room and so had to cope! At least the fare was only £9 a head, so one *did* cope!

Camel Riding

In 1973, I managed to get another indulgence trip to Gibraltar, leaving the boys behind, and this time was allowed to travel in the ship with Michael to Morocco, where I tried to ride a camel – uncomfortable, smelly and probably had fleas!

We stayed with a couple, both doctors, working at the Mission Hospital there and visited the man's sister, Patricia St Jean, who has written many children's books, including *Treasures of the Snow* – this has since been made into a film.

A friend, who was the Squadron MEO, kindly did Michael's job on board for him, releasing him to have time with me.

Travels Across America – 1978

On another occasion, the boys (now 8½ and 10) and I, leaving Ruth (aged 4) behind with family and friends, managed to get another indulgence flight out to the States. It was touch and go, as when our missionary friends, who were living with us at the time, took us to Brize Norton, I was told there were only two places and both boys had to have a seat. What to do? Well, we prayed, and lo and behold after a short time, the authorities said they had found another seat! So we all flew to Washington.

Through the Officers Christian Fellowship of America, we were told we would be collected by a family and given a bed for a couple of nights. However, when we arrived at the airport, there was no sign of anyone! I had no contact numbers, so asked at the desk if there had been any messages left for me. None had, so we waited. Eventually a man arrived, who turned out to be our host – he had had a 'flat' on the way to the airport, and with no mobile phones in those days, was unable to contact the airport!

The boys and I then travelled to Charleston, West Virginia, to stay with an American friend. We spent two very hot days with her. She was from Puerto Rico and did not suffer in the heat. Eventually, she produced a fan and we slept a little better.

We then took several Greyhound buses across the States to Seattle. It took three days and nights, and sometimes we had to change buses in the middle of the night. We ate burgers and hot dogs for every meal until I was sick of them, but not the boys, who so enjoyed them!

We then took a coach across to Vancouver, where we got a taxi to yet another house, owned by friends of people we did not know and never met! After a short time, there was a ring at the door and there was the taxi man with my camera, which I must have left on the seat – how honest of him! The brother of the owners of the house came to visit and insisted on taking us on his yacht to meet HMS *Birmingham*, which was arriving that day. Much to our embarrassment, he dipped his ensign at the ship and was upset that the ship did not return the sign!

He then asked a rating to get Michael, who was deep down in the engine room. Again, quite awkward for Michael, but he came! (You don't do things like that!) However, the boys and I had a great holiday. We were taken on board and sailed to Vancouver Island – the boys read books and played and weren't at all interested in the ship! There, Michael was given leave to stay with us at yet another unknown person's house. We also had use of their car.

Another English friend did come and stay with us, too. She kindly babysat while Michael and I went to a party on the ship. When we came back, we found she had trimmed the boys' hair and put the hair down the garbage disposal unit and totally gummed up the works. Happily, Michael managed to take it apart and mend it! We again did not meet the owners, who were away. On that occasion, Michael was away for six months, so it was great to see him in the middle of his deployment.

❧ LORRAINE MATTHEWS ☙

Lorraine is the long-suffering wife of Royal Navy radar operator, and later naval regulator, Eon Matthews. In his twenty-four years in the service of his country he went to most parts of the world and found himself in several hotspots. He served on two HMS *Ark Royals*, spent time serving with Prince Andrew, and was most embarrassed by the advent of ladies on board ships! Lorraine, ever the dutiful wife, made her own life, bringing up their children and enjoying her own career. For Lorraine and Eon separation started almost immediately:

Nine Months!

I met Eon at a mutual friend's 18th birthday party. He asked me to dance and then went away for nine months!

We wrote a few letters, and then he just turned up on my doorstep nine months later. I looked at this young lad and thought, 'I should know you from somewhere'! We started going out. I think he told me he was in the Royal Navy when we had that dance. Then he asked me for my address so he could write to me. He wrote from the *Ark Royal*, which he was just joining.

He went off, and I went out with a couple of people in the meantime. I had a couple of pen pals in the Merchant Navy as well. I used to work in a fish and chip shop and they used to come in there. I wrote to them, but that is all it ever was with them.

Getting Married

Eon and I got married in 1980. He asked me to marry him, and it took me six months to say, 'yes'. I had to think about it. My mum said, 'You are not just marrying the man, you're marrying the navy. He will be away for long lengths of time and you have to be able to cope with that.' I had to think about that. But, at the end of the day, it is one of those things. If you love somebody you have to think if you can put up with it. Can you cope with it?

I think we were quite lucky. We didn't have that long a separation – five or six months was the longest. Most trips were three months, so that was not too bad. When his ship hit a rock and had to come home, he had only been away for five months. That was out in the Gulf on HMS *Glamorgan* in 1981. They hit an uncharted rock, now called Glamorgan Rock. [The ship had been in an area of water that had not been charted for over 100 years. HMS *Glamorgan* hit a coral reef and had to be towed off by HMS *Ambuscade*.]

Three months is not so bad. By the time you adjust to them being gone, they're on the way back. I feel quite lucky they didn't go for longer.

My Life

It's my life, and it's what I chose. I just get on with it. I think if I hadn't married someone in the military I would probably have had a more boring life. Although you have separation, it does make it more exciting. In our case, it kept our marriage fresher. In all marriages, no matter how hard you try, you end up taking each other for granted because after you have been together for so many years, you just do. But, when they go away and then they come back, it is all sort of fresh. You delay the taking for granted, I think. You start afresh when they come home and that is good fun in itself.

We made the decision to have kids early. I was moving down to Portsmouth from Seaford and was leaving my job. It was either get married and find another job or get married and start a family. So we had our son, Carl, soon after we married and then a daughter, Kerry, who was a Falklands baby, born nine months after Eon came home from the conflict.

Carl was nearly school age when we decided to move back to Seaford. I was not really keen on the young kids down in Portsmouth. You go to the local swimming pool, for instance, and they use language I was not sure I wanted a 5-year-old to use.

Everyday Life

For Royal Navy wife Lorraine, life on a married patch was never dull:

Living on a naval estate you have these people who come around and cut the grass. I lived on a council estate before I got married, when I was a child. We had council grass cutters who came and then went.

On a naval estate, they don't always go … The van stays the night sometimes! I remember thinking that was quite amusing.

Family Support

We ended up moving to the same road that my mum and dad live in. My sister married Eon's brother and they live down the street. When I went to join Eon in Australia, when he was on the *Ark Royal*, I left the kids behind. One went up to my mum's, four houses along, and the other went down the road to my sister, Suzanne. After a week, they swapped over. You can imagine the kids walking down the road with their suitcases in hand, crossing halfway!

My parents were there, and it is hard to say but the children didn't miss Eon. They had enough people around. As they got older, they thought, 'Dad's coming home and that means he's not going to let us do this or that!' Even the dog barked at him at first when he came home!

Before I got married I was a receptionist/secretary. The first job I got, when Carl started school and Kerry was at playschool, was in Woolworth's, just part-time. I was only there a year when the firm I had worked at before I got married came and asked if I would go back. I went back as a secretary. I still actually work for the same firm, an accountants. About five years ago, they decided they needed a financial planning section, so they started up a separate company and asked if I would be an administrator for the financial adviser, so I'm his administrator-cum-PA.

When the kids were young, the company was really good. If I got a call from the school they said, 'Go home. Sort it'. I worked five mornings a week, so I would see them off to school and be there when they came back. Now I do three whole days as they are based in Uckfield now. Because it was so convenient, I could walk down there from my house as well.

When I could think about changing jobs, I'd built up too many perks – extra holiday and the hours I would like to work, within reason. I might have left if they hadn't brought out the financial planning part. I was probably getting a bit bored, but this is a whole new challenge. The firm were really good with Eon's job, accommodating, and that is another reason to stay. It was not always easy to find an employer that is as accommodating.

The Falklands Conflict

Eon had gone away on exercise on HMS *Glamorgan* and so he never actually came home before he went to the Falklands, so we didn't have the goodbye bit.

I still went on holiday. We had booked a holiday before he went, on the Thames with friends. At the time, he was still on the way to the Falklands, so we didn't know what they were going to or what it was going to be like. There were other people involved, so I went off for the holiday for a week.

I just put the conflict at the back of my mind and got on with my life. You can't do anything about it. The worst part was watching the news. You were compelled to watch it, but at the time, it was hard because they were releasing things before the next of kin were notified. That was the worst thing, especially as I lived down at Portsmouth on a naval estate, and my friends' husbands were on some of the ships that were hit.

By the time Eon's ship, HMS *Glamorgan*, was hit, the Ministry of Defence had got it right, and said that all next of kin had been notified before they released the information. It was my birthday. The strangest thing was that when they said the next of kin had been notified I thought, 'Phew! I haven't heard anything, nobody's come to my door.' Then Eon's aunt and his mum kept phoning.

'You haven't heard anything?'

'No, I haven't heard anything.'

Eon didn't expect me to be home in Portsmouth on my own, as he thought I would be with my family as it was my birthday. I can't remember why I stayed there now, but for some reason I did.

Homecoming

I was lining the waterside when *Glamorgan* came home. They got back on 10 July 1982. Looking back, I did not really think a lot. It was more emotion. I could see them coming back and there were lots of people on the jetty. You could see the damage to the ship. A hole. It was a shock. Damage to a ship is not what you normally see. The ship's company was lining the deck, but I couldn't see Eon. He was working.

Eon came off straight away, though, and came home. He had some leave. They had sent some of the crew home beforehand, so when the ship got in they went back on board and everybody who came home got leave.

I was just so happy to have him back. It was very emotional.

We went onto *Glamorgan* later to watch HMS *Antrim* when she came home. *Glamorgan* came home ahead of her because she was damaged. I remember that Eon was on duty that day and I took our son Carl to see the ship arrive.

Coping

Eon came back home to find that his mum was dying from cancer. They found out while he was away but, as much as I wanted to tell him, I didn't think it was right to do so while he was away. He had that to cope with as well as the effects of the war. He did change. He grew up, in effect. He was young when he went and he came back more grown up. He wasn't quite so happy-go-lucky. He was more serious, sombre.

It has been in later years that he has thought about it more. He is lucky that he has Kev, an old school friend who was also in the Royal Navy and who was in the Falklands. He is 4 miles away and they talk to each other. A lot of people don't talk about their experiences because they are surrounded by people who would not know what they were going on about. Kev and Eon just talk about it. That helps them a great deal.

You just have to cope, don't you? We call Eon a 'grumpy old git' sometimes in the family! He has certain things that trigger reactions. Military films, like *Pearl Harbour*, bring it all back and he ends up crying. I let him get on with it. I treat him as he treats me if I cry over something soppy! He has never been a great one for talking about his feelings.

Being Alone

I didn't think too much of it when Eon went to Bosnia. They were in warships, they weren't actually on land. They weren't really close to the fighting and none of the ships really suffered any damage or involvement in that conflict. It wasn't really too bad.

Then he was asked if he would go to Hong Kong – leave a war zone and go to Hong Kong. The only snag was that it was married unaccompanied for eighteen months. When I first heard about it, I was a bit upset, but when he explained it, it did make sense. He was out in Bosnia, which was a war zone. He was away anyway, so why not be away in Hong Kong rather than there. It was something he wanted to do. When you love someone, you realise that life can be pretty short and you have to let them do things they want to do.

Even if it had been married accompanied, I don't know if I would have been able to go. Our son was doing his GCSEs so I couldn't uproot him. I'm not sure I could have left him, either.

During the eighteen months, Eon came home twice and I went out to see him. I had never been to Hong Kong before. It was different. It was just before the handover and he took leave while I was there. He took me out on one of the fast patrol boats – that was FAST! Exciting!

My hair was so knotty afterwards I couldn't get a brush or a comb through it!

Falklands 30th Anniversary

In 2012 it was the 30th anniversary of the Falklands Conflict. They said that wives and families could go down to the Falklands at the same cost as veterans, a couple of hundred pounds, from Brize Norton.

I had no wish to go and see the islands particularly. It didn't matter to me that Eon had fought for them – it was something he had to do at the time. I went down for Eon. He wanted me to go and see what they were like. He went before, and unveiled the *Glamorgan* memorial there.

The main reason I'm glad about going down is that I got to understand the experiences of the islanders and how they felt about them. It was really nice that, even now, after thirty years, they are still so grateful. They cannot do enough for the veterans and their families. They come and they take you out. They won't take any money for fuel. They pick you up if you can't get to the lodge. They put the veterans up and won't take any money. The most the veterans can do is take them out for a meal. It's just so nice how grateful they are.

One of the islanders who was taking us around was locked into the hall in Goose Green. It was interesting to hear his story. He still, to this day, hates the Argentinians. They allow them on to the island now and they leave little badges and things. If he finds them he just throws them away.

It was an experience, off-roading around in a Land Rover. Seeing the terrain when I was up there I was thinking of the soldiers. It was a wonder that they didn't have more killed because it is so open. There was nowhere for them to hide.

ALIS GLENCROSS

When the Falklands Conflict blew up in 1982, it is easy to forget that not all service personnel were called to the front line. Without the men and women left behind to man essential services and provide the back-up and support to those at the front, there would have been no victory. One such serviceman, Peter Glencross, spent his war at the Royal Naval Air Station in Yeovilton, Somerset. His wife, Alis, was by his side:

The Falklands Conflict

We were living in married quarters in Yeovil and had been there for nine months. My husband was Peter John Glencross and he had been drafted to Yeovilton from HMS *Glasgow* flight. We had one daughter, who turned 2 years of age in the April.

I remember Pete was very busy at work and I believe much of this was making sure helos [helicopters] were serviceable and getting spares. I was seven months pregnant and obviously concerned about Pete going south, although he used to say that there was just as much work to do at Yeovilton and he had finished his sea draft. It might have been different if he had only just left the ship. I remember lying awake at night, Pete working, and hearing the planes taking off late into the darkness that he would have been involved in loading.

As the fleet was prepared, more and more of our friends were drafted to ships and the married quarters became a quieter place and certainly men disappeared daily. Pete was one of the few men left, and I remember being in a local shop and two women commented on why he was still home and used my pregnancy as a reason. I went home thinking we might get a white feather! All our neighbours went, including some Pete joined up with.

For me, it was hard, because I found that as the days went by, I no longer shared in the round of coffee mornings etc. The wives would meet and talk about letters that they received but that did not include me. I remember the day the *Atlantic Conveyer* was sunk. The husband of a woman living opposite us was on it and little information was forthcoming. It brought home to the quarters what was really happening. Her husband was fine. For Pete, and those at Yeovilton, it was bad because there were helicopters and so many spares lost, which were very necessary to keep the aircraft going.

Exocet Missile

The first casualties on the ships, and particularly HMS *Sheffield* and HMS *Coventry*, really upset Pete. He lost several good friends, and I remember when their names appeared on TV he found it very hard to listen to, although he had already heard the news at work. His old ship, HMS *Glasgow*, came back with an Exocet missile wedged in her side.

I was a homemaker, as it was difficult to get employment. I am a home economics teacher, and schools did not like employing navy wives in case we up and went. Pay was poor, but living in married quarters was okay. I do think that, although the Falklands was a massive undertaking at the time, we always lived with the terrorist threat that was a bigger everyday impact on our family life.

My son was born at the beginning of June and we stayed in Yeovil until July then moved to Weymouth, when 815 Squadron moved to Portland.

After Pete left the navy in 1994, we moved to Eire where we now have a smallholding, which I run with our youngest daughter, born 1996. Being a service wife makes you different, and certainly you learn a coping mechanism which helps me through every day.

He always felt he should have gone to the Falklands.

Pete got acute myeloid leukaemia in July 2011. The news was broken to him on our 33rd wedding anniversary. He was to have a bone marrow transplant in August 2012, but he relapsed and treatment failed. During the short time he had left, six weeks, his biggest regret was not going south. Although he was at home during that time it did impact on him that he had not been to the Falklands.

My husband served his twenty-two years, and I shared seventeen of them. It is a life so different to Civvy Street and I am now just realising, twenty years on, that the service link is never broken. I would do it all again.

❧ PENNY LEGG ❧
— A MILITARY SPOUSE AS WELL AS AN AUTHOR!

As well as being a writer, I am also a military wife as I married Royal Navy Radio Operator Joe Legg a few months after he came home from serving aboard HMS *Intrepid* in the Falklands Conflict. The weekend we were to have had a party to celebrate our engagement was the weekend Joe was recalled from Easter leave to get his ship ready to go to the South Atlantic. We never did get to celebrate our engagement!

Getting Married
Actually setting a date to tie the knot was difficult. Joe was scheduled to be at sea a lot, so when I would suggest a date, he would say, 'No, we will be away then'. It was late December, and we had been trying to sort it out for months. In the end, I got so annoyed with him, I just snapped, 'Well, when will you be around then?'

'I am free on 8 January, if that is any good,' he replied.

There was no time for Banns to be read in church and so I went to the local registry office and booked the only time slot that was on offer – 10.10 a.m. on Saturday, 8 January 1983. He sailed again on Tuesday, 11 January and was away for several months.

In 2015, we celebrated our 32nd wedding anniversary.

Tasteful

My husband, Joe, was a radio operator (tactical) in 1983. He was drafted to HMS *Andromeda* after his return from the Falklands Conflict and we moved to a married quarter in St Budeaux, on the outskirts of Plymouth.

I loved that quarter. It was a top floor, two-storey, two-bedroom maisonette with far-reaching views of the Plymouth dockyard and beyond. It had a small balcony off the living room, which was great in the summer as you could open the door and sit on the balcony to watch the ship movements. It was our first home together. It was one of the first generation of quarters where the soft furnishings were not covered in large orange flowers. We had some red and burnt orange plain furnishings, and it looked quite tasteful, although now I am describing them, I know they must sound pretty horrible to twenty-first-century ears!

The First Year

We did not see each other very much during our first year of marriage. I took to following the ship about if I could, just so that we might be able to snatch a little time together. We managed thirteen days in total during that first year, and most of those days were not consecutive. I travelled from Plymouth to exotic places like Liverpool, Newcastle and South Shields.

In June, Joe announced that he was off on a six month deployment on HMS *Andromeda*. Halfway through, the ship was to pull into Mombasa and there was an opportunity for wives and family to fly out to meet the ship. We had been married for only a short time. I had been unable to find permanent work in Plymouth as employers did not want to employ someone who could be posted away at the drop of a hat, and so we had no money for exotic foreign holidays. I waved him off, cried a lot, cuddled the kitten we had bought together on one of his rare visits home, and schemed as to how I could see my husband again during the deployment.

The last port of call was to be Gibraltar, which was far easier to afford than a trip to Africa. We decided that I would come out to meet the ship when it came in, prior to sailing for home. I saved and saved. I took every temporary job I could get, and soon got to know Plymouth very well as

I was buzzing about so much. I worked in offices, filing or doing admin; factories, where I built circuit boards for computers, and kitchens where I washed up and cleaned floors. Working and saving kept me occupied, so I had less time to mope because I was missing my husband. I was a busy bee and it paid off as I eventually had the money for the flights and for the accommodation. I had never travelled abroad by myself before and I was bouncing with excitement the nearer it got to seeing Joe.

It was just before Christmas 1983 that I flew off to Gibraltar. I arrived, checked into the little hotel I had booked and happily settled in. The plan was that I arrived on Monday, did the sights of the Rock on Tuesday, Wednesday and Thursday, and then went along to the dockyard to meet Joe on Friday. He had the whole weekend free, so we could be together. Bliss!

The weather was bright and warm and I remember that it was such a contrast to the cold conditions I had left at home. I was full of smiles as I explored St Michael's Cave and met the macaque monkeys. I puffed up the Rock of Gibraltar and took in the sights. I even flew over to Morocco and had a day in Tangiers! It was great. I had seen everything and done everything. Now I was free for whatever Joe wanted to do all weekend and could show him the sights, as I now knew where they were.

Then, on Thursday evening, I was in my hotel bedroom when the telephone rang. It was a friend in Plymouth calling to tell me that there was trouble in Beirut and HMS *Andromeda* was being diverted there and would not be coming into Gibraltar the next day. I was devastated! Beirut was a war zone, so my first thought was for the safety of the crew and, more particularly, for my Joe. The Falklands was not so long ago, and I had worried myself silly while Joe was in that war. How long would they be there and what would their role be? Just how much danger were they sailing into?

I spent a sad evening, and next morning wondered what I should do. My flight was not due to leave Gibraltar until the following Monday. Should I try to go home ahead of time, or wait in Gibraltar? Just as I was thinking this, there was a knock at the bedroom door and there was a welfare officer from the naval base. She had been alerted that I was there by a worried Joe, who had sent a signal from the ship. She came to tell me that the news was not as bad as I had feared. The ship was only to be in the Lebanon for the weekend, when she would be relieved. She was due back to Gibraltar early on Monday morning. I breathed a sigh of relief. Furthermore, the welfare officer went on to tell me that I would be given access to the dockside at the naval base, so that I could see the ship actually coming in alongside. Joe had also been given the day off, so, if we were lucky, we might get to see each other for a short time before my flight home. Super!

I immediately called my friend in Plymouth to tell her the news that the ship was only to be in the trouble spot for the weekend. She had not heard this, so spread the news around the patch. I am sure that there was a collective sigh in Plymouth that morning!

So, I then spent the weekend wandering around the shops, enjoying the novelty of English being spoken and the familiarity of household names on the High Street, but also looking through the windows of the duty-free shops, at the expensive luxuries I could not afford.

Monday morning came and I was up with the lark, dressed in a smart new suit I had bought specially, and was teetering in new high heels along the narrow streets with the burly dockers going off to work at the dockyard. I was not quite 20, had been married for nearly a year and was going to see my husband for the first time in five months. Even better, the sun was shining. Excellent!

As I was waiting on the dockside for the ship to come in, a very smart car swept up beside me and a tall officer in a lot of gold braid alighted and came over to me. Was I Mrs Legg? When I said that I was, he proceeded to apologise for the delay in the ship arriving and for the inconvenience it had caused me. Charmed, I beamed. I had no idea who this man was, but people saluted him, so he must have been someone.

The entire ship's company lined the decks of HMS *Andromeda* when she came in. I scanned the decks in vain for Joe. What I did not know until later was that he was below decks, changing out of his uniform into civvies. As the ship put down its gangway, he was the first off the ship, zipping down it to scoop me up in a huge hug. Our kiss, in front of the interested, entire ship's company, was met with a huge cheer!

My flight was leaving in four hours, so we did not have a lot of time to ourselves. There was time to go back to the hotel for a short while, pack my bag and go to the airport. This time it was he who waved me off!

Eventually, the ship arrived back in the UK, just in time for Christmas. I was on the dockside to welcome him back to Blighty. As we left the dockyard, Joe had his pocket picked and his wallet, containing his all-important Royal Navy identity card, was stolen. That is another story …

The Falklands After the War

We were expecting our first child when Joe heard that he was being drafted to the Falklands, this time to the peacetime base there. He would be away for six months. We were devastated. He would miss the baby being born. We tried changing the draft, asking if he could go earlier than planned, or later, but no. He had to go then. There was no budging the powers that be.

Joe was assured that welfare would keep an eye on me and that he had nothing to worry about. He did worry – we were on the married estate at Houndstone, 4 miles across fields from Yeovil. We did not have a car, there was only one bus an hour and that stopped at six in the evening, and the only way to get to the doctor was by Royal Navy supplied transport at specified times during the week. There was a NAAFI store on site that nobody used because it was poorly stocked and very expensive, so his leaving when I was seven months pregnant was a big thing in our lives.

My grandmother was nearly 70 at this time, and she said that she would come to stay with me until I had the baby. Joe and I were relieved. On a practical note, we had a cat and now there would be someone to feed him without bothering the neighbours while I was in hospital.

In the event, our son was reluctant to arrive. Joe was frantic with worry and 8,000 miles away. I did not see one person from welfare in the entire time that he was away, so when he sent messages to the Communications Centre (CommCen) at RNAS Yeovilton, asking if I was okay, of course they could not tell him because they did not know. I opened the door one day to a Wren from the CommCen, not welfare, who had been sent to ask if I had had the baby yet. She took one look at my enormous girth and realised that no, I had not had the baby. She did not come in, and the whole visit lasted less than a minute.

Thomas arrived on Boxing Day 1984. His father met him when he was 2½ months old.

Shortly after, Joe was offered the chance to join the Foreign & Commonwealth Office doing a similar job to that which he did in the navy, but travelling with his family, not leaving them behind, and with a higher salary. It was too good an opportunity to miss.

❧ SUE PIPER ☙ IN NIGERIA

Royal Navy wife, Sue, with a long pedigree of military service in her family behind her, was now in Nigeria at a volatile time in its history:

Coups

As a family we went to Kaduna, Nigeria, for two years in 1984–1986. Michael was on the British advisory team, helping set up the naval department of a junior staff college at Jaji. It was at the time of the coups. We were advised to take all our own food out, so had to pack boxes of everything we might need to last two years. Most survived, though we did get weevils in the flour! We were able to give food away, too.

It was an interesting time. Ruth, aged 10, went to the international school for the first year and then joined her brothers at boarding school in the UK for the second year, as there was no secondary schooling available for Brits. That was the hardest time for me – to say goodbye to my youngest. The house seemed very empty. However, the family were flown out to Nigeria each holiday. My parents were brilliant, and looked after them at half-terms.

Ruth got malaria very badly, and I, as a mother and a nurse, was very worried. It was the falciparum malaria, which is the killer. However, there was a kind Nigerian doctor who, I found out later, had trained at the London Hospital with my brother-in-law. He told us where to go for a blood test – run by two Lebanese. I actually saw the malaria parasites on the slide! They were then able to prescribe the right drug. It was so important that the needles were clean, as HIV had recently been discovered, so this laboratory was safer than a Nigerian hospital. Apparently, the boys told us later, Ruth started recovering as soon as she was on the plane returning to school! My parents' GP was so excited as he had never seen anyone with malaria!

The airport at Kano was about a four hour ride over ghastly roads, and the driving was atrocious. In fact, a dear missionary friend was killed in a car accident, on her way home from visiting us. The only contact we had with the family was by letter and occasional phone call. The phone calls were with those horrid phones, where you paid for three minutes prior to your call, and then you could hear the echo of your voice and there were what seemed like long gaps in replying. Ugh! It was traumatic for all of us, so we did not do that very often.

Executions

While in Nigeria, there was a supposed attempted coup, and dear Nigerian friends we knew were arrested and taken to prison, where they were all eventually executed. We went to visit some of the wives to try and bring some comfort. We later found out that all thirteen men had gone to their deaths singing Christian songs! One officer was not killed, and later Michael returned to Nigeria and visited him in prison. When his wife died, he was not allowed out to go to her funeral. We think the Nigerians feared that people would rise up and exalt him, as he was a fairly well-known figure.

✣ LIESEL PARKINSON ✣

Liesel's sapper husband, Rhett, retired in 2012 as a major in the Royal Engineers. Liesel is the author of *Coffee with God*. This was written in association with the Armed Forces' Christian Union, of which she is a member of the Ladies' Ministry. The book is a compilation of reflections on the Psalms by military women for women serving or connected to the military. The average length of a military deployment is six months, and there are 165 reflections in the book, enough for six a week, to cover the duration of the reader's time away. *Coffee with God*, CWR Publishing, 2012:

I am a Director of the Ladies' Ministry for the Armed Forces' Christian Union. I decided to put a book together of women's thoughts on the Psalms. Some of the women are military themselves and others have a connection to the military. I know that it would have been a help to me if such a book had existed when Rhett was away and I was by myself. I did not know what to do to get it published. I wrote off to a couple of publishers on the off chance and eventually got replies that said they thought it was a great idea, but they did not want to publish it.

Then I went online to CWR and filled out their application form. I did not hear from them for about three months and then, out of the blue, they called and asked me to come and meet them. They asked if I realised how rare the book was. They agreed to publish *Coffee with God* (2012) and, when I told them that instead of royalties I would like free copies of the book so that it could be given away for nothing, they thought this was a good idea. They themselves then gave away over 1,000 copies to the Christian Union. I have written a sequel, *Faith on the Front Line*, which is from those in the military. It came out in the autumn of 2014.

Meeting Rhett

We knew each other as children, went to university together and then got married when he was in Sandhurst. It was unusual to get married while still at Sandhurst. He still had six months to go there. He was not entitled to a married quarter so we got a flat. He had to leave at five in the morning to get back to the college, so it was quite a busy time.

Apologies

At the first mess lunch I was invited to when we had moved into married quarters, the CO made speeches and then said he had an apology to make to me. I thought, 'I don't know you, so why are you apologising?' He said that he had not realised that Rhett was married and so had arranged for him to go off for six months. So, Rhett went off to Belize and other places, and I stayed at home rattling around in our large house. Luckily, my old employer was only 30 miles away and they gave me part-time work, so I was okay. I tried to get involved by going to wives' coffee mornings and getting to know people. I made some wonderful friends, who are still friends today.

Familiarity

I knew army life, as my father was a Territorial in Rhodesia, where I grew up. He always had a distinctive smell about him and that was what I was familiar with. It was only when Rhett came home with the same smell that I realised it was the smell of gun oil. So, parts of army life were familiar – the smell of gun oil, the uniform, the military camaraderie but also the constant separation, fear and anxiety. There was continuity.

Privilege Versus Hardship

For me the army is privilege versus hardship. The smart uniform, the parades, the smart dinners, the feeling of pride on seeing my husband in uniform, but that is balanced by living with fear for them, living with being alone or with being a one-parent family, living with anxiety – will the next posting have a suitable school for the children, will they get in?

I am a teacher. The biggest thing that women sacrifice is career progression. Teaching is a portable career but I was always at the bottom, supply teaching.

❧ CAROL MUSGROVE ❧

Carol is married to army warrant officer, Richard. She is typical of most of the military women in this book. She has taken what service life has thrown at her and coped, whether it be with a new home, new area, new country or new job – or life as a single parent:

Old Style, New Style

My sister's husband joined the army and I went to visit Catterick, of all places, and met Richard. We will have been married twenty-one years this year. I have done the old style army and now the new style army. It is different now to how it used to be.

Maybe it was because I was abroad when we were first married that it felt more of a community. Our first posting was to Germany, Krayfeld, from 1994 to 1997. I had my first baby there. I worked in the NAAFI with the girls in the big warehouse in Kampen. Then we came back to Blandford for three years and I worked in the NAAFI there. Then we went to Joint HQ in Bulford – guess where I worked?!

Richard was away for four weeks out of every six, and that was really hard. He went to his bosses and said, 'I have to move, otherwise there will be trouble at home'. I was living as a single mum for a long time. My daughter, who is now 19½, used to run past him and come to me for anything when he was home. It was heartbreaking for me and for him.

I worked full-time, all the time, because I think it is important. My kids are independent and bright young girls, but I felt it was important that I went out and met other people. I could not be the person who stayed in the house and only knew the other wives.

I've got a friend who moved every two years for twenty-two years. Most husbands did something like seventeen tours in that time. It is hard. People reading this book will find it quite an eye-opener, I think.

Security

We had [security to think about] in Germany when we first went there. When I worked in the big house in Joint Head Quarters (JHQ), there were horrific photos warning us of what may happen if we forgot security. We were to check under our cars and vary our route – that was always a big thing. Don't always take the same route. Don't have a routine. When we were first married, we lived off the camp 6km away.

We had one of those torches with a mirror to look under the car. Most people left them sitting in the boot. If a device was under the boot, boom when you moved the car! 'Don't leave it in your boot!' We were told. I lived on the third floor. 'Do you want me to leave it there then take it back downstairs?' I used to ask.

They used to do lots of checks under your cars when you drove into camp when I was first married in 1994. Same when we lived in Cyprus as well. Until I moved into Bulford, I had lived thirteen years behind the wire, driving in and the guys were with guns and stuff. The kids thought it was great. 'Look at him, brilliant! He's got his gun out!' Then we moved to Bulford. That was quite strange that you were on the proper streets even though the heavy tanks used to drive round and shake the house!

The Wives' Brief

Richard went to Macedonia. Just after he left we had a 'wives' brief'. We went down to the JHQ and they told us where they were geographically and what they were facing out there, and how they could support us at home. I can remember this lady, the RSM's wife then, a newly promoted sergeant. We worked in the NAAFI together, and we were always giggling and being naughty. She sat in the front row at the brief. When we were asked if we had any questions, her hand went up. We thought, 'What is she going to say now?'

'Will our husbands be requiring psychological help when they get home?'

I couldn't wait to ring Rich because it was too good! 'His wife thinks he's going to need psychological help when he comes back.' It whipped round that day, and he was brought back to the UK quite swiftly. I don't know if they thought that he had some type of problem but he did not stay and do the whole tour.

Money

The first spell Rich did in Macedonia, we lost money for him to go away. This was because you used to get Married Living Overseas Allowance. If they are away, they only gave you Single Living Overseas Allowance, so you lost money when they went into the war zone. These days you get all the bonuses. We would be quids in now! That is why I have always worked as well. I never wanted to live on the breadline and wanted nice things for the house and the family. We lost money for him to go away. They did not have free phone calls or things like that then, either.

🌿 ANTONELLA DUNCAN 🌿

Antonella is married to serving artilleryman, Warrant Officer Class 2 Keith Duncan. They find life in Salisbury a far less stressful existence than military life in Northern Ireland:

Northern Ireland

We came to Salisbury from Northern Ireland. I know things have changed slightly, but it is still not good to mention there what your husband does for a living. Although nothing ever happened to me, I did not have any bad experiences and nobody ever made any comments, but I was always aware …

When I had a baby, I remember being in the hospital and I had to go three or four times to be induced because he just would not come out. I met ladies who were there at the same time and it was really weird because I could not really have a conversation. I did not want to get to the point where I was asked, 'What brought you here?' or a question like that. When I went to the hospital for my first scanning appointment, when I was twelve weeks pregnant, the staff were taking down our details.

'What do you do?' They said to my husband.

He said, 'I am in the armed forces.'

They said, 'We will just put your occupation down as unknown.' The local hospital did not have a paediatric department and so, if any problems arose, we would have to go to Belfast. If we went there with our notes, I suppose it could be a bit difficult.

🌿 DR CLARE SHAW 🌿 — A MODERN MILITARY MARRIAGE

For some military wives, being married to a serving member of the armed forces means having to be flexible, particularly if you are also in the military. Clare is a good example of this, as she fitted her training in with her husband's career and later had to retrain to keep her career alive:

I served as a doctor in the Royal Navy for three and three quarter years and was still serving when Kevin and I got married in 1995. We got married in December and had our two week honeymoon and then Kevin went to sea for seven months to the Falkland Islands. The result was that we had been married almost nine months before we both left the same house on the same morning to go to work.

I have been fortunate with my career, being able to move around and find jobs to complete my training, though we did have six months with me in Twyford, near Reading, while Kevin was serving in Corsham, Wiltshire. Our home moved to Wiltshire, as we were living in married quarters which had to be where Kevin was. Fortunately, I was put up by a kind naval couple nearby in the week and then went back to Corsham at the weekend.

Retraining

The greatest challenge to my career was when Kevin's job took us to live in America for three and a half years, which meant, on our return, I had to retrain to get back into general practice. I am now a partner, and the children and I are stable in our own home in Rickmansworth, but have had to accept Kevin commuting from Holland for the last two years so that we only saw him on most weekends.

Currently, he is in Wyton, so again we only see him at weekends, though sometimes in the week, if he is coming to London for a meeting, he comes home. We have chosen to be static and accept weekending to give our children, now aged 11 and 13, stability in their education rather than send them to boarding school.

SARAH KIFF

Sarah has been married to Lieutenant Commander Ian Kiff, a weapons engineer in the Royal Navy, for nearly twenty years. She works with children with special needs and the family live in Fareham:

When I first met Ian, in 1992, and we were courting in Bexhill, where both our families live, he was on HMS *Southampton*. I would receive letters with numbers, so if I had letter number three and the next letter was number five, I knew there was one missing in the middle. Some days, I got two or three letters all together but they had the numbers on, so I knew in which order to read them. There was no email.

I think they got one ten minute phone call a week. So, contact then was much less. You went for weeks and weeks and weeks without anything.

Now, you just use mobile phones, and so as soon as they get alongside somewhere ... I remember they used to get a little card with so many minutes put on it. They could use it in certain phones. That went again, though, because they all have their own phones these days. You can text and email too. It is all different. It takes away some of that anticipation of a call.

'I will try and call you, this time next week.'

You knew you had that call, that ten minutes, and you had to try and cram everything into it. You could never think of anything to say in that ten minutes! You want to use it to say all the important things that you want to say, and tell them everything that had been happening, but when it came down to it, you kind of went blank. It had all gone out of my head. I had to write notes. 'The children have been here and we did that', 'your mum phoned', and those kind of things. That phone call was so precious. Now, you can have a whole series of emails and chat, chat, chat. It's really great and I love it, but it takes away the specialness of that phone call. Perhaps that is really old-fashioned.

Starting a Family

We left it for three years before we started to think about wanting a family. It was quite a difficult time because I had a few miscarriages. Then we had our first child, Gemma, who was stillborn.

The navy were really good. Ian was on the *Manchester* at that time. It was a difficult situation. I had gone for a scan and things were not right, but the baby was still alive. This was a Thursday. I went back on the Monday, baby still alive, and we went like that for nearly six weeks. I was off work. How can you do anything in that situation?

Ian had time off for the scans, and then she was born. He had two weeks of compassionate leave and then he went back to work. I wasn't ready for him to go back. Then Welfare became involved, and he got another week and then he went back to sea. I was kind of ready then to try to start pulling myself together.

It is not easy, but you start to move on and let life carry on. That was a low time for us, really hard. Being left, he was not going out in the morning and coming back in the evening, it was complete separation, and then having to face everybody at work, it was a difficult time.

Matthew arrived a year and six days later. He was our blessing. Then Annabelle came along two years after that. Then I said, 'That is it. I am not chasing it again.' Even with Matthew, he got to thirty-four weeks and stopped growing. I had to go in [to the hospital] every day. I don't know what made me think I could do it again with Annabelle! She is a fighter, a tough cookie and was from the start. It was a really difficult time, but even now I look back on it and think that tragic time makes you stronger. If you can come through something like that on your own with the military support, and they were really supportive, then you can kind of do anything.

❧ JAY ARMSTRONG ❧

Jay met Scott, her Royal Navy helicopter pilot husband while she was serving in the army. As with other military wives in this book, she found it difficult to continue her career while married to a member of the armed forces, particularly as each was in a different service:

In the Army

He commands a helicopter force, which is based at Yeovilton in Somerset. He provided support for the UN, followed by S4 and I4 in the Balkans. I was deployed there as a commander in 1998, which was my first tour and he came out for a stint. The pilots do an eight week rotation. We do six months.

We met as colleagues. I was a single female officer and you kept your nose clean! People were waiting for you to trip up, but I was professional. We stayed in touch when we got home. Then we started seeing each other. I was in Tidworth, he was in Yeovilton. I don't think I'm unusual, as lots of people meet while they are in the services, but to meet while on operations is unusual.

❧ CHARLOTTE WOOLRICH ❧

Charlotte met her husband, John, when she was 16 and he was 20. He joined the Royal Navy as an aircraft engineer three years later, and Charlotte studied nursing at university in London. Eighteen years on, they have two children:

Meeting John

When John first joined, we didn't have mobile phones. I had to wait for a letter. I was in uni and the halls' phone was always engaged when he was at his official training down at HMS *Raleigh* in Plymouth.

He wasn't in the navy when we met. I had just finished my GCSEs, and his dad knew my dad from down the local pub in Havant. I knew his dad, but I didn't actually know he had children. He had won custody in a divorce – one of the first dads to win. I didn't realise that John was his son when I first saw him on a Sunday afternoon in the pub, when I was there with my dad at the age of just 15. I was 16 in the August.

In the October, I went to watch the pub play their Sunday League football and his father was in charge of the team. John was there watching. We kind of looked over a couple of times and smiled, and I didn't think much of it. Then, that afternoon, he rang me. He had got the number from his dad's phonebook. We spoke every day on the phone for that week and then we went out for a drink. Then love just grew. I think he told me, after about three weeks, that he loved me. I said I *thought* I did. I was only 16!

He was a window cleaner in his dad's business. He had been to college, and did about a year and a term of A levels and then dropped out because he didn't know what he wanted to do. His dad started the window cleaning business when his mum left, when John was 3.

I think we'd been together for just over a year, when he said to me, 'I'd like a career, and when I was at school I had thought of the navy. I felt that at 16 I was too young. What do you think?' I think I began to cry. I wanted to support him in what he wanted to do, and I already knew that I would move away to go to university anyway so I knew for three years I wasn't going to be in Havant. From that point of view, I wasn't going to say, 'no you can't go because I will be here on my own.' Well, you know, it's a good job, isn't it? A good career.

So, a couple of weeks after that initial conversation he went down to the careers office in Portsmouth. He spoke to a careers man who said, 'You can join up as an OM, operator mechanic', which John knew nothing about. He was asked to come back in a few weeks' time to sit the initial tests. He did that, and luckily it was a different careers bloke because John got 100 per cent and he said, 'What qualifications have you got?'

'I have my GCSEs.'

'There is no way you're joining up as an OM. You can join as a direct entry artificer.' Which is what he did.

He had to get his physics GCSE because he didn't have any sciences. He put himself through a year of home learning and, on my birthday, 31 August 1998, he joined the navy. I waved him off.

My heart was ripped out of my chest. I was going to university and was moving to London, so I knew we had three years of long-distance. His training was four years long and mine was three. We knew that at the end of my three he had one year left, which was going to be at HMS *Sultan* at Gosport. It was just awful. I had a jumper of his that I slept with for weeks and weeks and weeks. I took it to university with me and just waited for every letter and phone call. There were no text messages until he had been in for two terms. He got a phone because my mum bought me one to take to uni at 19, and then he got one.

Me, his sister, nan and dad went to the passing out parade. The four of us drove down in a car, immensely proud, and watched him pass out and he then came home with us for his three weeks' leave. He was horrible! He was moody, he didn't want to mix, was a bit grumpy, had stories to tell about the training and the things he did but you had to ask him. He wasn't basically willing, and that wasn't like him at all.

He is very chatty when he knows you, shy around new people, but chatty when he gets to know them. So I remember thinking to myself, he wasn't the person who went away. We had seen each other for four hours [while he was on basic training]. Halfway through his training he was allowed a Saturday afternoon off. I met him in Plymouth town centre for the afternoon. He was perfect. He cried when he left.

But he wasn't the same by Christmas. I remember thinking to myself, if he doesn't change and go back to how he was within a couple of weeks in the New Year, then I'm not sure he is who I thought he was. He did sort it out. He started on some of his training at *Sultan* and I went back up to uni after the New Year, so the rest of that time, the three years was seeing each other maybe once a month or once a fortnight. He went to Bosnia during his training, then Norway, and he was based in Yeovil a lot. The Sea King was the aircraft he fixed then.

As the old millennium came to a close and the new began, a new chapter in their lives was to begin …

5

A NEW BEGINNING

I met a wife who got married in February and then her husband left in March. I just thought, you poor girl, you don't know what you have let yourself in for, do you?
Sarah Hattingh, married to a man in the army, but resolutely not an army wife.

The turn of the century, the beginning of a new millennium, brought with it more conflict. Afghanistan became the theatre of war, and military wives saw their men off with their fingers crossed for a safe return, just as their mothers and grandmothers had done during times of conflict throughout history. Life, though, had to go on …

CAROL MUSGROVE

For army wife Carol, coming back to the UK was an opportunity to begin a new career:

I'd worked in Cyprus for a period of time in the Education Centre and it opened my eyes up because I had always wanted to do my nursing training. I did a lot of IT courses that gave me the equivalent of A levels. I came back and worked on a building site on camp for a few months, and then went to work in a local hospital. I was the site administrator for McAlpine. Admin is admin, and I've worked in education, in finance and the NAAFI. It's all admin, it's just different acronyms.

Then I went to the hospital, and I said to the girls, 'Next year I'll apply for uni.' They said, 'Why next year? Do it now.' So, in June I started filling out the form. I had it in with two days to spare to the deadline.

I started in September 2004, and I went to Bournemouth. We were living in Blandford at the time. It was on that understanding that Richard took the posting. Then we moved to Bulford, near Salisbury. My dad died ten days after we moved into our house at Bulford, and so I took a break from uni. I eventually qualified. Then I didn't want to work as he died where I worked as a student, so I went to the hospital in Swindon for a couple of years. I did the long commute. Either you work away, or you work from home. I've got a friend who is very super-talented, who works from home. You've got to make a choice really. You stay at home and become depressed, or you go and work.

There's a lot of wives who expect everything to fall in their laps and expect it all to come to them: 'My house is too small and I need a bigger house'; 'We need to move into a bigger house'; 'My husband's gone away and I can't cope'; 'Let's get him back then'. It does happen. In the old days when I was first married, I would phone up my mother, but you just got on with it. You didn't have the support then that you have now. So that's changed as well. It's better for changing. Some of the girls in our choir have husbands who are away for nine, ten or twelve months. That never used to happen.

The Salisbury Military Wives Choir
The Choir's Attraction

For Her Majesty the Queen's diamond jubilee our choir did it very differently. A lot of the choirs sent their committee, whereas we sent our best people along to sing.

Salisbury Plain is massive, and there is a lack of community here. I have been in Bulford. We moved there in 2007. The girls did not even have Guides or Brownies or youth club. We came from Blandford Camp, where there is a bowling alley and a cinema. Everything you wanted was on camp. The school was there. The guides were there, youth club, absolutely everything. You came to Bulford and there was nothing there.

We watched the TV programme with Gareth Malone, and there was a Facebook group that started. We all got chatting and we planned a little meeting, two years ago now, and six people turned up. We thought, 'well, it is not really a choir, is it? We'll publicise it and advertise it.' We had a big meeting in the local pub. We turned up about ten minutes before we were due to meet and the room was just so crowded. It was bulging. I have made friends with people I would never have met. There are people in the choir I met in the Accident & Emergency department in Salisbury, and they say, 'You looked after me!'

'Really?'

'Yeah, you put a needle in my arm!'

We would never have met. We became a community, and we hadn't had that. We had it in Blandford and in Cyprus, but never here. It was very disjointed in that respect. It has pulled us together. Rank did not matter, either. That was completely different from Wives' Club, where the CO's wife was always in charge, if she could be bothered. Rank does not matter in our choir, at all.

We have three groups in the Salisbury Military Wives Choir – Sops 1 [Sopranos], Sops 2 and Altos. So you have friendships in the choir and friendships within your little group that you go off and rehearse with, and then we come back together.

We don't do the same as Gareth Malone does with his choirs. We are very lucky that, in our choir, the musical director is the head teacher of the local school, and she wanted to make it something of a community within the school, based around the school. We have a lady who plays the piano, who is a music teacher. Then we have another couple of ladies who are super musically talented. What we do is we all warm up together. Have a half hour cup of tea, chin wag and catch up. Then we all do warm-ups together and then we split up into our groups and learn our section, and then come back and sing that song. Then we all rehearse at home.

We have socials, and people go to the pub after or when we go away on our little trips. We went to Sennelager, Germany, once, on the coach. We were away sixty-eight hours and a huge amount of that was on the coach, because it was a long journey there and back. You get to France and you think, 'are we nearly there?' Then you have another six hours ahead of you. That was when you got to know people quite intimately, on the coach. We slept in the bunk beds they used to accommodate the army in transit, all free, which we appreciated. The army paid for us to go over.

We have had amazing experiences, and the plans are still going on for some great things, but it has brought us all together and brought us back our sense of community, which we had lost.

Gareth Malone did not actually start the military wives choirs. There was a choir already in Catterick and the idea was shared with the BBC. For the programme, they wanted to show a choir starting from scratch. The husbands were deployed at the time and that is how it came about.

There are eighty-something singers in our choir, but you get about fifty at one time. Performances can range between twenty and forty singers.

Performances

We have done a couple of memorials. We sit in the choir stalls at the local garrison church and as you look out, that is the family right there. You feel the grieving. The first had died from a motorcycle accident. We sang at the memorial. It was really bad. You don't know them, but you know that it could be you and that brings it back. The second one was the funeral. They brought the coffin in and we were sat in the choir stall and they put the coffin directly in front of us. We were very fixated on a fly that was flying around, and a cobweb, so that we did not have to look at the coffin covered in the Union flag and the cap and medals.

They did not have any military choirs at the time of the Brit Fest in Germany, and our musical director knew somebody who said, 'Come on, then'. We went over from the Friday to the Monday. It was a great weekend away.

We were the first choir into the House of Commons. We take it for granted a little bit now. We went for the day. Some of us met up in Hyde Park, as they were to sing at the jubilee. The rest sat in a bar with our Gary Barlow and Boris Johnson masks on! We were on the coach with them on, waving!

We went to Portcullis House, opposite the Houses of Parliament. Being from the sticks, I had not done a lot of London and I didn't know where we were going. We went in there and we were all security checked and we went into a waiting room. In the next room was Ian Duncan-Smith! In one room there were all these portraits of Maggie Thatcher. We thought, 'Oh blooming heck, this is real stuff now!'

We got into our dresses, and Claire Perry, who is the MP for Devizes and Bulford, Tidworth and Larkhill, came in. She said, 'Right, we're going over now to the House of Commons.' We walked down the stairs, and there were these escalators down and it is like a secret little Harry Potter road under the street! You come out with Big Ben behind you. Then we went up and watched the Speaker in the House. There were not very many people there, but it was just the fact that I was there!

The Hill children in the late 1960s/early 1970s. Note the lamp is standing on lino. Rank was strictly kept, even at home. 'Other ranks' did not merit wall-to-wall carpeting in their married quarter, although colourful floral upholstery was considered suitable.

Kay and Alex Wylie, a newly married couple in 1961.

A 50th wedding anniversary celebration. Kay and Alex Wylie in 2011.

Anthea and Mark Fillingham on their wedding day in 1962.

Anthea and Mark at the Sungei Ugong Club in Serembang, Malaya, in the mid-1960s.

Sue and Michael Piper on their wedding day in 1967.

Lorraine with baby Carl at his christening on board HMS *Glamorgan*.

Eon and Carl Matthews watching HMS *Antrim* arrive back from the Falklands Conflict, 1982.

Eon and Lorraine Matthews on HMS *Ark Royal*. Families Day, 1987.

Lorraine and Eon Matthews with their Falklands baby, Kerry.

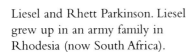

Liesel and Rhett Parkinson. Liesel grew up in an army family in Rhodesia (now South Africa).

The Portsmouth Military Wives Choir launching the Royal British Legion's annual Poppy Appeal, Portsmouth, 2013.

Gail Douglas, member of the Portsmouth Military Wives Choir, wearing her late husband Mark's medals.

Lorraine and Eon Matthews at Hooker's Point, Falkland Islands, paying tribute to the members of HMS *Glamorgan*'s company who died on Lorraine's birthday in 1982.

Kate Churchward with her two children Bella and Beth. (Photograph by, and courtesy of, Jay Armstrong: www.jayarmstrong.co.uk)

Laura and John Delahay's wedding. When she saw him in his uniform, she thought, 'Whoo!'

Charlotte Woolrich finished the 2012 London Marathon in five hours and forty seconds. She raised £3,542 for charity in the process.

Martial arts instructor, Nicola Laing, ready for anything!

We had photos taken and then we sang. It was the most amazing achievement. We sang in Portcullis House, in the atrium. It is built in a round, and our voices carried up. Apparently, even those who were in meetings came out and looked over and watched us, which we did not know at the time. The Armed Forces Minister was there. He had not seen a military wives choir so it was quite good for choirs as a whole for us to get out there and do that. Quite a few choirs have been there since, but we were the first.

The Chelsea Hospital

I can't remember the name of the man who invited us there. His wife died, and what I did not realise was that they are all widowers there. To see a whole group of women, who are military wives, brings it back to them who they have lost. One chap befriended us and took us around on a tour. Everybody was in their red coats. They only wear their red coats on ceremonial duties. He just said, 'You made me remember my wife in the most amazing way.' I did not realise that.

We have raised nearly £80,000, just our choir alone. We self-fund our trips to the Chelsea Hospital. They don't pay us to go up there. We do it because we want to.

Locally, we go into Salisbury. We did another concert in City Hall, an 800 seat venue. It is the second year we have done it with the local brass band. The year before, they sold 200 or so tickets. The year after it was a sell-out and I think there were only a couple of seats free this year. Salisbury is a city, but only small, and the concert is at three on a Sunday afternoon, but it is packed out. The audience talk to us and love us because there is a lot of ex-military in this area. It is so lovely.

I work in the public domain, and I had someone come up the other day and say, 'I think I've seen you on the TV!'

'You probably have.'

The choir has informed my kids as well. Both have done work for charity. One cut her hair off for a cancer charity and it was made into a wig and raised nearly £1,000, and the other one has jumped out of an aeroplane twice, raising money for cancer charities. I overheard Lucy say to someone, 'I do it because I watch my mum raising money and I wanted to feel like that.' I thought, 'Ooh. The kids love it, too.'

Security

It is funny being aware of security. We are aware now. When Lee Rigby was killed in London, we were travelling to the Cliff Richard concert to perform there, and we weren't allowed to wear our Military Wives advertising. When we went to Germany we had bunting all over everywhere, advertising who we were. After the murder, we weren't allowed to advertise that we were a military choir then. I had forgotten about security. It brought it home. I think that the security state was always up high, so you just joined in. I would go to university or go to work in Salisbury and come back in and it had heightened.

A Different Dimension

We have our own home now, so there is a different dimension to being a military wife. I do the choir and go to camp in Bulford or Blandford – Blandford most of the time.

Keeping in Touch

My dad died in 2007, just ten days after we moved. We already knew Richard was going away after Christmas. He had to do all the build-up, going to courses, but we were still really grieving. I was left on my own. I was not working because I did not want to work. Then he went away. Charlotte was 7, and coped quite well. 'My dad's gone to Iraq and everything is fine.' But Lucy cried quite often.

Communications now are better than they were when Richard did Bosnia and Macedonia. I might not hear from him for three weeks then. He always hand writes a bluey [flimsy, blue aerogramme letter].

I used to send him two or three parcels – we would go to the pound shop and get the padded envelopes. You can only do so much weight for it to be free, so you would get three a week to send him. I don't think, when he was in Iraq, that he had any for three and a half weeks. Then twelve turned up all at once! Then, when they had their post-tour party, a lot of the girls, more than the boys, came up and said, 'Thanks for everything you sent. I had no one to send me stuff.' He had shared it with them. I wished he had told me, I could have sent them something.

The best thing I sent Rich was a DVD of Ricky Tomlinson calling bingo in the *Royle Family* way, and a book of bingo strips. They had a bingo night in the bar and they raised over £100 for Help for Heroes. Instead of shouting 'House', they had to shout 'My arse!' They had not been able to go to the bar for quite a while. It had a tin roof and it was on the second night it was open they had the bingo night. I keep thinking of all these soldiers with their dabbers! He said it was one of the best times.

They were under fire for a long time – he came back grey, bless him, and it was quite … [Carol trails off, unable to say more for a moment]. You don't realise, and can't relate to it either. That is the sad thing. You can't say, 'It's awful', because you have no idea what they have been through.

When they are away, people don't realise that we are single parents. Okay, single parents struggle moneywise, but we are struggling with our emotions and trying to keep life normal for the kids, which is difficult, really. The kids always get sick while they are away. You can't say that the men are going to be all right, because you don't know. That sounds quite dramatic, doesn't it?

It is quite stressful, and you have to deal with normal life and work, all that kind of thing and it is really quite hard. Rich was in Afghanistan for my 40th birthday this year.

The general public don't realise. They talk to us when we are in the choir – 'Oh, I wish we had that [the choir] when we were younger. My mum was an army child. When her dad went away, they just moved away back to their grandparents for months on end. She was brought up mostly by her nan.'

I live off camp now and away from army people, and my life is different again.

Mess Life

When we first got married in 1994, the wives were seen and not heard, and they behaved themselves, whereas now that is not the case anymore.

If you go to the Sergeants' Mess for a dinner night, you are told what to wear and when you can go for a wee … The women can get up, but not the men. In the Signals' Mess you have a comfort break, and the only time you can get up otherwise is if you are pregnant. I did that once. What you find is a gaggle of women with a chap in mess kit between them as you walk out. Then he will come back and the men will have hidden his chair! So, he will come back to the table and will have to crouch down because he has no chair. He can't stand up, because then they will know he left.

There is a bell in the mess. If you ring it, you buy everybody a drink. We had one in the bar in Cyprus. The boys, if they messed up, had to ring the bell. Sometimes you would stay there for seven hours and not pay a penny for the drinks all night! Our kids would go in and the guys would pick up Lizzy, she is 19 now, but when she was little they would say, 'Ring the bell, daddies like that when you ring it more than once!' She would reply, 'My daddy said I am never allowed to touch that bell and you are very naughty to try to make me do it.' If she had rung the bell, every time it rang that is a round Rich would have had to pay for. The women are not allowed to touch it in the Signallers' Mess.

When Rich first got promoted it was an honour to go to the mess. You are proud of your husband, but once you got in there it was, 'Well, is this it?' I have more choir dresses than mess dresses now. I could wear a choir dress to the mess!

Nowadays, they get a grant to pay for their mess dress. Well, we used to pay for our own mess dress. They give the promotion, yet you have to go out and spend £600 on this mess dress, but surely, if you got promoted and they think you are good enough to be promoted, shouldn't they pay it? I don't think I will ever be in to the army way of thinking. If someone gave you a job and said you have to wear this, a uniform, your employers would supply you with everything you need to wear.

That first day, though, seeing him, he looked so handsome.

A Big Mystery …

Rich is a warrant officer class 2 in Signals. I have learnt a few buzzwords, but I have no idea what they do. He gave me an example of what he did once. When he was in Iraq, in Baghdad, he was responsible for communications as a whole in the city, and if they went down, it was his responsibility to reinstall it. That is his job. That is the example I use. I suppose it is project management, equipment care and communications.

Moving On

Rich is out of the army next year. He has done twenty-two years. He wants to go to Dubai for a couple of years to pay the house off. We bought late in life, so our mortgage is huge. He will do in Dubai what he does in the army – communication, project management, repair equipment! He has done an electrician's course as part of his resettlement so, if all else fails, he can be an electrician. They earn more than nurses, which is a low-paid job.

I work in A&E. I did my training while he was in the army. That is a new thing. You would not have been able to do that in the olden days.

He managed to get postings to accommodate my training. As I can't empathise with him and what he does, he has no idea what I do either, and he does not want to hear about it either. He is squeamish. If I come home and say that I have had a really shit day, he says to me, 'Dear, I had a really crap day the other day'. For me, that means that the worst has happened, someone has passed away, sometimes in tragic circumstances and you have helped the family. He has been stuck in a meeting for six hours! That is the difference in our bad days.

He said to me three years ago, 'I have this course.'

'What is that about then?'

'Breaking bad news. It's awful. You have to go and tell the family someone has died.'

'Welcome to my world.'

'Oh no, it's different for me.'

He is in a little bubble. Two or three years ago, my mum said something about somebody dying, 'Yes, but you don't deal with it.'

'What do you mean, I don't deal with it?'

'You don't deal with it, do you?'

'Yes, I do, mum.'

'Well, what about the people who deal with the dead bodies?'

'Yes, they are called A&E nurses.'

You sit in a small room and you tell the family the most awful news, and you take them through to see their loved one and you deal with their emotions, and the police come along – and my mother had no idea. Richard is the same. I thought of saying something, but he does not really listen – he is squeamish.

❦ Penny Legg ❦

25th Anniversary of the Falklands Conflict

Veteran Royal Navy wife, Penny Legg, has found that, like so many other military veterans, her husband Joe had never really let go of the armed forces:

I remember that Joe was very keen to march with his old comrades in London on the 25th anniversary of the Falklands Conflict. As time has passed, he has become more and more involved with military organisations and helps to raise funds for several military charities. At work, he often has cause to work closely with the military and so I knew that he would want to mark the anniversary in some way.

We were on a diplomatic posting to the tiny Caribbean island of Anguilla in 2007. I had a column in the local newspaper, *The Anguillian*, and so I thought I would cover his attendance for the paper. The island, although only 3 miles by 16 miles, is a British Dependent Territory, and Joe was there as part of the governor's staff. The editor thought the idea was a good one. There had been a changeover of governor just a few months before, and the outgoing governor was now in charge on the Falklands. This brought more Anguillian interest in the story.

We flew home and stayed at my parents' home in Kingston-Upon-Thames, conveniently close to London. Joe had got tickets for both me and our son, Thomas, to attend and so, dressed in our best, Joe sporting his South Atlantic medal, and wearing his beloved naval beret (which he had had a flap about just before we left, as it was not where he thought he had left it!) we set off. I remember that it was a scorching hot summer day and I was wearing a lime green linen suit and low stiletto heels. It is funny what you remember when you think back on things. Thomas was in a suit and was not quite sure what he was going to. He was born at the end of 1984, so had only heard of the Falklands second-hand.

We split up in London. Joe went to join the hundreds of service men and women gathering in preparation to march. Thomas and I joined the long queue to get through the security and then find our seats in the stands erected at Horse Guards Parade. I remember being amazed at how big the event was. There were hundreds in the stands and, soon, hundreds of serving personnel from all three services standing on the parade ground. There was a royal presence, of course, and a live link-up to the Falklands, where Alan Huckle, the former Anguillian governor, looked splendid in his white, feathered uniform.

The drumhead ceremony was as moving as ever. The march past, which took many minutes, was quite emotional for us watching. I took lots of photos and was fortunate enough to find Joe in several when I reviewed them later. One made it to the newspaper when I wrote the event up later.

I realised that each of the sections of tiered seating was from a specific ship. Joe was on HMS *Intrepid* during the conflict, so all the people seated with us were family members of that ship's company. I had seen the ship, but it was not until I was there that I realised just how big the *Intrepid* family was. It was quite sobering.

Somewhere among the carefully arranged seating plan were families from unluckier ships like the *Coventry*. She lost nineteen crew, and Joe has always thanked his lucky stars he was elsewhere when she sank. *Coventry* went down carrying Joe's boots, as he had left them there when he went on Easter leave just as the conflict blew up.

When all the men had marched out of the parade ground, they carried on down the Mall to Buckingham Palace, and we left our seats and followed them. I am not old enough to remember the end of the Second World War, but I have seen the photos of the celebrations and the huge numbers of people gathered outside the palace at the end of six years of conflict. The mass of people around the Victoria statue and engulfing the Mall reminded me of those images. There were thousands of people there and it was a humbling sight.

Even now, several years after this event, long after the newspaper article has been used to wrap fish and chips, it still chokes me up to think about that day, as it does when I think about the conflict itself. It took me a quarter of a century to be able to write about it and I was just a loved one anxiously waiting for news, not even there. No wonder then, that so many of the service men involved have not been able to talk or write about their experiences, and no wonder too, that there are so many welfare organisations that still work with Falklands Conflict veterans.

Thomas went off to find his father and I caught up with them both eventually. They had been talking to some of Joe's former shipmates. It was a good day.

❧ LORRAINE MATTHEWS ❧

Twenty-fifth Anniversary of the Falklands Conflict
We went up to London by train, Eon and Kerry (our daughter), and I, with Kev and Nicky McDonald, our friends. I remember there being lots of people. Kev and Eon went off to march and we found our seats. Kerry and I had to go up towards the palace and we were going to meet Eon somewhere there. I remember we waited for ages for Eon. As usual he was chatting somewhere and took ages to find us!

The strange thing was, we were with the rest of the *Glamorgan* ship's company and I actually don't know many of them. A lot of the people I knew at the time don't go to these events. A lot of Eon's friends at that particular time don't go. A lot of the ones who do go are more officer's wives and family than rank and file.

❧ GAIL DOUGLAS ❧

Gail describes her Royal Navy late husband, Mark, as 'a stick of rock with HM Navy running through his core'. In an emotional interview, she speaks about her life with him and how she has coped following his sudden death:

Meeting Up

He was my next-door neighbour in Newcastle. I had been married before and I swore I would never do it again. My twins were 7 when I met Mark. We met at Christmas. He knocked at the door and asked if I had a tape measure. They were just moving in. He had a share of the house with his mate. Bizarrely enough, for once in my life, I knew where the tape measure was!

We were really good friends straight away. He was only home for Christmas leave, a few weeks, and then he deployed until May, but he kept in touch with emails and messages. We were best friends but nothing else. We did everything together when he was home. We took the kids out, went out to eat. We used to joke because he'd do the cooking in his house and I'd have a little stir, as you do, and he'd joke that I couldn't keep my hands out.

People kept saying to me, 'Really? No, I think there's more to it.' Mark told me afterwards that there *was* more to it, I just didn't pick up the vibes! He used to keep a bag of rubbish by the front door, so if he saw me walking by he would have an excuse to go out and talk to me.

Seventy-four days later we were married. We didn't tell people in advance that we were getting married. We just rang people up and said, 'What are you doing on Thursday?'

'Going to work, not much else.'

'We're getting married.'

'What?!'

'If you want to come you are welcome. This is where it is. We're not doing invites, not doing presents, not doing the big wedding. We're just going to get married, have a meal and everyone's welcome.'

It was 2004, and it was a lovely wedding, very low-key.

My family thought I was mad, considering how adamant I had been about not getting married again. I had been on my own with the twins since they were born. I had been in relationships, but as soon as they were getting serious I finished them. Then I met Mark and literally everything changed. I loved him and so did the kids.

He was just a junior rate in CIS (Communications & Information Systems). He dealt with computers, signals and emails, stuff like that. Friends would say they couldn't understand it as the email's been down for weeks. Yeah, right. Their husband just hadn't been in touch.

Deployed

I had my own house in Newcastle and we stayed there. We got married in the August and he deployed in the December. He joined HMS *Endurance* and they used to deploy every year. They would go in what was the austral summer, our winter. It was always December or January. I was pregnant with Dominic, and Mark deployed. He came back in June and I had Dominic in the August.

It was hard, being pregnant and him not being there. I had the twins in an awkward relationship. I felt that it was very quick – getting married to getting pregnant and then him going away. What had I done? This could be a complete repeat situation, but it wasn't. Those fears prey on your mind a bit.

I don't have easy pregnancies, they are high risk and Mark was very worried. He came home, I had Dominic by emergency Caesarean section and he deployed again. He left a 6-week-old baby and was gone for nine months.

Dominic was 10 months old when the ship came back, and I had lost a lot of my baby weight. I had long hair when he went. I had my hair cut really short. He walked down the gangway and straight past me! I laughed, and he said that he recognised my laugh. I had changed so much, which I thought was quite funny.

Meningitis

Dominic got meningitis and we were still in Newcastle, although Mark was in Portsmouth with his ship. I was constantly on the phone.

'I can leave, they've said I can come.'

'Stay there.'

In my head, the minute he got in the car to drive up it would all go horribly wrong. I just kept thinking, 'if you stay there and I stay here, it will be all right'. He came home anyway at the weekend. He was driving to the hospital and his car was hit by a huge piece of timber that came off the truck in front. He said he saw it coming towards him and thought, 'This is it!' It hit his car and bounced on the floor. He looked in the rear view mirror and it was carnage behind him. Eventually, he got to the hospital. He said, 'That is it, I have used up all my luck. I either need to leave the navy or we need to move. I can't keep doing this journey.' I knew the journey was horrendous – a six hour drive on a good day. He was doing it on a Friday and getting in sometimes in the early hours of Saturday morning and then getting in the car again on Sunday afternoon. So we said that we would fill in the paperwork for a married quarter.

Moving House

We thought it would take a long time to be offered a house. We didn't think it would be quick. He handed the paperwork in on the Monday morning and they rang on the Monday afternoon and said, 'We have a house for you but you need to say yes by tomorrow morning.' It was at Lee-on-the-Solent, on the brand new married patch there. Mark asked if he could have a look at it and was told no, the builders were still there. But he was shown a plan of the house, which he took a photo of on his phone and sent to me. I wasn't sure, but he said, 'Look, it's a brand new house, it has four bedrooms and, from what I can gather, Lee-on-the-Solent is a really nice area.'

We took it and moved down on the Saturday. On the Monday, he got up, kissed me and went off to work. We had been married for over a year and we had never done that! 'I'll see you later,' he said. It was very strange!

An hour later, I got a phone call. 'Gail, I'm really sorry. We're going to sea for a couple of weeks for sea trials. I'll see you in two weeks' time.' It hadn't mattered before because we had been apart anyway. He got on board, and suddenly thought, 'Oh my God, I'm not coming home!'

The quarters were still being built. We were only the second family to move onto the estate. It didn't feature on any maps or sat navs. Even local people did not know it was there. I couldn't find my way home! I managed, though. By the time he came back I knew my way around.

The ship came alongside and he was in his cabin. People were coming and getting their bags and going-home stuff. He was on his bed settling down to watch a DVD. A friend came in and asked if he was going home. 'You have a quarter now, don't you?'

'Oh God, yes!'

It took some getting our heads around. We had the August and then he deployed at the end of September. Most of the time there I spent alone with the kids.

Keeping in Touch

People don't understand. When I was in Newcastle and expecting Dominic, I worked as an administrator/receptionist in an old people's home. Mark rang me at work and the girl in the office answered the call.

'Hiya Mark. What's the weather like? Is it cold? Have you seen lots of penguins?' She was chattering away to him, and I was saying, 'Give me the phone'. She kept whispering back, 'Yeah, yeah, yeah'. Then someone else came in, and they had a chat with him, too. He kept asking if I was there, bless him. I finally got the phone and said, 'Hello' and then got cut off. The girls said to ring him back, but I couldn't ring him. That was it until the next week. We had had our twenty minutes. They were sorry when they realised, and after that whenever he rang they put a message out on the tannoy: 'GET TO A PHONE!'

Family Life from Afar

Mark adored Dominic. He had a draft to Northwood. Dominic was only little, pre-school, and he loved *Chuggington*. It is a train cartoon on children's TV. Dominic and Mark loved it. It used to be on at six o'clock every morning. Dominic was an early riser and Mark would ring him every day at five minutes to six and they would put their televisions on and watch the programme together and talk about it. I would usually run and jump in the shower. They would watch that daft programme together.

Memories

Mark did not believe in buying gifts for birthdays and Christmas that would clutter up the home. Instead, he brought memories I would keep forever.

I was a zoo keeper for a day at London Zoo. I went everywhere, the entire zoo. I fed live locusts to meerkats and helped with the animals' enrichment programme – they try to make the animals look for their food, as it is more natural than just giving it to them. Who knew that warthogs liked boiled eggs?! You obviously can't go in with them so you throw hard-boiled eggs at warthogs! I was standing in London Zoo, throwing hard-boiled eggs thinking, 'that's just wrong! I should be told off for this!' I cleaned out the giraffe house and then the giraffe came in and kissed me.

Then they took us into the lion enclosure. You are in a cage, in effect, and the lion is roaming. The cage is about the size of my hearth rug. It is not good to sedate them every time the animal needs to be checked over, so they train them to respond in certain ways so that the vet can check them out, which is really, really clever. We were in the cage and a big lion called Lucifer came over. He has ear problems. They do clicker training with the lions, like they do with dogs. They clicked and Lucifer put a paw on the front of the mesh right in front of my face. They gave him a tiny little bit of meat. Then they clicked and he did the other one, reward, and they clicked and they checked his ear, reward, clicked and he opened his mouth. They have to keep doing it to reinforce it to him. And you are standing there thinking 'that is an animal and they have trained it' – no, they haven't! That animal is not stupid. At the end, they have done it and no matter what that animal does, they're wrong. That animal is in charge! He did not go away. He got up on his hind legs and he put his front paws up on the sides of the cage and he roared! That is the one thing that I remember. He was not happy. Most people who see a lion that unhappy, that is the last thing they see.

I am terrified of butterflies, and I ended up in a butterfly house with huge ones. Mark took the kids around so that wherever I would be they could see me. The baby was about 10 months old and this big butterfly came down and landed on his chest. Dominic crushed it and tried to eat it! There was a huge big butterfly on my back and I did not even know it was there. I nearly freaked out when I realised!

Held Captive

I used to complain that I was being held prisoner by sleeping children. They were in bed at seven o'clock and I could not leave the house. Sometimes I used to email him and say, 'I just want a bar of chocolate!'

He would tell me to go and buy chocolate but I couldn't, if I had, I'd have eaten it! He never said it was getting on his nerves but … The next time he deployed and the chocolate email came through, he replied, 'Have you made bread since I left?'

'No.'

'Look in the bread maker.'

There was a little bar of chocolate he'd hidden there. He had hidden little bars of chocolate all around the house so that when I was complaining that I was being held prisoner, I had chocolate. He had been dead six weeks when I went into the car for something and found a bar of chocolate.

People say it was a hard life, but I missed it desperately when it was gone.

Made Redundant

Mark got made redundant in the first tranche of the redundancies. He got a letter. If I remember rightly, if you had been in less than five years you were safe. You were the cheapest. If you were nearing your twenty-two years, you were safe as well. It was the bracket in the middle, because they cost the most.

Mark was told it was because he had done so much sea time. Not that he had asked for it. He was told 'this is your draft and off you go'. He cost them more, though, because his sea time was more than was legally allowed and so, because he was over the limit, they would have to pay him more for every single day he was away at sea. Obviously, the cost of him, compared to the cost of anyone who hadn't been doing any drafts was significant. It was all financial for them.

Equally, Mark was just short of his twelve years, and I know a lot of people that this has happened to in the same position. If he'd done his twelve years they'd have had to give him half his pension. As it stands now, because they made him redundant and he died a day before he'd been out six months, I am not even entitled to his pension. I have to wait until he would have been 60. Twenty-one years I have to wait, which is a double kick in the teeth, I think.

It was very callous how they told him he was being made redundant. He was on his way home from a six month draft in the Falklands, waiting in the departure lounge. They handed him the letter telling him. Everyone had to get the letter at the same time. It devastated him.

He was trying to get on the rigs. He did lots of courses. He was finding it frustrating. He would see the jobs and he would say he could do them standing on his head, but they always asked what experience he had. 'I've been in the Royal Navy for eleven years and been at sea for most of it.'

'No real experience then.'

He was struggling.

Rest in Peace

Mark Douglas died on 29 March 2013. He had been gardening with the family when he suffered a ruptured aorta. All efforts to save him were in vain. He was 39 years of age:

> It was Good Friday and it was a sudden death, so the police had to be involved, and the coroner. Apparently, nobody dies on a bank holiday because coroners don't work over bank holiday weekends. Then, they have a big backlog of all the people who've died. So, he was in the hospital for ten days for autopsy and they couldn't release the body. The girl who worked in the morgue said, 'I am so sorry. Nobody should have to be here so long.'
>
> We had his funeral at HMS *Collingwood*. The Portsmouth Military Wives Choir sang. I wasn't a member then, because when it started it was just as Mark was being made redundant and I didn't see the point. He loved the military wives choirs, and thought the whole ethos of it was brilliant. He was a big one for tradition, history and knowing where you are from. It was lovely when the choir said they would sing. Dominic wanted them to sing a song he knew from school and the twins sat down with him to coax the words out of him. They found it on YouTube and the choir learnt the words.
>
> Dominic was 7 when his father died. He completely understood what was going on, but I think because Mark died on 29 March and the funeral was not until 15 April we had time to get things right and Dominic was involved with all the funeral planning. I just think you need to normalise it, because when I was at school I had friends who lost their parents and they were traumatised by it. I didn't want him to look back and say, 'Everything was fine until then.'

Joining the Military Wives Choir

> A friend phoned me up and said that she had found out that it was not too late for me to join the Portsmouth Military Wives Choir. We joined the choir together. We turned up and then discovered that it was in the chapel at *Collingwood*, which was where my husband's funeral had been held. I got to the door and said, 'Oh, my God', She went to hold my hand and I said, 'Don't be nice to me. Tell me to get in there and sing.' She did. I went in and have been going ever since. Dominic tells people, 'My mum's in the choir.' It's nice to hear him.

❧ Antonella Duncan ❧

Army wife Antonella loves to sing, and the formation of the Salisbury
Military Wives Choir was just what she was looking for:

Joining a Choir

We moved in the October and I remember that there was a choir started
in Darington, just a normal choir. I had said to my husband, 'I think
I might join'. I wanted to sing. Then I saw the Salisbury Military Wives
Choir on Facebook. I told another wife, Caroline Board. She said, 'If you
go, I will go.' We went there. I did not know anybody else. It was good.

The Chelsea Pensioners

We do a medley of war songs. There was a couple of pensioners in
wheelchairs at the front and they were enjoying it. I was watching them.
When the medley of war songs came on it was like they were buoyed,
they woke up. They were back there and all of a sudden the foot was
going and the hand, and I just looked and I shed a tear. There was a
woman, one of the carers, she was crying. So it was lovely.

We have done a lot of fancy stuff but really, the loveliest were the smaller
events. For BLESMA [the charity for limbless veterans] or local charities, you feel the people and if you are raising money and you can see the
people that money is helping, it is the proudest thing. As a wife, you do
your bit by following your husband and keeping the family going. On top
of that you can see you are raising money and you are helping others.

Role Reversal

Sometimes it is role reversal. 'You have to look after the kids this weekend, the choir are away,' I say to my husband. He did a tour in Iraq just
after we got married then he went off to Afghanistan, so he was away for
seven months. I say to him that he still owes me. If we wrote it all down,
all the exercises on top. It is not just the tour, then you have the months
of exercises, four or five weeks at a time. He owes me.

Sending Parcels

There are a lot of charities who send parcels to service personnel. They
try to do it in an orderly fashion, because otherwise it gets to the point
where there are so many that our regular parcels don't get through. It is
nice for their morale.

After a while you get a bit stuck for what to send them. I would ask Keith what he wanted. He would say, 'Nothing.' I would say, 'They do Irn-Bru in little plastic bottles, shall I sneak one in?' (There are not supposed to be liquids sent in our parcels.)

'No, I'm fine.'

Then he would phone and he'd say such-and-such has been sent an Irn-Bru bottle and it's lovely. I don't think they know what they want! Anything.

Watching the News

I think everybody's experiences are different. For me, I never watch the news. My husband's mother, she would watch the news constantly. I don't think she quite understood how I couldn't. He is there. I know he is there, but I have a baby. I can't sit in my pyjamas all day and worry. If anything happened, we would know before anything came on the news.

You still see families that are devastated by things that have happened. Inside of you, that selfish bit says, 'Thank God, it's not me.'

I just couldn't, but there are some that constantly watch the news and are obsessed. I just couldn't, because I think if I started doing that I would not be able to function.

Mess Dinners

I never could conform. I never got up just to prove a point, but I always said to my husband, 'I am sorry, you are in the army. I am now in the mess, but if I need to go to the toilet, I will get up and go to the toilet.'

The other thing you must deal with if you go to a mess dinner are the name cards on the table. Every soldier will go in and take the name tag and put it in his pocket, because what his mates will do is pinch the name tag and write a message on it and give it to the RSM (Regimental Sergeant Major). It would say something like, 'I really fancy you sir, from Sergeant Duncan', or whatever. Then everyone would be laughing and the person gets fined a bottle of port.

I remember our first mess do was not actually in the mess back in North Yorkshire. It was a country home thing. They had been golfing all day, and I said to him, 'This is my first mess do as well, please don't get too drunk.' I was upstairs and I heard this noise downstairs. I thought, 'Oh-oh!' I sobered him up a little bit with coffee, and he got dressed, but a button had come off his mess dress so that is a fine – a bottle of port. I think he had about three or four fines that night!

When they get to the port they do the toast to the queen, and in some messes the port decanter can't leave the table. You can't lift it from the table, so when you get to the last bit, there are people pouring it off the edge of the table.

You have a mess leader and you have to wait until he starts his dinner before you even pick up the cutlery.

Working

I work from home, and Keith does not get it. I do beading embroidery and make decorative picture frames and cushions. He thinks it's lovely because he loves me. When I get orders for things, I think he is quite surprised. I can feel him thinking, 'Someone wants to buy?' It's not that he does not think it good enough to buy, but he is a bloke and this is girl stuff. It's personalised and special.

❧ HELEN MALCOLMSON ☙

Helen is one of the few ladies in this book to have been on both sides of the fence. She was in the military when she met her Royal Navy husband, Lee:

The RAF or Canada?

I qualified in the NHS in 1998. I trained in London, but couldn't really afford to stay in London so I thought, 'How can I earn a similar amount of money but not live in London?' The two options were to emigrate to Canada or join the RAF.

I went to the careers office and they said, 'Oh, no, we don't take nurses. We don't do nursing in the RAF.' A guy in the corner of the careers office put his hand up and said, 'We do! We do!' It turned out to be the navy. Thirteen weeks later, I was on a train to Plymouth. I never quite got to Canada. Three days into basic training I met Lee. He was in my class. Thirteen years later, we are married with a 9-year-old.

No Fraternising in Basic Training!

Because we were slightly older, the PO who took us through our training and our CO knew we were together, but they sort of left us alone a bit. Then Lee passed out, and he got based in Portsmouth and I got drafted to Plymouth. We were told it would never work.

Distance does work, as we know! Lee had a bit of training in Plymouth, and then went to Portsmouth. Six months later, he was on HMS *Newcastle*. He was on there until she decommissioned in 2005 and was on that ship when we got married.

I was working in Derriford Hospital in Plymouth, and I was living at HMS *Drake* and trying to commute at weekends. He was doing the same thing, until I finally said that I needed to move and got drafted up to Portsmouth. I started working at Hasler. That was in 2001.

In 2002, just before Christmas, I got called into the office and told, 'Have a nice Christmas, we don't know when you are coming back'. I got sent on a ship that we thought was going on an exercise but when we got to Cyprus we carried on going and we were in Iraq. I was out there from January, to four weeks before I got married in August. We planned the wedding while I was out there.

Wedding Planning

I got emails from my mum with samples of the different things I had to choose. At two o'clock in the morning, when you have your down time, I was going through favours and emailing my mum back and forth, saying, 'Yes, I want those colours and can you get the bridesmaids to try these dresses on because I've seen these ones that I like'.

I don't know how we managed to do it, but literally we planned the whole wedding while I was in Iraq and Lee was on firefighting exercises, so he wasn't at home either! I chose my wedding dress in a size 14 and then sailed for seven months. By the time I came back, I was a size 8. I tried the dress on four weeks before I got married and said, 'This is not going to work!'

Getting Married

Then we got married. It was the perfect day. We had a complete military theme to the wedding. Our cake looked like three navy hats put together. My mum commissioned two glass anchors with rope twisting them together, which went on the top of the cake. We couldn't find a man in navy uniform to go on the cake and I didn't want a man in a suit because Lee was getting married in rig [uniform].

We had three days in Paris and then Lee had to go away again. He was away doing a tour of Europe. I came home for the weekend in November and that's when I fell pregnant with my daughter.

Lee sailed on an eight month deployment in January. He got back on my due date. I had a huge bump. I had a 10lb 10oz baby! I remember standing on the edge of the dock waiting for the ship to come in and thinking I don't know how he is going to recognise me. I was huge. I couldn't get up the ladders or anything. He did recognise me but probably because of all the family around us. The pregnant one's the wife!

He was there for the birth. I was two and a half weeks late. He had been given three weeks leave from the ship so he only got one week of paternity as he then had to go away to do his Killick's course [leading hand]. I was left with a week-old baby with no family down here. Now my parents are retired so they help and have moved down to Portchester from up north. That is five minutes away.

Leaving the Navy

I left the navy when I had my daughter. Lee and I barely saw each other as it was, with me in the navy. I was told that, pretty much as soon as I came back off maternity leave, I'd be sent to Afghanistan. Three of my friends had all ready gone. I couldn't do it. It's easy for me to get a job as a nurse, so I decided to leave. I got a job back in the NHS after that.

I think Iraq really affected me and I don't know if I'd have been able to cope going out to Afghanistan. Iraq was, for me, very, very difficult. I was on the ship all the time. I got stuck in a shower with a prisoner of war with a needle, and he was by the door and no one could get in. I got threatened and spat at, and things like that. It wasn't a pleasant experience and I don't think anything can prepare you for that.

We lost a couple of friends while we were out there, too. They died in a helicopter accident. That was really hard. I lost someone else that I knew while they were out in Afghanistan. I just don't think I would be able to cope with that.

Leaving was easy with the pregnancy. They just got rid of me. I left on maternity leave and that was it. I went in and signed something to say that I wouldn't be back after my maternity leave. There was no handshake, no nothing. That was it, done. They are not very good at the end bit. They are really good at getting you in. They look after you while you're in, but the moment you want to leave … I was in the Royal Navy for six years.

I was really lucky, because the place that I was working at when I was pregnant and still in the navy was a civilian day surgery unit. They employed me as a civilian nurse after my maternity leave. I carried on working for the NHS. I knew the system, I knew what I was doing and they knew me, so it was a case of, 'Are you sure you want to work for us? When can you start?'

I was working full-time. I had no support or help from family. I was spending between £700 and £900 a month on childcare. It was hard, but you get on with it. I can't imagine doing it any other way.

The Military Wives Choir

I've always loved music. It took a lot of confidence to try and write that first email to say I wanted to join. I'd seen it on TV and thought I'd really like to do that. It's been amazing ever since.

They are all so friendly. When I had my back surgery they were such a rock. I honestly don't know how I would have coped this year without the Military Wives. I have friends for life. It sounds corny, but they've been amazing and lovely people. Plus, I get to sing in fantastic gigs and do things you would never expect to be doing. Singing for 5,000 people at the Rose Bowl; singing for God-knows-how-many people at the South Coast Proms in Portsmouth; going to London to do the poppy launch; we were at Gunwharf Quay in Portsmouth to launch the Poppy Appeal there. You have bits going on all the time.

It's great. I love it. I love singing. I'm musical anyway, but I didn't have self-confidence. I wasn't sure if I could do it or if they would accept me. I felt so isolated. That first email – I think I must have written it about ten times before I sent it. I'm just starting to become my own person again. You become a wife, you become a mum, and I've lost everything else, so now I'm me again, with the Military Wives. I feel like I'm getting myself back after so long, probably since Iraq. Now I'm becoming the person I always was.

I think, because everything sort of just happened, I never really had time. I got back from Iraq and I got married and I was pregnant and then I left the military. Then you just live. You deal with your child and life.

I realised that I had no support when Lee is away. You almost switch off and don't really live. You sort of exist. I don't know if that makes sense. You close the door, and just wait for however long it is until the door opens again and then you start living again. With the choir, now I don't just exist, I feel like I have a little bit of me back. Without them, I'd still be closing the door.

My daughter is my life and I love her dearly but sometimes you just need *you*, an identity rather than just being a wife, a mum, a nurse. What am I? I want to be Helen sometimes. I think that is what the choir has done for me, made me realise that I am something and I'm part of something that is so huge, so amazing and I love it.

Spine Tingling!

At the South Coast Proms, singing in front of 7,000 people in Portsmouth [HMS *Excellent*, Whale Island, Portsmouth, July 2013], I was petrified! It was so hot. It was spine tingling; an amazing experience. We've done little gigs in front of a couple of hundred people, and the Rose Bowl, for a cricket match, was in front of 5,000 people. Then we do the poppy launch. You get the little gigs, which are quite intimate and then you get the huge ones. It is such a surreal experience.

I sang at Romsey Cathedral a couple of months ago and it was beautiful to sing in such a fantastic place. The Royal Marines Band was there. Even though you are singing, you think, 'We sound really good!' You don't notice it, and then you get into it. I remember I couldn't remember the first word of one of the songs! I was right at the front, too. Even through the intro, I was thinking, 'I can't remember the first word!' I had to whisper to my friend next to me, 'What's the first word?'

'Are.'

'Oh!' Then I knew what I was doing! My mind just went blank. What if I had opened my mouth and nothing came out?

Understanding?

Lee is very supportive, but he does not really understand about the fact that I now have a life outside, rather than being the lady that doors close to. That has taken a bit of getting used to for him, especially with the South Coast Proms. The day he was due to come home, I left him at a pub because I had to do a rehearsal. He got home after a deployment and I was off singing with the Military Wives! He was not massively impressed with me. He understands that I originally needed the support as I had been ill, but now I think he gets that it is more than that. He is very supportive, but I can't get him to come to a concert yet, although he did come along to the South Coast Prom.

Dresses Galore!

We have a dress code. At different gigs we wear different things. We've got a black Military Wives tee shirt with the Military Wives logo. With that, we wear either black trousers or a skirt and boots. It is informal.

Then, the next step up is a black, knee-length dress for smart casual. Then, for the big gigs, it's cocktail dresses. I have different ones for different things. It's great because you get to go shopping! I have three different black dresses. I've never worn so much black! Now, because I've worn them so many times, I need new ones.

We can't really afford to buy another couple of hundred pounds worth of dress each time we do a concert. We're trying to do a clothes bank together, so, as we are all completely different shapes and sizes, if we all put our things together then we can wear each other's dresses and swap. I've got a three-bedroom house, but there is only me, my husband and daughter, and our spare room is full of junk, so I've volunteered to buy a clothes rack. In Argos you can buy one. They are not expensive and we can stick all the dresses up there. Then, if you say, 'I am this size, what have you got?' it is there.

Surgery

I've had spinal surgery for an injury from when I was out in Iraq. I lost the feeling in my leg and had back pain. The doctors thought it was a disc. It turned out I had damaged the nerves. I fell through a door and went down a couple of stairs while I was on the ship. Then I damaged a nerve and, apparently, two nerves had joined together so that there was not enough space for the nerve to come out of my spine. They made the hole bigger in the bone where the nerves come out and have taken away part of the bones and joints in my spine to give me room for them again. Hopefully, I'm fixed now. This year has been a complete write-off. I'm on the mend, and hoping to go back to work soon and put it all to bed.

Lee has been back for four or five months and helped me through the surgery. The navy have been really good. When he is home, he is able to help. He doesn't work long hours when he's back in Portsmouth. He is the PO stores accountant.

When he was out in Bahrain, I was on my own, trying to hold down a job and things. It brought me down, but I tried. So many other people have more problems than me. The girls have been brilliant, coming round and making sure I'm OK. Even just popping in, 'I'm on my way to Portsmouth, thought I'd pop in and have a coffee.' One did my washing up for me!

Then they turned up in the hospital to make sure I was all right after the operation. Before the surgery it was really difficult. I was on crutches, and they were brilliant. I would turn up for a gig and they would help me up the stairs. I tried to carry on with making myself do the stuff with the Military Wives, even though I could quite easily have closed the door but I wanted to keep that.

Now one of the group's father-in-law passed away yesterday, and we're helping her. I feel like I can help somebody else. Do the same for her that they did for me. We're just like a complete support network of friends. They all understand. Friends who aren't navy wives don't understand what it's like when your husband is away. You don't need to say anything to them, they just know. You don't need them to say anything, you just need them to be there.

Lee is not going to be here at Christmas, so the gigs we do at Christmas and the do that I am making myself go to will help – just seeing other people. We wouldn't have done anything this Christmas, otherwise. Having the girls makes you realise you have to do other things as well. You can't just be a military wife. At my job, if I say, 'Lee's away', they say, 'Oh! I'd love that! Six months away from my husband. It would be brilliant!' I think, 'You don't know what you are saying.' You have to just say, 'Hm, yeah. I'm pretty sure you wouldn't.' Whereas if I say to my military friends, 'Lee's away in a couple of weeks', I just get a hug. They understand.

Limelight

Wives are a complete nonentity. Without the choir, I don't think anyone would have known anything about the wives. Your husband gets the limelight – evacuating people from Syria and it's on the news. Fantastic.

What you don't see is that, actually, when he was doing the evacuation the first thing I knew of it was when I turned on the news and saw his ship. I saw him shoving people onto the ship and thought, 'well, he was due home tomorrow, I guess that's not happening'. I'd planned a couple of weeks leave because I knew he was coming home. Things like that are not newsworthy though, are they?

SARAH HATTINGH

Originally from New Zealand, Sarah Hattingh lives in the army garrison town of Tidworth, with her REME lance corporal husband, Rouvierre, and Percy, the dog that idolises her:

Not an Army Wife

We got married in April 2011. I met him when he was straight out of basic [training].

When I first moved here, to Tidworth, I hated it. To be honest, I used to be quite rude about the persona of a military wife. I would go on Facebook and there would be other military wives that had that as their job title. So, they would have where they are from, where they live and their occupation would be an army wife. I thought, 'There has got to be more to you than that.'

It is what they thought they had become. I used to take the mick all the time! You would see them getting their nails done, their hair. They were 'ladies who lunch'. And that was who they were. I am educated, and I am a primary school teacher, and I get up and I go to work every day. I have a salary and I have my life at home and then my work life, and then my personal life is separate.

Whereas, for these ladies, when I got here, the army was their life. Their husband was their life – his stripes, what he wore, his rank – and they just didn't seem to have much more to it. But it has been since my husband has gone away, and I have had to meet these people and socialise with them, that I know there is more to them. *They* just don't know that there is.

It wasn't until my husband was away that I had no choice but to get involved with the welfare then. Our welfare was really good. They arranged all kinds of things, and I met people. I feel as if I have friends now, among the wives. I have some who are best friends and I have some who are acquaintances. So my view of what an army wife was when I first got here has changed loads.

I remember that, just before they were deployed to Afghanistan, I was sitting beside a lady I had never met before and she was telling me that they were looking at sending their children to boarding school. She was saying that she did not know about it, as she would be left at home by herself.

I said, 'Why not go and find a job?'

She said, 'Oh, I don't think that my husband would ever let me do that.'

I just thought 'Ahh! You make me feel so sad.' I asked, 'Why don't you study something?'

'No. I was never very good at school.'

They are 'just a wife' and they see their role, and their husbands promote their role, as being a good wife and keeping the home happy so that he can do his job.

Military Life

I had no preconceptions about what military life was, or what I was letting myself in for. It was awful. I had no idea! It was just a job. Just like any other. I had not considered what it would involve at all.

Up until we moved here after we had been married, I was living in London and I would come down on the weekend. I had never been to Tidworth. We would do touristy things and I had no idea, until we got married and I moved my stuff, and then it was like ... 'Oh, my goodness!'

It wasn't that I didn't like it. It was because the community is so tight and everybody is really cliquey, not in a bad way, it is only until you find where you fit in. When you first get here it is really intimidating. Actually, now I have been here long enough, I make an effort that people did not make with me. So when new neighbours have moved in, I make sure that I go over there, because nobody did that for me. They would be out on the street with the other wives gossiping. Every single house here is military.

Sarah, the Teacher

I love my job. I have no problem whatsoever getting up every morning and going to work. Clarendon School is the garrison school, and when I first got here, I got a job there. I lasted a year before I resigned.

Nothing was wrong. I just found it really difficult being professional and keeping our lives separate. That was important to me. I found that really hard.

The other thing I found hard was because I had just moved here. I was meeting people through work, but you can't be friends with them because you have professional boundaries. I could not go to Tesco's or go to the pub and walk home because I would run into parents and kids, and it was hard. They were really nice families, but I could not have my own life. I lasted a year there and then moved into Amesbury. It is only a fifteen minute drive so it is not too bad.

I teach 7 and 8-year-olds. They are old enough to be able to get on with it but not so old that they are cheeky.

My husband cops it at work because I earn more than he does. I think his friends take the mick a little bit. He does not seem to mind, though. He knew when we met. I think he likes that. When we first got here, I remember asking him – there was a wife thing that came up, at Christmas, I think – if it made him look better if I got involved in these things. He did not actually give me an answer about whether it did or not. I don't know. I have met wives who are too involved and a little bit busybody, and going in and asking why their husbands did not get promoted that round, and I will not be doing that!

Afghanistan

When they leave, people who aren't involved with the military in any way say, 'Wow! How is that? How can you put up with it?' I have spoken to other wives, and they agree with me that they just want their men gone!

The kit is all over the house for weeks before. They are not the husband that you know because they don't know what is going on and work is busy. Stuff is just everywhere. People say that this must be really hard, but I say to him, 'Just get out, leave, go', and then we can start the countdown to him coming back. Other people don't understand that. It is the same with him coming back. The people at work say that I must be so excited. But an army wife is like a parent. You don't get excited, because he is not the same person who has come back.

R&R was awful. He was just horrible. I said to him, 'I just want you to go back to Afghanistan'. It is awful to say this. Only another military wife would understand. You just want them gone. They are not here. My husband is a really sensitive, gentle type and he came back really bossy and really controlling and I have never seen him like that before. So much control is taken off him out there, because they are told to do everything at certain times, because there is an order to their day at all times. They don't make choices about what they eat; they eat what has been cooked. There is no control. When he came home, he was over-compensating. Trying to gain control over everything. You think it must be amazing to have them back, but it isn't.

Readjusting

I got used to being here on my own. Doing what I wanted when I wanted. Then, all of a sudden, there is somebody else. Little things get on your nerves. Silly things like he puts the ketchup in the cupboard, not the fridge. They are non-important things that I just have to get over. It takes a while to retrain them. Last year he went to Canada for four months. When he came back it did take three or four weeks for him to learn how to recycle and where the washing goes – normal day-to-day things that they just forget.

You Obsess so you don't Obsess About the Worst

He is a bit of a balancing person. Before he went, he sat me down and said we needed to sit down and talk about all the things that I found tricky while he was in Canada, and solve them before he left. Canada was the first time he had left me. I had only been here for six months and so I had not made a good circle of friends that I could just pop around to their house. I found that really hard. We sat down and spoke about Canada when we knew he was going to Afghanistan, and he said, 'New things are going to come up, but let's eliminate all the things that we already know are going to happen.' So we did that. It was much easier.

He does really well at his job and, from what I understand, he is well liked. He actually got awarded a gold medal while he was in Afghanistan. I don't know what for, but he has done really well and he does work hard. He seems to enjoy it. He really wanted to deploy. It was like a teacher who trained for three or four years and then realised that they would never go into a classroom. He really wanted to go. I asked my husband if he wrote me a farewell letter. He said he started one but couldn't finish it.

To be honest, we had a welfare department that was really good. We had a meeting, and they put everybody's nerves at rest. They said that, if you see it and it is bad on the news, you know it is not your husband. It won't be on TV until you have been told. If someone tells you about something bad that has happened, it has nothing to do with you. From what I understand, they weren't told that before, and every time they saw something the wives went into panic mode. We did not have that when my husband went to Afghanistan, so we were really lucky.

Actually, at these meetings, they are also making sure that everything is in order. Who knows how to check the oil on their car? I was the only person who put their hand up. There were three of us who knew where the fuse box was in the house. That is another thing that these wives have trouble with. There are men's roles, and there are women's. It is very traditional. Welfare had to hold mornings where a mechanic showed them how to check their oil.

Welfare had something on every weekend free of charge that you could opt into. From shopping in Winchester, they took us to Bournemouth beach or to the zoo. There was something different every weekend. The welfare staff were really good. The whole time that they were in Afghanistan they were running these events and making sure that all was okay. Sometimes they held a DVD night for the kids and ordered in a whole load of pizza and put on a movie and the kids could go in and watch. They took videos of the men out there and they sent us all DVDs. So my husband was giving me a tour of his workshop and his room. It got screened in front of all the wives. It was fun.

Planning Ahead

When asked what she planned to be doing in five years' time, Sarah was stumped, revealing the fundamental uncertainty that is never far from a military wife's mind:

You don't know where you are going to live. I don't know if we will have children in five years, because in five years I will be old! I don't know. I could still be here or in New Zealand. We could be out of the army. With all the redundancies, we just don't know. That is another choice that is taken away from you. A lot of military families volunteer, but my husband didn't. It would be such a scary thought. It is the uncertainty in the current economic climate, you don't know if work is going to be around the corner.

❧ JADE LEAHY ❧

Jade lives what she terms 'my crazy life!' Brought up as a military child, she is now married to Sam, a Royal Navy air engineer:

I went to a boarding school in Somerset as dad moved so much. A lot of military people were there. There was a local boarding school closing down, so they all started coming to our school but they were all army children. It was like an army and a navy school coming together.

That is how we met. His dad's still in the army. We have known each other since we were 11. We hated each other then – as you do! We've been together since we were 15. It's crazy because we have two completely different lives. His dad wanted him to go to Welbeck Defence Sixth Form College in Leicestershire, but no, he followed me to sixth form and decided to join the navy. It was the best thing he did. His dad is so proud of him now. He went off and did it himself.

Joining the Navy?

I was the one who wanted to join the navy. I had seen my dad go through it and I loved it. I think it has been part of my life. Between me and my husband, we have worked out that we have had thirty-five house moves. As much as I hate it, it is part of my life. I love moving. I love the excitement. So right, I'm joining.

So, I was down the careers office and in the process of doing my AIB (Admiralty Interview Board) and going through to Dartmouth. Then me and Sam started getting serious, and from then on I thought, 'I don't need to join the navy because he's doing it!' It was scary, though. It came about because dad was talking to Sam when he came down from a weekend off from school. My dad was saying, 'Oh, yeah, this is what I do in the navy'. Literally, a week later, Sam says, 'I'm joining, doing your dad's job'. My dad was in a complete panic. 'Oh no, your dad's gonna kill me! I've just converted you to the navy!' It just appealed to him. He's now at Dartmouth doing officer training but he's an air engineer. He spent most of his time down at Yeovilton.

Sam was halfway through sixth form, doing his AS exams, and he just decided there and then, he didn't want the army because they move a lot. He's spent a lot of his life in Pakistan, in Northern Ireland, Cyprus and Germany. I think he just got fed up with being in boarding school and in education. He wasn't ready for uni and what his dad wanted for him at the time. He just wanted to work and earn money. He joined the navy, and from day one he went on to a fast-track scheme. So for eight years he's been sat in a classroom to get to where he is now. Actually, it has worked out very well for him and his dad. He has done two Afghanistan tours, Iraq and Kenya.

Afghanistan

We had been expecting Afghanistan. I was pregnant.

My dad goes away. I remember coming back from school one day. Mum had just picked me up and the next-door neighbour ran in the house and said, 'He's gone. He's left a letter for you. He'll be back in six months.' I was used to that type of lifestyle anyway. When I was a child I was in boarding school and I was quite protected from it.

When it's your husband, it's completely different. It was horrible. I was pregnant, but I was working full-time. I wasn't really in a community where I met naval people. So it was tough. I don't think you expect the navy to go to the places that they do. You don't hear about it.

He loves it, but you don't get to talk to him. This is the hardest thing. When he did make the odd phone call, I can remember the alarms going off in the background and then him just saying, 'I got to go, bye'. That was in Iraq. I didn't speak to him for a week. Iraq was awful. You just have to wait for a phone call. It's horrendous. They watch what they say on the phone as well, and you try to get conversation out of them and all he could say was 'yes' or 'no' half the time, so it's hard, but more difficult when children are involved, I think.

Crazy Life!

He didn't go away for two years because he was on courses. Then Afghanistan was the first trip when we were married. He had two Afghanistan tours, and Kenya in between. They go away, they come back and then they have three months back at home, but Kenya was in between that, and then they go away again.

When they are on a front line squadron you just don't see them. It's not until they are on a second line squadron, or on a course, that you see them. He went away when I was twelve weeks pregnant and then came back when I was heavily pregnant and looking completely different. He didn't know how to act. He felt even too scared to hug me because he didn't know if it was going to hurt. It's things like that, when they haven't been there to see you grow, for a man is a real shock. He came back to a bump and he had three days with me and was gone again on a course. It's just crazy. I don't know why I let myself in for it after my father. Dad did tell me not to marry a sailor!

I was a bookkeeper, training to be an accountant. That's what I had just qualified as before I had Oscar, my first son. I've had my children really close together. I had Oscar and was on my own for five months, then he was doing a course, and then we moved here when I was seven months pregnant again. I went back to work for three months, and then I wasn't very well so I've been off work for eleven months.

It is not worth me going back to work with two young children. Childcare is just through the roof. Staying at home looking after children – I would prefer to be at work. I love my children, but I think that is the hardest thing about being a forces wife. If they are going away for such a length of time you don't really have a choice, sometimes. You have got to stay at home whether you want to work or not. Childcare is fulltime – there is no one to take over in the evenings.

I Just had to Run!

I try to have fun. My biggest thing is fitness. When my husband has been away in the past and I didn't have kids or I wasn't pregnant, then I just had to run. That's what I did to keep fit. It's just brilliant stress-relief and when you're on your own it's an amazing thing to do. My idea of fitness used to be putting on my clothes and going out. I was one of those annoying, naturally skinny people, so I never had to do anything to keep fit, whereas now I have to – my metabolism is starting to slow down, so I'm having to be careful.

Now it's a bit more difficult because I have two children. I used to go running with Oscar in his running buggy, but the new baby is too young so I can't do it yet. I don't have a lot of hobbies.

I like working, but I can't work at the moment. I miss working. I think that's what's hard because you make a lot of sacrifices as a wife and the biggest thing we sacrifice, in this day and age, is a career. Most people work now, don't they? To have a decent kind of income you need to both work. That is the big sacrifice I've had to make, to leave my career, accountancy. I'll pick it up one day, hopefully. I purposely picked accountancy.

I saw what mum went through – the endless struggle she went through. Even though she was never in the services, employers only have to look at the address and they know, so they don't recruit you. It happens to this day. Everybody knows where the married quarters are. They only have to look at the address and they know you'll be moving on. I know it sounds daft, but work's my 'me' time. I think that's what I find hard with children. I'd appreciate them a lot more if I was back at work. Just to have a little bit of a break.

Sacrifices

I know I had to make sacrifices when it came to career, but Sam had to make heartbreaking decisions for both of us because he needs to go and do things to support our family. With your first baby you think it will be difficult, but you don't know how difficult it is until you have the baby. Everyone tells you and you say, 'Yeah, it's fine.' Oscar was a planned baby, but in the military there's never a good time, as we found out because Sam was in Afghanistan, and then he was on a course. He came home for the delivery in hospital and had twenty-four hours with me and then went back. He drove me home and dropped me with my baby and left. You are kicked out of hospital so quickly now. They don't show you anything. I'd never held a baby.

He talks about it now, saying it was the worst thing he'd ever done. He felt awful for having to do that, and so responsible for what I had to go through in leaving me. He had a choice. He didn't have to leave me but he would have sacrificed his promotions. We made the joint decision that it was the best one for our future and our children. I'm left with the children. They're not going to remember that bit. I thought I'd be brilliant at this because of my parents. I grew up and dad wasn't there. I was shipped off to boarding school and did not see my family, so I thought I was the perfect candidate to be a forces wife!

The Future

He'll be back in eleven months and we have decided, because we've had a lot of house moves, and we do love moving, but we've come to a point where we want to settle. So we're going to stay here and buy a house here in Hill Head. They are always back and forth here for training, so it's our home. The schools are better. Things like that, I'm starting to think about now. There's a lot of downsides to going through boarding school. Me and my husband haven't had a childhood. I know my mum and dad did what was best for us, and I thank them, but there was a lot of things we missed out on and I won't be sending the children to boarding school, maybe when they are older, but not young. So we need to be settled and have a home and some family time.

❧ STEFFI HUGHES ❧

Stefanie Hughes, known to all as 'Steffi', has been married to soldier husband, David, for twenty-one years:

All New

I was very much aware that he was in the army when we met. It was all new to me, coming from a non-army German background, but all *very* exciting! Especially when he was telling his stories from his times abroad …

In the beginning, it was all new and sounded like one big adventure! And, to start with, I guess it actually was, as obviously I was living in a new country, although I had been to England on a number of occasions before, and even spent part of my studies in London. Life takes over, though, and I realised that things were not that different from Germany. The things I have missed over the years are mostly things that I either now can get here too, thanks to more international products available

throughout – supermarkets such as Lidl and Aldi do help in these mat-
ters – or, due to years without, I might have either forgotten or learnt to
do without.

The Best Thing

The best thing for me is, what a lot of my friends would have classed as
the worst bit of being an army wife, the constant moving around. To me,
it was just a chance to see more places and meet more people. It never
bothered me that we moved very frequently to start with (in all these
years we have now made it to house number twelve). The only part of
life that got affected by it, and caused some grumbling at times, was the
work side of things for me, as I have had a number of brilliant jobs that
came to an end far too early due to a move too far away for commuting.
I think I managed to keep a job over two postings once in that time, but
generally, having a job any longer than one year always was a virtue and
did not happen too frequently. But on the other hand, it gave me job
diversity too and that is never a bad thing!

Once children were on the scene things got a little trickier, especially
once they started school, but with the opportunity to have them go to
a good boarding school, something we could never have dreamed of
without the army's financial support, and with that came a very good
education and stable friendships, things became easier again.

Unfortunately, the longed for overseas postings did not happen
as much as I had hoped, although we did make it to Heidelberg and
Münster in Germany, but with those postings I almost felt a little cheated,
as it was home ground for me. You can't have it all, I guess!

The Worst Bit

The worst thing about being married to the army has to be the housing side and the moving issues that families have to put up with in line
with postings. Family issues are, in most cases, never really taken into
consideration, and planning your move around your family with all that
involves, such as finding new schools etc. is not always made easy.

As the army wife you do, at times, feel at the mercy of the powers that
be, with tons of frustrations included. However, in our case those occasions were rare, although we did have one incident where David was
already in his new post up in Scotland and we were meant to join him.
All had been made ready, schools cancelled and movers were booked to
come on the following Monday morning, when David called me on

the Friday afternoon, just before I was going to get the kids from their school, and told me that the whole move was cancelled. I admit I did lose my temper slightly with the phone flying across the room and me shouting abuse at the top of my voice. As I said, though, that was the once and, in general, we have been all right in most of the cases.

With regards to the housing issues, again we have had some nice houses along the way and generally it hasn't been that bad, in comparison with other families' experiences, but the system leaves me baffled on quite a regular basis. I do appreciate the fact that a house comes with each posting, and I can only imagine what an administrative nightmare it must be to ensure there is sufficient housing supply. However, when it comes to the state of the houses, I do sometimes lose the will to live. The thumb rule seems to be *as cheaply and little as possible*. Well, if money is tight, that is a logical approach, but if they did a quality job from the start, their maintenance costs henceforward surely would save money, as things will last longer. This is a theory many wives share, as far as I know. You learn to make do and to sort a few things out yourself, even at your own expense, in order to get an improvement.

Playing Second Fiddle

I have always worked, only with short interruptions due to moves or having children. My original calling was as an international PA. That is, a personal assistant with languages, but over the years I have worked in all sorts of offices as a secretary, an administrator, a PA, as a swimming instructor and even behind the till at Sainsbury's. Whatever I worked as, or for, has always taken second position in our lives and as soon as we are on the move, I have to leave one job and find a new one. As mentioned above, that is one of the frustrations, however, I knew that from the start and therefore cannot hold that against David. His is the main income and it is the bit that dictates our lives.

Good and Bad Times

We've had good and bad times, as every marriage does, I am sure. It's a working relationship and it takes two to tango, so you constantly evolve and adapt. Over the years, we've had plenty of laughs, some tears and some nice holidays.

One trip was through David's one year posting to Sierra Leone. We met up in Cape Town, South Africa, and then travelled along the Garden Route all the way across to Port Elizabeth. That was a fabulous holiday!

Our postings abroad, to Heidelberg and Münster, were a great experience and we made a lot of friends with whom we are still in contact. Indeed, over the past twenty plus years we have made a lot of very good friends! Keeping in touch with them and with family isn't all that difficult, as both the international travel opportunities and the social media technology have really shrunk the world!

The Children

Of course, there are our two children, Kimberley (16) and Timothy (12), who we are very proud of (even if they do drive us round the bend on a regular basis) and who have brought us tons of lovely memories and anecdotes over the years. The most surprising army fact currently is that Kimberley has been enjoying the Clayesmore Cadet Force (CCF) very much, and is now looking at possibly going down the military route in order to finance her studies to become a vet. Who would have thought that?

Being a military wife has meant I was able to give my children the chance to grow up with two languages, which, in my daughter's case, has worked out very well as she is pretty much bilingual, like me. I am still working on my son …

The Salisbury Military Wives Choir

I had followed the programme on TV about the first military wives choir, thinking, 'if only we could have one of those here'. Then I found out via the local radio station that a choir had been formed. I always wanted to go and lots of my friends had joined and urged me to come along, but it never really worked out over that first year.

When I finally joined in January 2013 (a New Year's resolution!) I absolutely loved it and haven't looked back since. I have made some lovely friends. Every week I look forward to our Thursday night gatherings, as it is a time to laugh, sing and have fun with a whole group of lovely ladies who are all in similar situations and with whom you can have a chat and a giggle. Plus, there is the performance side of it, which is exciting and so rewarding! I wouldn't want to miss it and I always look forward to returning to rehearsals after a break.

Do it all Again?

I ask myself if I would do the military wife life again if I had the chance. Even though there are times where you ask yourself why on earth you are doing it, and keep on doing it, if it came to it, I think I actually would do it all again. Maybe next time it would be with a few variations though, following things I have learnt on this journey.

❧ Lauren Bray ❧

One of Lauren's grandfathers saw service in Aden and Kenya and was awarded the Air Force Cross for bravery. Her other grandfather was a submariner. She is happily married to Royal Navy Lieutenant Commander Andy Bray and they have two children:

I enjoy being Lauren Bray.

We met at college when he was 16. I was in all my first year classes with his brother, his twin, who is now in the Royal Marines Band Service. Then, in my second year, I was with Andy. He was the only 16-year-old who would literally say at every opportunity, 'I'm going to join the navy, I'm going to join the navy!' We didn't know what we were doing tomorrow! He did.

We stayed friends. I went to Winchester University to do business, he joined Dartmouth and we officially got together in February 2003. He was already in the Royal Navy and I knew from the beginning that he was in the services.

I don't mind my own company, but I did not know what I was letting myself in for – you don't at 19. But it didn't really matter because I was in my home town. I went to Winchester University, my family are here, his family, at the time, lived in Surrey, so when he went on leave he went to Surrey. I would go and see him, or he would come to me. He drove from Surrey to Winchester one day when I was working in the bank, just to spend my lunch break with me, then he drove back to Surrey! Bless him. He was my best friend and he still is. It was not really a decision I had to make. It was just going to happen.

He was the most junior officer at our wedding. He was a sub lieutenant and everyone else was a lieutenant. I didn't mind. We got married at St Ann's Church in the dockyard, Portsmouth. We were 22.

He joined the navy straight from college. He did not have a degree. His family see the value of education as much as the next person, but we are massively into education. We are life-long learners and my mum went on and on at him from day one, 'Why don't you get a degree?

You can do it.' My mum signed him up to a level one Open University course whether he liked it or not! Six years later, he got a law degree. He sat exams in Iraq and Afghanistan.

Heartbreaking

Andy leaves me alone a lot! He should be here now, bless him. It was awful when I realised he wasn't coming home when he should have come home. Heart-sinking, because we had already lost my mum.

She was ill before he joined the ship, and the captain was lovely. I think that he went through something similar a couple of years ago. He was able to empathise with Andy. He said, 'If we can get you home, we'll get you home.' It was good to have that in the back of my head. He was not even supposed to be on the ship now. He was not due to join it until it came home later this year. He is always away. That is difficult.

My mum had gone into the hospice on 8 July 2013 and she did not pass away until 28 August. Andy joined the ship on 3 August and I think, in my head, I thought he'd be here. There was no way she could hold on, and she did, which was amazing, good for her! But, this was quite inconvenient really with Andy going away! The captain was even going to move the ship nearer to land so that they could get the helicopter in, but it just didn't work out like that because Syria happened, which was fine but it was really difficult.

Harder for me to think about how hard it was for him. For me, because I had enough going on, and I really wanted him here. Your mum only dies once. He was very, very close to her. I felt worse for him because I had all my family and friends around me and he didn't. He had people he met two weeks previously. A select few knew what was happening, but they were not people he knew forever, and he felt so far away. That made it harder for me.

I was dealing with our daughter, Phoebe – she did not really know. Our son, Thomas, had his own idea about what was going on and I was trying to make sure that he was okay, talking to the school and helping my dad and my sister and my granny, and then I went back to work. It was busy, but I just really missed him. Of all the things we have been through together, I just needed him here for that one thing, and he wasn't. It was not his fault. He thinks I blame him. I don't. I am not cross with him. Everyone understands. I don't mind. It is just that I wanted him there. It was the hardest thing we have been through.

Lucky

We are really lucky, as he was here for the babies being born. He was here for the first ten days of their lives, which actually is nothing, but you are in that state of shock, or whatever it is, after you have a baby and you just get on with it. I have met lots of other wives and people who are not forces wives, and people who cannot comprehend what it must be like and I think, 'What a weak person you are!' Then I think, 'Hold on, they are just different to me.'

I just go with the flow, really, and take it as it comes. I have never sat there counting down the days until him going away, and have never really counted down the days to him coming home, because I am too busy thinking about today. The separation doesn't really bother me – it does bother me! I would love him to be here. He is very big and he is very loud and he puts coffee in the wrong place! He's been here two days, and I think 'When are you going?' [She says this while laughing] I just think, 'I hope that when we are 80, I don't look back and think "that was rubbish"', because when you are in it, you just have to do it. There is nothing else you can do. You get depressed otherwise. I am not that kind of personality.

Iraq and Afghanistan

I was worried, because you see it on the news and you know other people who go and it is massive. It is in everyone's mind. Whether or not they are in the least interested in the armed forces, everyone knows what Iraq is, and Afghanistan. You talk to people at work and you say he is going to Afghanistan and they say 'Oh, my God!', and that makes it worse because they are panicking for you. How is that helpful? I can't endure the time he is away with them saying, 'Are you all right?'

'Yes, I'm fine.'

'Have you heard from him?'

'No, I haven't heard from him.'

Then *they* panic because you haven't heard from him! I was lucky because when he went to Afghanistan he never went for a massive long stint. He did shorter periods at a time. I think the longest period he went was six weeks as he is in an air squadron, 847, and he is their logistics officer, so he will go and set up and then he will come home for a little bit, and then he will go and do something else, and when the squadron eventually came back from Afghanistan, he went and packed everything up and sorted it out and came home.

It was never a massively long stretch, but I was pregnant with Thomas when he joined the squadron, and the first time he went Thomas was 10 days old. So, it was in the back of my mind. I can't think of the worst case scenario because I just can't. But, I thought, we have just had a baby, please come back. He did. Then he went, and he came back again, so you kind of get used to it after a while. 'Oh yeah, he's going again but he'll be back.' I never did that dramatic good bye, I just said, 'See you in four weeks', or whatever it was. He wasn't here anyway, he was living in Somerset when he was in England, so I don't necessarily think I missed him any more because he was there.

I missed talking to him all the time. It was really difficult on the satellite phone. He would always start the conversation, because he worries about me and he clearly thinks I am an idiot! Every time he phones he says, 'I MIGHT TO HAVE TO GO AT SHORT NOTICE. IF THE PHONE GOES, DON'T WORRY!' Every phone call! 'I know,' I say, 'you are wasting minutes telling me this. What do you have to say?' We are really lucky to be in this generation because we can do blueys [flimsy, blue airmail notepaper] and I can send him parcels, and he gets to phone me every week and I know that is relatively new. We are lucky with what we have. People say that thirty minutes on his phone card is not enough, but it is quite a long time and we can email every day, long rambling conversations. That is what we do. I do it at work. By the time the evening comes, I have a whole day's worth of stuff to tell him and so I do it ad hoc at work to build up an email for him.

I wasn't happy about him going to Afghanistan. When he came back, he told me that one of the other guys from the squadron was in the room next to Andy and he got up to go and have a shower and his room was bombed, so if he had not got up to have a shower, that would have been it. Thank goodness he told me when he got back! Then Andy had a Land Rover and he parked it where he always parked it in the car park to go in to breakfast and when he came back, the entire car park had been bombed and his Land Rover was the only car still standing. If he had parked it three in, or whatever, or had been sitting in it … It was not his time to go. I believe in that fate stuff.

Then he went somewhere else, which was big, massive. He was out there for seven months in a really dangerous place and no one really knew they were there. That made it a lot worse. That is when I had Phoebe. I was very poorly when I was pregnant with her and I was due to be induced. She was not even late. I went into a major meltdown in the hospital thinking, 'Andy's not even here.' He managed to get home, and he came home on the Friday and she just appeared herself on the Saturday, which was really nice. He did come home with a ginger beard, which went very quickly!

She was 10 days when he went back and she was 4 months when he came back. That was the longest we have done. He has been away a lot, but we can't really complain because when he has not been here, apart from those three times, he has been in Somerset or in MOD in London, which was the job he did before this, which he really loved, and so it has not been too bad. He is home at weekends. I feel sorry for Andy. He feels sorry for me. He misses everything. Even when the children are annoying me, I think, 'At least I have seen them.' Phoebe says something new or comes out with some bizarre thing and I think, 'Ah, he's missed that'.

The Children

The children just love Andy! From the first minute, even when they were babies, they knew exactly who he was. Thomas had a picture in his cot but I never did that with Phoebe. I am not sure why. Perhaps because it was the second child and I just did not do it. Phoebe and I went up to the airport to collect him when he came back, when she was a baby. He obviously was absolutely gobsmacked by this massive baby I was holding – she knew who he was, though, and was perfectly happy to be passed over. She snuggled.

Thomas was just bouncing off the wall by the time we got back. My mum and dad were looking after him, he was 3½. For a week or so, mummy may as well not be there as they just want daddy for everything, which is fine by me. He can get up in the middle of the night and do the nappies, and whatever. So we have never had a problem with that. This time is the first time they have noticed, because Thomas is 6½ now and for two years daddy has just been here at the weekends. That is quite a long time in a 6½-year-old's life and he had got used to that. Not so much now, and a lot has happened.

Phoebe is old enough to realise. 'I really, really miss daddy.' She says it every day, which she never has before. They do miss him, but they love talking to him on the phone. He told me a story of Dartmouth, of the commodore's children. They weren't particularly happy on one of the passing out parades. They wrote on a massive bed sheet, 'We hate the navy', and hung it out of the window. I hope my children are not like that, you hope they won't be, but you just don't know.

My Work

I work as a special educational needs officer in the special needs section at the education department of Portsmouth City Council. Our bread and butter is in assessing children for additional needs at school, from babies up to age 19, and writing their statements of special educational needs, which is a legal document, which lists what they need and what the school needs to provide.

I started there in 2006, the week after I got married, as a case worker – an admin role. I had never worked in education before. I actually worked in the Ministry of Defence prior to that, but it looked quite interesting. My mum was a teacher and she saw it in the newspaper and thought that it looked quite good. She said to me, 'Why don't you go for it?'

'Don't know.'

'Give it a bash.'

So I did, and I got it – unbelievable. I worked my way up. So now I am middle management level in the team and I have my own case worker. I really love it, a niche job. Since I have been there, and 100 per cent because of my mum, I got my PGCE, just to have it really. Why wouldn't you? [She says this laughing.] I always wondered about teaching. Mum said I should have been a primary school teacher and she is probably right – she was rarely wrong about anything.

I went and did post-16, so when I had Thomas and I went part-time, I had time to do it. I was doing three days for the council and then two days being a trainee teacher. Every year I say, 'I am going to qualify in this now'.

I have done a bit of event management and my SEN BTEC – I did not need any qualifications for SEN, but things are changing so I went and got my BTEC. I play the piano. I like to teach myself things like that. I will take on any sort of project. After I had Phoebe I actually left the council after my maternity, in a great dramatic flair, and just said I am not coming back and went with an events organising company. I was at HMS *Warrior* for a year, which I now view as my extended maternity leave, because my best friend, who I worked with at the council, phoned me up and asked, 'Do you want to come back?'

'I don't know, I have not really thought about it. I quite enjoy what I do now.'

Thomas was starting school at that time, so I could be there to take him. She said, 'Seriously, we have lost everybody and all the new people in don't know what they are doing.'

'Oh, go on then!'

So now I am back. Actually, people did not know I had left, I was so memorable! People just thought I was on maternity leave.

I need my own identity. Even if Andy did something else, I would not be a stay-at-home mum. I am not maternal enough. I love them, but I am also enjoying being Lauren Bray. I am good at what I do.

The Portsmouth Military Wives Choir

The choir – I love the choir. Everything is fun! I love singing. I trained as a singer when I was at school. I appear to have some kind of aptitude for it, which is very fortunate. My dad is musical as well, and it is something that I have always done.

My mum and my sister saw the notice in the *Portsmouth Evening News* that the choir was being set up in HMS *Collingwood*. I hate new situations, and my sister made me go. She just appeared and said, 'I am here to look after the children. I have arranged for you to go to *Collingwood.*' So I went.

They are very friendly, and there is no 'officers and ratings'. We are just 'the wives'. I don't even know what half their husbands do. I don't want to know, because I am not that interested. We see it on the Facebook page, that 'so-and-so is on HMS *Daring*' and they can see that Andy is on HMS *Dragon*, and things like that, but I don't really know what they all do and I don't really understand every job going.

I know the girls I sit next to in choir. I know that, lots of times, we get told off because we are laughing too much! We have had our moments – you get eighty women together – we are a big choir in the chapel at *Collingwood*. There are bound to be fallings out. They last about five minutes and then you move on.

Our musical director is absolutely amazing. He is the deputy head of Portsmouth Grammar School and has a very musical background. He loves the attention of all those women, but is very inspirational. I am fortunate that I can read music, and when we get a new song I just give it a while and we see what happens. But then there are ladies who have never sung before and who can't read music, can't read a note, and it doesn't really matter because we have performed in Portsmouth Cathedral together.

We went up to London and did the Poppy Appeal launch last year and are going again this year. We performed at Ely and, of all the women, only half have some musical background. The others just qualify to be in the choir and come along, and I have made some of the best friends I have got at choir. You won't meet anyone who does not say the choir is brilliant.

I don't know everyone in the choir. I am a soprano 2, so I sit in the middle. We have Sop 1s that side, and altos that side. I couldn't tell you who half the altos are and who half the Sop 1s are. I know them to look at and can say hello if I bumped into them in the street. We get together, have an amazing couple of hours, we always have fun, it always cheers you up even when you have one of those days.

Recording

We made two albums. We were just so lucky that anyone wanted to be interested in us. I watched the Gareth Malone choir and I felt it was a good idea. I just thought 'That is fair enough, they have chosen one choir from one part of the country and set it up', but I think, as well, you are never going to get a fair representation of all those linked to the forces. That just won't happen. I think it was a good decision of theirs to make it of a bunch of guys who were away at the time, so that was linked onto the public's consciousness.

I had only been on the choir for a couple of weeks, maybe, and the lady who set it up said, 'They are going to come and we have to learn some songs to go on an album.' So we had to learn it, oh my goodness! We recorded it in the *Collingwood* Chapel, which was so much fun, because how often do you get to be in the middle of a recording studio with this really clever man recording you? Then all the advertising came out. I felt, 'That is me, I have done something and I have got it!' It is there for the children to see.

Before it was released, John Cohen came back and played the entire album to us. This was the chap who was the producer. So we heard all of the other eleven tracks, including ours. It was just our choir, it was lovely and bizarre to see, sitting in *Collingwood* Chapel, all facing the front. We were just listening. We clapped every performance. We all cried at every track. We were just so pleased for all of the other choirs and when we heard ours, all hell broke … It was amazing. He made it sound good. We were so proud of us. We all bought it. That was Christmas sorted, fantastic!

Then we did a second one, with a much bigger choir and it was a much bigger thing. Then to get to number one – I just thought, 'No one knows I am a military wife, I don't need them to, no one knows I have done the Military Wives Choir, or an album, but I bet you've got that album.' You know, if you pick out ten people, seven of them will have it. Then to go to number one and to think, actually, we are not alone, someone cares.

I always watch the Festival of Remembrance. I cry every year. More so now, because I always say to Andy, even if the worst happens, I would still love him. I would go and would be so proud to do that. I hope I never have to. I love Hugh Edwards, and he comes across as really interested. It will be a sad year when he does not do it anymore.

Ignorance ...

I am astounded by the ignorance of people in Portsmouth, who don't know anything about the naval base; who don't know what's in it and they don't know what goes on.

I had a lady at work the other day say something about the military and about the country saving money. 'I don't know what the forces *do*, you know. We are not really at war now, are we? So if they are not fighting a war, what *are* they doing?'

I thought, 'Oh my, how ignorant.' I said to myself, 'I am not going to say anything, I really am not going to speak for the entire armed forces.' I did send a little prayer up to all of those people who died for keeping people like that safe. I honestly don't know, I am not a political person, I am not going to get involved.

Andy has been to Iraq and Afghanistan, but he, and lots of people in the navy, if we are talking about the navy, are also catching pirates and they are stopping drug smugglers and keeping international shipping lanes open, and they are keeping international relations open, because we do not really want to fall out with America or Europe, or anything like that. We don't have to be fighting to be doing something of value, and just because it is not on the TV all the time doesn't really matter.

Andy was in the MOD in London, which I think was probably not his most favourite job, but certainly the biggest eye-opener and the most interesting. He was not at home but he was not fighting anyone. So does that not count?

❧ FIONA JAMESON ❧

Royal New Zealand Navy officer, Fiona, is married to Andrew, of the Royal Navy. They have an infant daughter, Amy. Fiona is in the UK as

part of an exchange of personnel between the two nation's navies. Fiona
is unique in this book as being both military herself and a military wife,
as well as belonging to an overseas navy. She may possibly be one of New
Zealand's future first female frigate commanders:

I think in the space of a year, we got married, had a child, moved house,
got a dog – and we were only together for six weeks!

Andrew and I met at a dinner, at the home of a mutual friend of
ours in 2010. She'd been on an exchange in New Zealand. She had met
Andrew through work. We ended up sitting next to each other at dinner.
I wasn't enjoying my time here, I was too enthusiastic for the classic
British culture.

I struggled when I first arrived here, because me saying, 'I'm from
paradise', people didn't know I was joking, and they thought I was putting their country down! I hadn't had a good time, and hadn't made any
friends, and I was 30 so didn't want to go to the bar every night with all
the young kids that were staying on base. All of my course mates were
using their twelve months ashore, like all good warfare officers, to do
nothing with the navy, because they had been at sea for ten years: 'It is
really nice to meet you, but this is my family time.'

I utterly respect their decision, but I wasn't prepared for it. I thought
that, like every Brit who arrived in New Zealand, they would wrap you
up and take you home. So, anyway, Andrew was the first person who
invited me over for coffee and I thought, 'He's just another Brit. He
doesn't mean it.' He is someone who is saying to me, 'do please come
over for coffee, just pop in anytime', but actually, of course you don't just
pop in any time to someone's house in England. You do in New Zealand,
but you don't over here. You don't mean it, why do you say that to me?

We almost had an argument over dinner as I complained about all the
things that I was not enjoying about England. He got sick at listening to
this! 'I will tell you why England's a good country.' We got into the classic Gallipoli discussion. This is big in New Zealand. It turned into not as
painful a night as I thought it would be. He sent me a book on Gallipoli,
to teach me the facts!

We also had the same last name. I was Jamieson with an 'ie' and he is,
and I now am, Jameson with an 'e', like the whiskey. So he knew my last
name and popped into *Collingwood* to leave the book for me and it kind
of went from there. I found his phone number through our friend and
texted him, and said that I was going for a bike ride at the weekend and

if you want coffee, we can. I didn't have to change my name when I got married, so I was really pleased! We got married in England.

I was here on a course and Andrew was on a course. We got to know each other over the weekends. Then he deployed a couple of months later, and I finished the course and our deployments were opposite deployments. So, the following January we met in Singapore, and he came home at the end of July and I deployed in September. We met again in South Africa the following February. I was there when he proposed, and my ship got back to the UK in May.

Getting Married

It was a choice: either get married that August 2012 or plan to get married in summer 2013. With all good laid military plans, we knew he would be around that August because his ship was due to deploy in September, so we gave ourselves three months to plan our wedding and get married. I was not really a white wedding dress girl. I would happily have eloped! That would have broken his mum's heart, so the 'get married in England' decision was pretty straight forward. My mum passed away when I was 11, so there wasn't really that pull for me.

So, we got the back of a fag packet out and pulled it off! It turned out really well. Andrew set a budget of £5,000 and I said, 'Okay, I'm happy with that'.

'When I say £5,000, I don't mean it in your warfare approach! I mean it would be great if it came in less.'

Unless you home grow, you can't achieve a wedding for £5,000. We were living in Wickham at the time and Wickham church is lovely. So we decided to get married there. Our first official date was at a pub called the Rising Sun in Swanmore, which does fantastic food. I loved the idea of walking into a pub and the landlady knowing your name, and there is a dog by the fire. We went and saw them and asked if they would do a marquee and cater, and it was quite cool.

We did not come in on budget! Marquees are insane! £2,000 for a marquee! We spent more than we wanted, but planning for three months' time meant that there were a few decisions that we had to make. It worked out OK, but it was an expensive day. We had already planned our holiday before we had planned our wedding. So, we went off to Greece on a yacht with four mates.

Then, he deployed late September 2012. I fell pregnant the week before he deployed. He was away for two weeks, and then I said to him that I was pregnant. We had two really difficult miscarriages beforehand. It was good news obviously, but it started the waiting game.

He laughs about the fact that he found out that I was pregnant when he was deployed. He was due home three days before she was due. They knew how the pregnancy was going, luckily, and they let him come home two weeks earlier. He was here in time. What every military wife would say is there is no point in thinking about them coming home or in not coping. You just crack on. I didn't want him to come home early because I wanted him to take the leave with us as a family.

We weren't talking crutches and wheelchairs and bedridden. I would have to stop work early, he would have to come off the ship, take up leave, and if I stopped work early then my maternity leave reduced and I don't get as much time with Amy. I have found the Royal Navy supportive throughout, and the choir was, too.

Andrew's ship decommissioned and they finished up a little bit early, so he was going to have some weeks off before he was due to start his new job. We hoped to go to New Zealand in February 2013, but the new job meant that he was on courses pretty much until January. February would have meant that he had been in his new job for two weeks, and so his first question would have been, 'Sir, can I go to New Zealand?'

Although I would not recommend to anyone to fly five weeks after a C-section, it was our only real opportunity to get to New Zealand. Andrew hadn't seen the country, and I was supposed to go home in the November but had been ill, so we jumped on the plane and off we went. We did a camper van tour of New Zealand. Staying in one place would have been too much as we were there for five weeks.

Seeing Family Life

I was really lucky, when I was fairly junior I became quite good friends with my first commanding officer's family. He deployed on a ship. I then saw them at church on a weekend and they were talking about their son struggling with statistics. 'You're studying statistics at university aren't you, Fiona?'

'Yeah, I am.'

'Would you help him out?'

'Absolutely.' So, over the course of his deployment, I would go around on a Tuesday night and I became really good friends with the family.

The ship had then been deployed eight months in Asia. They made it to Western Australia on the way home when Iraq 2 kicked off and they got told to re-store and turn right. So they had had an eight month deployment and were now being turned around two months before Christmas to go for who-knows-how-long, and so I got to witness this through the CO's family. I got to learn a lot by seeing things I would not normally see.

While we have moved with modern times, I think the military wife link has got weaker, which is where I think military wives choirs are brilliant. There is no phone pyramid that they used to have in the bad old days, and so the support network has almost dissipated as technology came up. I think I have seen in New Zealand and here in the UK that the support network realises that it needs to be there and build back up.

Last year, when Andrew's ship deployed, I had said to the wives, 'Do you want to get together?' I had never been left at home before without a ship to go on, or something to do. So we all got together. They had been away a month or six weeks and the wives were saying 'They are having a great time, they're having cocktail parties and this and that!'

I said, 'What? They are in Morocco, it's a dive. They are not having a good time. It's the worst part of the whole trip.'

'What do you mean?'

'First two weeks they have all fought and hated each other because they have just left their families. They don't really know why they are grumpy, but they are. The next two weeks they will have just started taking malaria tablets. Now they are doing cocktail parties in all these horrible places. Andrew doesn't get a day off – he didn't step ashore in the last port. He is miserable, they are all pretty miserable.'

'They aren't telling us that.'

A Different Perspective

Because I am in the military I get a different perspective. I told them, 'I have bought some really stupid envelopes today.'

'What do you mean?'

'A My Little Pony & Friends envelope and a Teenage Mutant Ninja Turtle envelope.'

'What for?'

'Andrew joked about buying me a *My Little Pony* magazine. Now he is going to get letters for the whole wardroom to see and open in an envelope with *My Little Pony* on them! You all sort the mail for each other and you all look at each other's mail. Mail is morale.'

'Really?'

Mail is the most important thing. If you sent them a pencil, it doesn't matter because that pencil is going to be the conversation of the wardroom. I remember that my CO never got mail for the entire deployment and the look on his face as time went on. I was really lucky, I had a friend in the UK, and his parents also sent me stuff. I would get boxes of ridiculous Christmas decorations or Marks & Spencer's boiled sweets, which sat on my desk – no one eats them! But I was never, ever going to say no to Andrew's mum, who was doing her best to think, 'What can I send to this girl I barely know who is marrying my son?' It turned out that I saw one of the senior rates in the NAAFI asking for some boiled sweets. I said, 'You know what, I have a deal for you!'

Wives don't have a connection to the military and I had a grasp of all of that at a young age, just by having been able to see it myself.

The Military Wives Choir

One member of the choir lost her husband. He loved the first song they recorded and wanted it at his funeral. We sang and she joined the choir. She joined the choir for the same reason as I have.

The pregnancy knocked me for six, and I spent fifteen, sixteen weeks off work sick. I got lots of emails from wives saying 'What can we do?', but with a bad pregnancy there is not much you can do at all. It was nice to know that they were there and I could call on them if I needed to. As I started to turn the corner, the choir was singing. I can't play sports now and I have always played a lot of sport. I need a club or a hobby, something to do.

I thought, 'Maybe I will join a choir because that is a hobby I can do when I am broken.' I need a team. I am a New Zealander, I need a team and to be part of a team or to build a team. So I went along to their Christmas performance, passed out at the back because it was the first time I had been up beyond 7 p.m. in about fifteen weeks, but then joined the choir in the following January.

I think I was three weeks into it when I realised that I really couldn't do rehearsals regularly and I was starting to miss them. I turned around to one of the ladies and said, 'Look, I think I will pull out because I can't commit, I'm not very good, I'm not able to attend practises and I am certainly not able to commit to performances.'

She went, 'It doesn't matter.'

What? If you play sport you have to practise. They accepted that I would come some weeks. I never made the full rehearsal, I only made until the break, and that was fine. They still seemed to get to know me and care about me, even though I was barely there. I certainly wasn't performing.

The Military Wives Choir does what it says on the tin, and I have to say, I doubted it, particularly being a female in the military, because sometimes there is that funniness if you work with their husbands. I can understand why it is, so I tend to be a bit cautious because I am not quite one of them, I'm one of the others, but I *am* a military wife.

In the Future

I will come off my maternity leave and go and work at HMS *Collingwood* again. Andrew's time in the Royal Navy will be up in 2015. Early on in our career we had discussions, and we had to look at the practicalities of deciding which country we wanted to be in. Our first question was, can we give up our country? One of the reasons our relationship works is that neither of us has answered that question. I can't give up NZ, but who am I to expect someone to give up their country?

As time went on, a couple of things happened. He got his career commission, which was good in terms of pension, but he is a little bit of a square peg in a round hole in terms of warfare. He is far too reasonable and has strengths in too many broad areas to fit the warfare mould that the Royal Navy seeks. Whereas I am an alpha kind of girl, so there is a natural career path.

He has done a variety of jobs, and he changed over to warfare because he was too stuck behind a desk. As we got to that point in his career, we also got to hear from New Zealand saying that I could stay on and I also got a better idea of where I might be going. Command started to look a bit more obvious. I want to do it for various reasons.

If I can have it all ... can you have a career and family? I'm not convinced, but I will give it a shot. I can't face being 60 and not having had that. A ship is not going to be with me at retirement, a family is. So that is my choice. If I can have it all, I will. I have since had some good chats, and my hope is that my goal of command is a bit more realistic.

So, how does that work for the two of us? New Zealand is willing to let me stay here. I should have returned now and been an XO (executive officer). I said, 'a) I think I am too young because I have shot through quite quickly anyway, and b) I want to have a family.'

There is no better time. I am not going to choose to delay a family so I can go XO.

They have been pretty good about it. There are still some negotiations to go but … To some extent, I am breaking new ground. They haven't had a female frigate captain. They certainly haven't had a female in command with family. The Royal Navy did that as well, she took command of one of the Type 23s and had a baby. I can't wait to have a chat to her!

The plan is for us to go home to New Zealand at the end of 2015, because you can't carry on forever between England and New Zealand, and we have been lucky so far, even to the extent that Andrew is now based ashore for two years, which is brilliant.

❧ SARAH KIFF ❧

Iraq

He did Iraq in 2003. It was frustrating because he was on HMS *Edinburgh*. My husband is a weapons engineer. His career, in terms of being on ships, has been on the Type 42 fleet. He has done quite a lot of them. They were the first ones to go out there. They had gone off in the January, the conflict kicked off in the March when we saw them launch things into Baghdad and he was involved there, supporting the American ships that were firing. They were the last ones back. It felt at the time like they were the forgotten ship. They went out first and came back last.

There was a carrier there, too. There is a pet name for the carriers among the seagoing men. They call them 'death stars'. They take all the glory. They go out there and they sit there and they take all the glory because they are not fighting ships. They are just there to carry helicopters and they say, 'Oh, we are just very big and special and important' and they come back and crowds wave the carriers in! Then there is the rest, 'We did everything, we get nothing for it!' There has always been rivalry, though.

HMS *Edinburgh* did not come home until the end of June or the beginning of July. They did the full six months, whereas everyone else did about three or four months. It didn't go down too well. I received emails such as, 'We think we're coming home', and 'It's had been put back'. In the end, I just said, 'Don't tell me when you think you might be coming home. When you have a definite date and you know it is set in stone, then tell me. I can't bear this up and down. Great, he's coming home in a month! It will only be four weeks tomorrow and he's coming home! Oh, actually it is six weeks, oh, eight weeks. Don't tell me until you know for certain, then I can start looking forward. It is depressing.'

The Letter

I remember writing 'The Letter'. There is a letter you send off with them in case they never came back. I didn't anticipate that, but you don't know what is going to be fired from the other side, do you? So the letter says everything you want to say. It is a bit of a hard one. He hasn't been in any real war zone situations. That was his only real conflict.

They were going off onto a deployment into that general area, and Iraq sort of crept up very shortly afterwards. I do remember thinking, at the time Annabelle was 3 and Matthew was 5, 'How will I manage if he doesn't come back? How will I explain it to the children? How will it be for us as a family if he is never around again?' So, actually, I think it is more a case of what impact that [Ian's death] will have on you as a family. You don't really think about it as your own person, as a wife.

I am lucky, he is a very practical man. If you want a shelf or something fixing, he can do it. He is really brilliant at that kind of thing. I probably sat there and thought, 'Oh my God, I'll never be able to have another shelf, ever again!' I don't remember being scared. I think you have to be philosophical about it. That may be me. Others may react differently.

I went to the dockside and met him. His mum and dad came too. It was a lovely day and we were very pleased to see him.

There have been long periods of separation. He has done two six month trips. He was the decommissioning officer for HMS *York* in 2012. So he did a South Atlantic trip, to the Falklands; that was six and a half months. The last deployment he did was very different to the previous one because we had Skype. He could go on shore and Skype us. Interestingly, it was really weird because he would call and there was a bit of delay, so it wasn't the easiest thing, but it was good to be able to see him and chat with him and Anabelle was thrilled. But Matthew, who's 15, my eldest, tried it and said, 'I don't want to do that again.' It was too hard for him. He said, 'I can cope talking to him on the phone but actually seeing him …' It really upset him.

No Idea

People will say, 'Well, you knew what you were doing when you married!' No, you don't know. You have no idea. Nobody can prepare you for it.

I always used to call the ships 'his mistresses'. They are grey with very large bottoms! Ian is due to come out in October 2015, although there is a high chance he is going to get offered an extension because they are a bit short of people. It's likely that we may get to 2020. It is unlikely he will go back to sea. HMS *York* is probably his last ship, so it is quite poignant for him, but he was so dedicated to that steel thing. He loved her like a … I don't know. I suppose she can cook him nice dinners – he rings up and says 'We have to get rid of some food as we're going off, so we're having lobster tonight!' I look at my chicken breast and steamed vegetables and think, 'Yeah, lovely! Oh, it's a cocktail party tonight, hmm.'

Sometimes I was resentful of the fact that he would be waited on and had all these lovely meals; that his washing was done for him, that in the evenings he would go and drink wine and whisky with his fellow officers. He had a huge amount of responsibility, so in the practical day-to-day running of the ship his job was very important, but the downside of that was that all these people were running around after him. How nice!

My job, very important in terms of what I do, but when I come home I carry on working. So, I suppose I get quite resentful of that aspect of it. I was never jealous of it. It was only ever a temporary thing. It was not forever. Let him have his fun, do what he has to do, go to all these amazing places but he'll always come home to me. He doesn't really want that. They have a really good time and there is that bond that you have with your ship and your crew that no one else can understand unless you have been there and done it. But they always come home to us, and that is quite nice.

I Have Never Been Anywhere!

I do get jealous of the places he's been. We got married in April, and he said 'I have to join HMS *Manchester*.' Then he was a chief.

'OK, when are you joining the Manchester?'

'8 April.'

'That's our wedding day.'

'Yeah, I've spoken to them.'

'What did you say?'

'Can I join on the 9th?'

'What did they say? No?'

'They said they would give me three or four days. I said, two weeks with my bride and then I will come.'

He flew to Singapore to join her out there. While he was there, he rang me up. They had done everything they were doing up there and had come back up the Suez Canal around Egypt. He rang me.

'Guess where I'm going?'

'Where?'

'To the pyramids at Giza!'

He knew it was a place I have always wanted to see. My dream of a Nile cruise is yet to be. He has promised me he will take me sometime, so for him to ring up and say this was desperately upsetting.

'But you can't go!'

'Why not?'

'Cos you promised you'd take me.'

'But I will take you.'

'It won't be the same because you will have already seen it.'

He just didn't understand that at all. He has been to some great places. Last year he went to St Petersburg and that is another place I'd love to see. I have never been to any of the places he has been to. It has never worked out for us. Whenever he has gone somewhere really great, he has always had to join the ship halfway through. He has gone over at the same time as the wives all go over, so that is no good. When it has been a long period of time, it has been Iraq or South Georgia. I didn't fancy going down there, really. So, I have never been anywhere.

Playing Second Fiddle

I started working at the school when Annabelle was 4. I had never worked at a school before. I fell on my feet really. I work at a school in Stubbington, Hampshire. It is a school for special educational needs, a secondary school. I am the family and student support worker. I do a lot of liaising with family services and transition students, those coming into the school mid-year. It is a pastoral role. I really love my job. I really, really love it. It is never a chore to go there. I never, ever wake up thinking, 'Oh my God, I've got to go to work.'

The kids are amazing. They all have particular needs: those who have low ability and difficulties learning; some interesting autistic characters; youngsters with Down's syndrome, who are just adorable; but they are all unique and special in their own way and we all know each of them. It is a big school in terms of special needs, but it is small in terms of second-ary schools. I really like my job, although it is not nearly as important as my husband's! Not important at all if something needs to be done out-side of school. If one of the children was ill, when they were smaller, he would not dream of taking the day off to look after them. It was always me, and I think you will find that from any service wife. Whatever we do, it always plays second fiddle to them.

We have been really lucky, we have not really moved around a lot. We have always stayed in this area. I think the employers in this area are geared up to the fact that they have a large proportion of military fami-lies living here. I have never found being military to be a problem.

When the children came along, I stopped working and I waited until Annabelle was school age and then, getting employment in the school, in terms of holidays their holidays were my holidays, so the only prob-lems were when they were poorly. Annabelle had chicken pox and I had to have two or three days off. My mum would always come down if I needed her to. It is easier for her to come now, as she is retired, but when she was working she would try and see if she could get a day or two for me. It wasn't too bad.

Accommodation

There used to be a rule that you couldn't have a married quarter if you owned your own home if it was in a 60 mile radius. Then they had a lot of empty quarters, so they relaxed that rule. I said, 'Let's sell this house and move to Stubbington.' We started looking. Someone asked, 'Why don't you get a married quarter over there?'

'We can't have one as we own this.'

'No, that rule has gone out the window.'

So, we put in for one and got one really quick. We have been here ever since, nine years. This is home. Magnolia woodchip is not every-body's thing, but I can't be bothered to try to change it!

I know people who have been in the navy twenty-five years and still don't own their own home, and you think you will leave and you will have nothing – you have been earning money all these years and have nothing to show for it. It's a bit scary. We were lucky, we bought our house in 1997 for £66,500! It's a three-bed semi. We will wait to see what happens next year.

We should know soon whether Ian is staying in the navy or going. If he is staying, we will hang on here another couple of years probably and get Matthew through his GCSEs and then we might decide to buy something over here, and sell the house in Lee. Ian is due out in 2015, on his 50th birthday. At that point the mortgage ends. The question is, do we wait and sell it and have all the capital – capital gains tax, not sure how that works – or do we sell it and just move on and buy another house locally? We don't know yet and will wait and see.

Portsmouth Military Wives Choir

We have been going now for nearly three years. It was started by my neighbour, Kim, who saw it on the telly when she started watching the Gareth Malone series. She thought, 'We could do that'. She has a music degree so she stuck a note on the local Facebook group for the ladies in the area, saying 'anyone interested?' I have loved singing and have done music festivals, although I am not qualified. I can't read music, just like to sing.

So, she and I got together and went out one day and put flyers through all the local married patches on a wet December day. I got soaked and it was freezing. We went all around Gosport, all around Fareham, up to Titchfield. We just parked up and tramped streets, putting flyers through doors. We got a group together, started rehearsing at her house, and then there were too many people. Some people wanted to do it in the daytime, because they have little ones, so we did a couple of sessions at the community centre in Stubbington.

Then she had a phone call one day. The man on the phone said, 'Hello, Gareth Malone here'. I think she nearly fell over. There had been something in the paper and he had wind of it and asked her to tell him what she was doing, how many people she had got and what song she was singing. We had started off with a simple song. The next day she got a call from someone from Decca [Records] who said that they were in the middle of putting together a Military Wives Choir album and asking if her choir would like to be on it. It was so exciting! On the first album there were five choirs and we were one of those first five.

I have done some amazing things with the choir. We went to Abbey Road and recorded the song for the diamond jubilee with Gary Barlow. Twelve of us went up and did that. We sang at the jubilee, outside Buckingham Palace. That was surreal. I can't describe it. We got home really late that night and watched it the next day. Watching it, it did not feel like I had actually been there. Yet I had stood on the stage, had come back on and did the National Anthem at the end. I had a chat with the

Prince of Wales and Camilla; shook hands with Sir Paul McCartney and Sir Elton John and Tom Jones, and chatted with Annie Lennox; said hello to Kylie Minogue, it was the most bizarre thing! I stood and watched will.i.am greeting the queen and had been in close proximity to her (she is beautiful), and it was a really weird experience and I just can't believe I did it.

Some of the best things have been with our choir. We did a really beautiful concert at Ely Cathedral, which was fabulous, and that was with the band of the Royal Marines. Twenty-five ladies from our choir went to Biggin Hill for the 70th anniversary of the Dambusters' Raid, and we recorded *Friday Night is Music Night* for BBC Radio Two. We did a concert at Portsmouth Cathedral, which was lovely.

We've done some really nice small concerts. Recently, we went to Romsey Abbey and were performing with the Royal Marines Association Concert Band, which was great. We've done cocktail parties and things like that. We've had lots of opportunities that we would never have had and I have found myself in situations that I never thought I would. For me, choir is about going and enjoying the music, enjoying the singing, seeing everybody, saying 'hi', chatting. For other people, it's about the support network outside their weekly rehearsal, the friendships they've made. It's, again, more to do with the fact that I go to work every day. I don't have time to go and do the networking in the daytime. The ones with little children do more of that. It's less of a support thing for me and more of a joining-in thing for me.

It was weird because, for once, I was doing something much more exciting than my husband! My family are at home watching me on the TV in London! You haven't done that matey, have you?

𝔍 Jay Armstrong 𝔍

Army officer Jay reflects on the compromises she felt she had to make when she became engaged to her Royal Navy husband, Scott:

I left the army in 2004 after seven years. There is a book called *Lean In* by Sheryl Sandberg (Virgin Digital, 2013), the CEO of Facebook, about overcoming the obstacles facing women in seeking to be leaders in business. I read a chapter last night, about how a woman came to her before she was even married saying, 'Tell me about how you manage to do family and work.' When I met Scott, I was on my own career path and then, when I got engaged, the compromises started.

Actually, looking back, I was doing well in a medical branch as medical support and a troop commander. I'd done a training job and pushed a bit, and the next step would have been adjutant, but it would have meant moving to Catterick. I had already been in Lichfield and we'd commuted for a year, and also it was a peacetime army, so there was a lot of money in development and training because everyone was getting a bit fat and lazy, to be honest. It wasn't a lean army. To see action was uncommon. Within that, I decided I would go down the training and development branch because the jobs for that would be around the Salisbury Plain area.

Immediately there was that compromise. What I didn't expect is that, when you compromise and you change your cap badge, your loyalties are questioned. You are seen as not sticking at something. So, I came across to the education branch and I remember, on my course I was going to get best student, but they decided not to give it to me because I had already had training experience. You think, 'Well, actually, that's not fair!' Then the education branch were saying that they wanted people who had experience and I came across with that experience. They said I didn't have credibility within the branch. I felt as if the doors were shutting.

One thing that Sheryl Sandberg said is that Harvard have done a study that shows that men are promoted on their potential, but women are more experienced. That explains a lot in the military. Aptitude tests are how you get in, so it's all about potential and any new job you get they say they take a risk in case you fail. It's felt that, as a woman in the military, you're being assessed on what you *haven't* done. 'You haven't shown that yet, therefore you can't …' That rang true when I read it. Very interesting.

So the compromises started. We got married, and I just looked at women who had had children and they were so stressed, it was awful. The marriages were falling apart. A friend had twins at age 38 plus and they were born at twenty-six weeks in Germany. They had medical intervention. She was up hoovering at two in the morning. She was just running on adrenaline the whole time. Her husband was off doing what he was doing. I saw this again and again. I just thought, 'I can't do this.'

Scott, being a pilot, was on a better pay grade and for him to leave didn't make sense. I think I just began to grow a little bit weary of the sexism in the army. It began to be unrelenting sexism. I think that is definitely an issue – jobs for the boys.

I went to staff college and was doubted for my credibility because I wasn't an infantry officer, yet if you were a male combat officer it was fine, and it became such a fight. You have to look at the big picture, and this wasn't for me.

So I left, and I became a photographer. I taught myself. I think I just wanted to do something for me, and I was getting fed up being told what to do by other people. I wanted to be self-employed and to be flexible and I don't want to be bitter and twisted. This is the way life turns out and you take it at the time. You can't have everything. You have to make compromises.

It has been challenging. We have a place in Dorset. My husband is based in Hampshire with the Special Forces lot from the RAF, which is a story in itself. The day we moved in, he got a phone call to say he is deploying in two days' time. He had two weeks' leave booked. It is in these situations that you say, 'Oh, for goodness sake!'

Working

I am left to do everything, with no support network. If you were to ask what had been the biggest challenge, it would be to do everything by yourself, with family who generally don't have a clue how hard it is. It's all the other girlfriends, who are themselves professionals, who say, 'My husband could never understand why I could only work part-time because the rest of my capacity was taken up supporting him.' That is more and more of a trait that I see on the married patch. I gave up my business to come here and support Scott, so the family could be together. I've attempted to start it up here but, to be honest, you have to be in an area for more than three to five years to get established and gain contacts and customer base. I might be a good photographer, but no one is going to pay me unless I am established. In the end, I was paying myself less than I was paying my cleaner.

I had always had photography in my life. I had my first camera when I was 8 and my 21st birthday gift was an SLR. I spoke to the photographer where I was based and I really enjoyed the challenge. Ten years ago it was not as accessible as it is now. The challenge was of teaching myself the editing and pretty much everything. I had the opportunity to do something different.

The trouble is, I come from a service family. They are all in teaching, service or medicine, so you get into business and you are in that service mentality – giving more than you get. From a business perspective, people will part with money at a book party, but if you try to sell yourself and a skill there is sucking of teeth. Women don't support each other. Men fight, women are at war!

When I set up as a photographer, I wanted to do weddings. I met a navy guy and his fiancée, and Scott was in Iraq at the time. He was working on the Chinooks with the RAF. Weddings, to me, were always nerve wracking. It's so complex technically. I was doing this wedding in Sherborne Abbey, where we were living, and it was a Saturday morning. I was all set to go and I arrived at the bride's to find that she was still at the hairdresser's. So I went next door to a friend's house. He was just back from a tour in Afghanistan with the Special Forces and he completely got it, what Scott was doing. He met me at the door and said, 'Mate, I'm so sorry.'

'What?'

Basically, I hadn't had the telly on. A helicopter had been shot down over Basrah that morning. Obviously, that was in the days when news was sent quickly with no news blackout; the journalists hadn't been briefed at that point on what to do, what not to do. Nobody knew anything at that time. There were only about twelve British aeroplanes in theatre at that point. It was like when you walk into a crowded room and your eyes can't quite focus on things. I was very calm. It was odd. I didn't panic, but what I did do was go back to the bride's house and pace up and down. It was lucky she was late.

I phoned my mum and said, 'Please don't ring me, I'm working.' I phoned a man who's a minister and said, 'This has happened, could you pray for Scott?' It was so strange. Then I phoned my good friend, a doctor friend, who had Sky and I said, 'Could you please switch on the telly and when you know what aeroplane it is, can you let me know?' Those were my three phone calls.

The bride was late and, because it was a high-pressure day, I was trying desperately to pull myself out into what I had planned, so I started taking pictures of shoes and door handles to try to get back into it being all about the bride. Her day. I couldn't. She was marrying a navy Harrier pilot. Just before the bride got back, my friend phoned and said, 'It's a Lynx helicopter.' I knew there were four who had been in the air crew. It was somebody we knew, but there was a blackout at that point.

Most of the people at the wedding knew the news, knew a Lynx had been shot down but didn't know who it was, so it was quite a strange day, yet it was somebody's wedding. The bride had said to me that the shot she wanted was 'me coming down the aisle'. I got to the church, braced myself against this pillar, went to take a photo and my card was full! It was because that capacity I have had been completely taken over by the events of the morning. I hadn't checked, and had taken pictures of shoes! I completely missed that shot, adding to the stress.

Then, just before the signing of the register, they did the *Eternal Father* hymn. I stood by the pillar and cried. It was so awful. It was such a moving hymn. I think that what had happened is that you have prepared yourself up to that line. You have got yourself ready for that news, but what you haven't prepared yourself for, because you can't, is that step over the line. When someone else has to cross that line, the awful feeling is that someone out there was going to have the worst day of their lives. That really got me. I thought, 'I'm okay', but there was a commonality there that was quite moving.

Is it wrong to have chosen hymns? To plan what we would sing? Who will carry the coffin? Ironically, Scott's brother, who is in insurance and drives up the M25 every day, is probably statistically more at risk than he was. The thing is, if it goes wrong, it goes horribly wrong and that is the trouble with helicopters. They don't tend to crash land nicely. It shook me, because I realised just how ready I was for that news, had it come.

After I finished doing the church and then the shots in the garden, before the reception, I just went home, just to touch base with myself. Scott had left a phone message so I got that. He rang his dad, who was worried. Scott had lost his mum a year before and that was a heart-wrenching time. You could empathise a little bit with what the families were going through.

The next evening, the Sunday, I was coming down the stairs in our house and through the glass bit over the front door I could see a police car pulling up. I opened the door and my legs were feeling a bit wobbly. They were doing a little patrol and turning around. Our neighbour opposite used to be a prison governor where the Krays were. He was under security. I was quite shaky after that. I didn't know the people in question who had been killed. My husband did, as did the wider group.

Frustrated

At the moment I feel frustrated intellectually. Wives have branched out and done artistic things and their husbands have not been supportive of it. That has driven me nuts. My husband *has* been supportive. The dining room is my office, our dining table is in the kitchen.

He says to me, 'I don't like the idea of my wife cleaning toilets, let's get a cleaner.' Releasing me from these jobs gives me time to spend doing other things, and it helps another woman in her employment, but it is challenging to see these women having to ask for permission. I live in a married quarter and you need permission to run a business in a quarter. I had a token letter to write. I had to write one when I took the dog to the base as he needs public liability insurance there!

I am considering doing an MA in professional writing. It is a one year taught course. One thing about self-employment is that it is very lonely, and to be in a taught environment with a structure would be a good thing. My cousin is a social worker and has set up a street children's charity in Congo. His aunt-in-law is 71 and is a missionary midwife in an outstation in Angola. I see the Sunday supplements and think 'I could do that'.

Esme, my daughter, has started school and Scott has started his conversion to Sea King helicopters course and will then go to HMS *Collingwood* to do his CO's course. I have time to take a year out.

❧ KATE CHURCHWARD ☙

Kate has been married to royal marine, Matthew, for fifteen years and they have two daughters, 10-year-old Bella and 6-year-old Beth. They met in Bristol, when she was studying economics at the university there and he was at the polytechnic:

Midshipmen Together

We met in the University Royal Naval Unit (URNU). We were midshipmen. My flatmates went along and I went too, but didn't know anything about it. Matthew was very committed. He knew he was joining the Royal Marines.

The first year, I didn't really know him because he was rugby playing and was always drinking. I was incredibly shy and nervous then. My last year at university was when we met properly, when I was 21. Everyone knew he liked me, and eventually he got around to inviting me out. I didn't know he liked me! Everybody else knew he was head-over-heels for me the entire first year. The drinking was just bravado because he was shy as well. I knew he was joining the Royal Marines and he was not the sort of person that I would want to be meeting up with.

We got together in the final year and it was instantly, 'I love you'. I was adamant that I was doing my Masters in economics and I would go overseas to Africa, which I did. I thought that there was no way I could be serious about my studies so we split up for a while, after we did our finals. I went to Warwick University to do my Masters and I was doing my interviews for the Overseas Development Institute, on the Fellowship Scheme.

I got sent to Fiji. I went to Africa later. He was joining the marines as I was doing my interviews. He had not stopped writing to me, saying, 'I still feel the same – I know you're going to Africa, I still love you. I'm joining the marines. Look, we can still make this work but we'll just be apart for a very long time.' Even my sister said to me, 'You're made for each other. You are daft not to be together.'

'Yes, but he is in the marines! I am going overseas.'

'It will work.'

Literally, I decided then. He met me at the airport when I was going off to Fiji. I finished my finals for my Masters and Matthew was at Lympstone and was doing his initial training, so we never saw each other. He met me at the airport with my family and he said, 'Let's get married! Whenever you get back, I'll wait.'

I said, 'OK!' And flew to Fiji.

He said, 'I'll wait for you, however long. I'll fly out.'

So we had the most bizarre early years 'courtship', as my father would say. I flew back for his passing out parade. I got the same thing again, 'Will you marry me? Shall I buy an engagement ring?'

'Not yet, I still need to get to Africa.'

We knew that we were never going to see each other much. Then I came back from Fiji early because I was poorly. We got engaged. He went overseas, did Norway, went to Brunei and did his jungle training. Then I started my job at Reading University and among all that we got married.

I think that, by that point, I was ready to settle down. We soon realised that it would be very difficult to arrange and his job was changing every year and a half, two years. That hadn't fully sunk in, in all that time that we were darting around the world. When I flew back for his passing out parade, his boss's wife came up to me on the dance floor and said, 'Don't do it. Please. It's awful.' As clear as that. 'It's awful being married to the marines.'

'It will be fine, I have my job.'

She said that their first child was born while her husband was doing his training. 'It is the only stability we have had in all these years. Run away, run away. Don't do it.'

So I had a warning from somebody, but when you are 23/24 you are not thinking about marriage and children and what life would be like. I was very much focused on my career and Matthew was very support-ive of that. He wasn't trying to hold me back. He knew I wanted to do some development work.

I was working at Sussex University, at the Institute of Development Studies. I was in Zimbabwe [for the university] and he was actually organising the invitations and present lists. We got married, and when we came back from our honeymoon there was a note on my desk to say that the chief economist at the Cabinet Office had got hold of my name and wanted to interview me for a project. I started an intensive year in London, doing the project. I got very run down again. I get run down easily. We never saw each other for the year, so at the end of the project I said, 'I need to move where my husband is and actually see him'. So I moved to Plymouth – and then Matthew went to Norway!

I eventually got a job at Plymouth University. Within a couple of months Matthew came back and said we were moving to Brunei. I said, 'I don't want to move to Brunei! I have this job.' We moved to Brunei. I carried on doing some consultancy for Plymouth University, which was handy.

Brunei

It was such a culture shock for me in Brunei, it really was. There was nothing for me to do. Most of the women out there had children. I didn't have children. I volunteered at school and at the Gurkha lan-guage centre, and I did projects for the university as they came up. I swam; I made cards; I learnt to play the violin. We had been there about five months and it was my 30th birthday.

'What shall we do? Shall we book a nice hotel in the capital?'

He said, 'Well, I am in the jungle for five weeks. A tracking course.'

'Well, in that case, I'm going back to England.' So I booked a flight and I came home for five weeks and I was here with my family. I think

Matthew was a bit concerned that I wasn't actually going to get back on the plane and go back to Brunei, but I went back. He was in the jungle, teaching jungle warfare the whole time. I made the best of it but it was lonely and a bit boring. It wasn't that I didn't enjoy it. I made the best of it. I made some lovely friends in the army.

Jungle Warfare

I had my first baby overseas, far away, no family, in this very decrepit hospital. It was the most bizarre experience. I felt as if I had earned my first medal!

I did used to have a career, a lovely career. We went out to Brunei and I thought, 'I have a decision now.' We knew we wanted to have a baby. I went back to Brunei and was pregnant instantly! I had quite a few problems, and I was not allowed to travel. Usually you go to Singapore, but the midwife took my passport off me and said I couldn't travel as I had nearly had a miscarriage. I was basically confined to Brunei, which was okay, but he wasn't around – he just wasn't around.

When Bella was born she was a month early and my husband was in the jungle, where he used to live all the time. I went into labour, went into hospital and, because I had to have an emergency Caesarean, the Muslim hospital wouldn't perform the Caesarean until my husband signed the consent form. The RAF midwife, who was absolutely lovely, said, 'It's all right, everything is under control. We're just going to phone for your husband. It's all right.'

I was thinking it was a false alarm because it was a month early – I didn't know what labour was all about! I remember the conversation when the nurses said, 'Where is the husband?'

My midwife said, 'He is in the jungle, with the trees. I will get him a helicopter to fly him out.'

They said, 'Oh!'

The midwife said, 'It's fine.' She went into the corridor and I could hear her shouting, 'Get the helicopter and get Matthew here now!'

They would not do the operation until he'd signed the forms. The baby was breech. I had gone into full labour straight away. The midwife whispered to me, 'I'm so sorry. They wouldn't do this to you in England. If Matthew can get here now, that would be good.'

They were going to land him in the hospital, but because he had a weapon he had to go and hand it back in and he came flying through the door, with his beard and his machete and the smell, he used to smell being in the jungle, and they thrust this form at him for him to sign and they just literally threw me into the operating theatre and knocked me out!

Looking back, it was an incredibly frightening time for me, but I can smile about it now – Matthew was in the jungle and had to have a helicopter, so now I smile and I think I was incredibly brave.

I had Bella and he said to me, 'I have good news and bad news. I have the adjutant job at 40 Commando in Taunton and the good news is that we can leave a bit earlier, in April rather than August.'

'Oh great, I can see my mum!'

'But the bad news is that I will have to go straight out to Iraq.'

'That is fine. Just get me back to England!'

We landed, my suitcase was still open and he said, 'We are going to Iraq earlier. It might only be three or four months.' Of course, it ended up being six months, so he wasn't here for Bella's first Christmas. It hasn't really stopped since then. Bella is now ten.

Afghanistan

We moved to Taunton, he went to Iraq, and I moved in with my parents. It started off I was to stay for the summer, and then I just stayed. I have a lovely family who are very supportive. He came home in the January, ready for Bella's 1st birthday. He had eight weeks' leave. It's called POTL – Post Operation Tour Leave – and in those eight weeks he said, 'Right, we're buying a house, we're moving in. We've saved so much money in Brunei, we need to buy a house.'

So, we bought a house in Taunton, lived in it for about six months and then he got a job in Portsmouth. So, our house has been rented out for the last seven years. We moved here in the May, and in the early June I knew he had something to tell me, I could just tell. He said, 'I'm going to Afghanistan.'

'When?'

'In a couple of months' time but I have a lot of training to do before then.'

We moved in here literally the same as we did in Taunton when we got back from Brunei, opened the cases and off he went. Luckily, I have my family here. I have aunts and my sister in Fareham. He left in September 2006.

We managed to get Bella christened and then off he went, and halfway through his job he got moved into another job as a lieutenant colonel because this chap's wife had become seriously ill. He took over somebody else's job, so his tour got extended. He was supposed to have been home in March, he came home in April. He promised Bella that he would be home for mummy's birthday in April and obviously he wasn't home. She turned 3 and found it very, very hard.

She doesn't like change and wasn't very good with moving. She took ages to sleep in a new room. She was 2 years, 8 months when he left and she honestly screamed every day for six weeks. When he phoned, he had a twenty minute phone card and she would be screaming. I would be saying, 'Daddy's on the phone,' and she would say, 'That is not my real daddy. I want my real daddy.' She couldn't understand. That deployment was very hard. It was easier when she was a baby because she didn't know.

I was living with my parents, and the first trip to Afghanistan he was working incredibly long days, so when he phoned, as the tour went on, he was so involved with what he was doing that he was losing track of what I was doing here. We didn't have email access then. He would say, 'Is it Easter yet?'

'We had Easter last week.'

'Oh, right. Is Bella at school?'

He wasn't connected, whereas now we know how to manage it, we know how to keep things ticking over, but then, because he was so entrenched in his job and Bella was just a nightmare as a toddler, it was a stressful deployment.

Keeping in Touch

When Matthew deploys he gets given a welfare phone card which used to be just twenty minutes long per week. It was then discovered that inmates in prison were getting thirty minute phone cards! So, on his last deployment [again to Afghanistan] we had thirty minutes each week, which we tried to divide into three or four phone calls each week. Obviously, with both girls speaking to him as well, it wouldn't last very long and would run out by a Thursday. I would then have a very long weekend without the chance of speaking to him.

🍃 Laura Delahay 🍃

Laura is married to royal marine, John, who, among other deployments, has had four tours in Afghanistan. They have four children. For Laura, life as a military wife has meant constant house moves:

Meeting John

I lived in Bahrain in the Middle East. That is where I met John. He was a wet-behind-the-ears young officer. I don't even know his job – I'm one of those wives!

I was working in Bahrain and he was working in Faslane doing fleet protection for the navy and I just met him out and about, as you do, in a club. I was cabin crew for Gulf Air and, when I met John, I was also teaching English at the British Council. The embassy said there was a do aboard ship. He was there again on the ship, in his smart uniform, just chatting and I thought, 'Whoo!'

I went to boarding school. My dad's non-military, and I grew up not actually liking military children very much. They were a bit brattish and a bit 'My daddy's the CO of So-and-So'. I thought, 'I don't like you.' My dad said, 'You just tell that child, I pay all your school fees. The military pay for yours!'

For three weeks, John said, 'Oh, give me a chance!' Because of my impression from boarding school of the military, I thought, 'Oh, I don't really want to get married and have my children growing up thinking like that.' It wasn't because of the going away. I just thought, 'I don't really want to get married to military.' I had been slating it for years. I couldn't then go and do it. Then I fell in love with John. He is a lovely person. He is an amazing dad. We have four girls.

Moving

My husband was adjutant at the Royal Marines base in Chivenor, Devon, and I was pregnant with Molly, our first child. He was deployed, and the CO's wife there, Antonia, gave me some advice. 'If you want your marriage to last, go with your husband. Move around with your husband.' Separation puts pressure on your marriage, so I took that advice in when I heard it. Antonia and her husband are now in Australia, very happily married and having a wonderful time!

We moved from there, and John went to do his major's and we moved down to the married patch in *Daedalus* in Lee-on-the-Solent. He did an office job and we were there for a year. They get extra money when they get deployed. A year in Afghanistan came up. He said, 'Shall I do it?' Poppy is number three and was 3 months old.

I said, 'OK, I think I can do this.'

We did talk about it. He didn't come home and say 'I'm doing this.' We have always had excellent communication. I said, 'Yes, we can do it, so long as I can chose to move to where I want to.' My parents are in Torquay, and so we moved down there. It was hard that year, 2010, but it was doable because I had made the right decision to move.

I used to go and pick him up at Brize Norton when he came home on R&R. I turned [his absence] into a positive. I had gained weight after having three babies very close together, so I lost weight, had my hair cut, picked John up from Brize Norton, and I was a different woman! He said, 'Wow! Look at you!' It was nice. He could have got the coach, but I always went up to pick him up with the girls. The two weeks they're home is just fantastic.

Then we found out that he had got his company up in Scotland. He came back [from Afghanistan] in February 2011, by which time, during his R&R, I had conceived Amelia, and he said, 'Oh by the way, we are moving to Scotland and I have to deploy again.'

That was quite hard. I was pregnant and the houses you get in Scotland are big, old ones. The lawns are, like, 2 acres – massive, like fields! I was there, heavily pregnant, mowing a lawn that took three hours to mow! There are only four commanders' houses in a row and then the commanding officer's house, so you are very on top of each other. That is one of the drawbacks, but you just become a family. The other wives say, 'Hello. What you doing?'

I have homebirths and, because I kept so active because John was away while I was pregnant, my pregnancies and births were all easy, no complications. I was lucky.

Recognition

I suppose that the Military Wives Choir is recognition. I thought, 'John has done all that' and I have thought, 'Hello? What about me?' Someone in Whitehall, or wherever, saying, 'Laura Delahay, well done'. We don't get that, and it is such a shame.

John says it, but some husbands don't. I went to Marbella for a week's holiday and John said, 'Spend this money, you've deserved it. You have basically been a single parent for the last four years.' He comes back, I conceive, he goes away again. Literally.

The icing on the cake was when John came back from Afghanistan and then got called up for the Olympics. I must be the only woman in the entire UK that hated the Olympics! Every one of my friends was saying, 'Love it, brilliant!' My husband had just come home and had gone away again, and I was thinking, 'Grrr!' John was texting me from

London saying, 'I want to be with you. I want to be with my family. I've missed you.' He was doing security because of the mess the security company made [at the last moment, security company G4S could not supply enough security guards for the London 2012 Olympics, and so troops were called in to fill the shortfall].

Chicken Pox

When John went back after Amelia was born, all four of them had chicken pox. I had a 2-week-old with chicken pox. I had to go to the doctor with them all. I have never actually had a bit of a meltdown, I have just kept going. My mum is a bit old-school – it will make you stronger!

I was at the doctor's surgery and I was in tears wailing, 'I can't do any more!' It was peeing it down, there was sideways rain, thunder and lightning. Luckily, I had a 4x4 at the time. One of the mums from school said, 'I'll take them home and feed them, don't worry.' I thought, 'I'm a military wife,' but I just said, 'Oh, God, thank you!'

I managed to get hold of John in Afghanistan and he was saying, 'It's all right.' John is my calm, I am his storm. Just hearing his voice was enough.

'She'll be fine, she'll be fine. Don't panic.'

I came here to live, and people say, 'You're always so calm! So cool and collected. The girls are lovely.' They have no idea what I have been through. Somehow I have survived no sleep for two weeks, having to get up, putting up with crying – they couldn't sleep, didn't feel very well – trying to feed a newborn, then putting her down to go and tend one of the others. No family to help me, nobody. It was hard work.

Going Home

On drives to John's parents, when we were in Scotland and I was really heavily pregnant with Amelia, John's brother would get the train up. He would help me with the girls and we could drive back down together so I could have a couple of weeks with his parents. He was just amazing. He sort of stepped into John's role, but after I had had Amelia we did the journey on our own. From Arbroath it takes three hours just to get to Glasgow. We stopped at service stations because they have to be fed, watered, changed nappies, the dog has got to go out and have a wee. I would be stopped [by passers-by] all the time:

'Yes, I am doing this on my own.'

'My husband's away.'

'Yes, in the marines.'

Some service stations would get to know you, 'Oh, you've come back down! Off to see your family?'

'Yes.'

You became a character, the crazy lady with the four kids and the big dog, a German Shepherd. Ben is lovely, the calmest, easiest dog. Everything was planned in my head so I became this organisational person. I would drive up to service stations and I already knew who I was going to let out first. Ben would go for a wee, a sniff around and some water, while they watched a DVD in the car. Then, Ben back in the car, feed Amelia, then get them all out of the car. 'Hold hands everybody, we're in a car park,' as we walked up. I was like a school teacher.

'You sit there, don't move. Molly, you're the eldest, you watch them while I go and get the food.' You have to leave your children to go and do the simplest things. People who have never done this, logistically they will never know. I am stuck there while they are eating, four of them, on my own, and then one says, 'I need the toilet'. I can't say, 'Off you go', I have to get them all out and off to the toilet.

Now John is back, I back off. He needed to feel part of the family. We have had to sit down and I have said, 'You have to understand, I have been in charge. This has been my job. This has been my environment. I have been in charge of them, choosing what I pack, where to stop, what goes where.' I am quite a dominant person. It is not natural for me to stand back and watch him come in and take control. He comes back and says, 'It doesn't feel like I live here. It doesn't feel like I'm at home.'

'I know John, you've got to learn.'

They get a little booklet when they deploy – a little pack. Something from the church about bereavement that you have to go through, then the little book – it is almost like a little old Scout Guide – dib, dib, dib, dob, dob, dob! It needs to be modernised a bit. Up at 45 Commando they have a meeting and they are told, 'Don't forget your wives are going to go through it too, and there will be that adjustment when you get back. A list of DIY for you to do, but they will be in control, just step back.'

CHARLOTTE WOOLRICH

For Royal Navy wife, Charlotte, the twenty-first century brought the excitement of the beginning of her career, several new homes, heartache and joy:

I graduated from uni on my birthday, 31 August 2001, and John had one year left of his training at *Sultan*, so we then moved in together. I went to the flat in Southsea for a year. I had a great year. I worked at the Queen Alexandra Hospital in Cosham and it was my first job. I worked every other weekend. When I wasn't working we went out in Southsea and for meals with friends.

Then he got his posting, which was going to be Yeovil or Cornwall, because that is where the aircraft were. It was Yeovil. So, all guns a-blazing, 'Let's buy our first house!' we said. We went down there in the September.

My job was awful at the hospital. On my first day, the matron called a meeting to say that in the nine months to date they had had twenty-eight complaint letters. They were eleven staff members down on the one ward. It was an orthopedic trauma ward.

It was dreadful, and very stressful not being near my mum and dad. I had been away at uni but mum would come up at weekends. I was only in Kingston so she would drive up the A3 and see me.

It was horrible in Yeovil, and then came the tragic phone call on 17 December to say that John's dad had been rushed to hospital with a heart attack. We threw a bag in the car and whizzed down the motorway, and there we sat, waiting for him to die. He had put his knife and fork down in the restaurant he was in with his brother, said he didn't feel right, went grey and dropped down. The first-aider came out with a plaster, didn't even attempt CPR.

We should have been at that meal. I have obviously gone over this many times. We can't do anything about it now. We had other commitments, and we were coming home to spend Christmas with family. Who knows what would have happened. We were there [by his bedside] with John's sister. John's sister's son, Liam, had just been diagnosed with cystic fibrosis and his nan had died six months before.

John's dad died about eight o'clock the following evening. We were in the hospital. I decided it was my turn to go out for a walk, so I did, and then I went into the quiet room in the intensive care department. John came in and collapsed on the floor, saying his dad had gone. That was the first person who had died, who was close to me. I had known his dad from when I was a child. I had seen him in the pub and was John's partner for nine years. It was very hard.

We stayed down until the funeral, which was the beginning of the year, and then we went back to Yeovil. We had been in our house about a week, and we were in bed reading our books and we almost simultaneously put our books down and said, 'Let's go back home.' That is what we did. A week later, we put the house on the market but it took until July to sell.

I left in the March because I couldn't handle my job anymore. The guilt feelings, with no staff, not being able properly to look after patients was just awful. So I left and came to work at the Intensive Care Unit at the Queen Alexandra, which seemed a bad move. I had flashbacks about his dad. We went to a flat in Fareham for a year and we got married.

Getting Married

So, we had the flat, we got some inheritance and we went to Las Vegas and got married, had a honeymoon in Hawaii and then came home. I think I never really wanted to have a church wedding. I'm not religious, and I didn't want to do the whole church thing. I wanted to do something different. Something funky. I had a normal wedding out there. I took my dress out. We had five guests who came out – my mum came. Unfortunately, his sister didn't come out. Liam, by then, was 3 and she didn't know how he would react to the heat. It was 104 degrees out there in August.

Before we got married, John was home weekends. He was away quite a lot. He was due to come and do a month's course at *Sultan* for the whole of May, so I thought, 'How lovely, that will be nice'. He got out the car and he only had a backpack, like a rucksack.

'Take a seat. Someone's off sick, and because I have been allowed to have a bit longer leave to go to Vegas to get married, I have volunteered to go on HMS *Ocean* for a three month trip.'

'Right, you have no suit, no wedding rings, we have nothing and you are telling me that you are going to be home three days before we go to Las Vegas?'

So that Saturday we went to Southampton and we bought the wedding rings, his suit and shoes and the invites were ordered online. They came on the Tuesday or Wednesday and that was him gone. He left the weekend after. That was his one and only trip on a boat. He is aircraft.

We then got married, and the week after our honeymoon we bought our house. We had some inheritance, so that was a good deposit to put down. We didn't make anything from the house in Yeovil.

He was still based in Yeovil. I had to take a year out from nursing. I was in intensive care and I needed to chill. I had some grief counselling myself. I worked at a local college, assessing NVQ students in care. I went out on their placements. It was very boring, but what I needed. I used to come home and do my paperwork.

Then I knew I wanted to go back to nursing again. I worked at Haslar, the naval hospital, for four years. In that time, John had about three trips to Iraq, went to Bosnia again and to Norway for his arctic training. He was in Iraq when I told him I was pregnant with Oscar. He rang up and he said, 'Any news, anything to report?'

'Yes, the car's been playing up,' I said. 'Nigel, at the Citroen garage, sorted it. Oh and I am a few weeks pregnant!' There was a deadly silence. 'Hello? Are you there?'

'Yeah. There's no chairs to sit down, hang on a minute!' He was quite shocked. He went the beginning of July and it was the beginning of August. 'That hasn't taken long, has it?'

'No.'

'That's a good one to tell the lads …!'

He then came home. His Iraq trips were about nine weeks long, so were bearable, not like six month deployments as they do on ships. I have been quite lucky in the navy, he hasn't done long trips but he has been in war zones. He went back to Iraq.

I leaked my waters at thirty-five weeks. It was a Wednesday. I was due to go to a breastfeeding workshop. I had finished work the week before. I had a shower and I thought, 'Something is not quite right'. So I phoned up the midwife and she said, 'Go to your breastfeeding class and then when you come back, call me again and let me know if you still think you are trickling water.' I put the phone down and then a load just trickled down my leg. I thought, 'Oh no'. I phoned my mum and she came and collected me.

At the hospital they did a test to see what was going on. My waters hadn't gone but a slight seal had, so I was trickling. This was the Wednesday and John was due home on the Monday. So, I thought, 'What do I do?' I couldn't believe how calm I was. My mum wasn't calm. John had given me this card for emergencies, a number to call. I had this lady on the phone taking all the details. 'Obviously, I don't know when I will give birth but my waters are holding on for blah, blah. I would like my husband home for the birth.'

She was tapping away. Then she said, 'I can tell you now, we won't be sending him home. If anything changes, if you're in danger, or the baby, give us a call again.' I put the phone down and the midwife behind me said, 'They did that to me when I was going to give birth. They didn't send my husband home.'

I went back into my little room and I said to my mum, 'What's going to happen to me now then? I have the number for the squadron in Yeovil, I wonder if they can speak to anyone?' So I rang, and this chap answered the phone. 'Hi, I wonder if you can help me? I am about to give birth at thirty-five weeks and my husband is not home, he's in Iraq.'

'Okey-dokey, is there a number there for the ward that he can ring you on?'

Twenty minutes later, John rang me:

'What's going on?'

'I don't know!' I think I just broke down then, having heard his voice.

'I have the credit card, they are telling me to come home, but because of all the injuries from a bomb that killed some soldiers, I don't know how many seats there are on the plane.'

'OK.'

They took me up to a ward and staff came up to me saying that they had such-and-such on the phone asking if my husband should be sent home. Of course, I told them 'yes'. I didn't know when the baby would come. I stayed overnight on Thursday and I hadn't heard from him. Then in the morning he came walking up the ward. My hero! All in camou-flage. He was absolutely shattered. He had obviously been travelling all the night.

He stayed for about an hour and then said he needed to get some sleep. He came back in the afternoon. I stayed in that night and they did another scan. Then I went into labour naturally on Monday teatime and had Oscar on the Tuesday morning. I was exactly thirty-six weeks.

Military Wives Choir

When the Military Wives programme was on telly, John was in Afghanistan. I had not watched any of Gareth Malone's other stuff. I remember my sister telling me about it. I watched half of the first one and was in floods of tears. I was feeling sorry for myself. I was stuck at home on my own with my two children, Evie had followed Oscar four years later, and my husband was in a war zone. It was no good him tell-ing me he was safe, he was in a war zone.

Some women have their husbands away for six months and I think they are lucky, as their men are on a ship and they go to nice countries. They are not having to worry quite so much. I know that sounds a bit selfish, but countries like Iraq and Afghanistan are not nice places. Look at all the people we've lost. The programme was on, and when it finished, I went to a family day at HMS *Collingwood* – I used to go to the gym and the children to the crèche – and the ladies from the patch were talking about it. One of them said that they had had a flyer through the door.

One of the wives was going to start a choir up. She showed it to me, and I rang the lady called Kim and said I was a bored housewife with my two young children and I wanted to give it a try. I went to a meeting just before Christmas and met a couple of the ladies. It was all talk about how they were going to go to *Collingwood*. Initially it was a daytime rehearsal but it then became a Tuesday evening.

Gareth Malone saw the photo of us in the *Portsmouth News* and Kim answered the phone and it was him saying that he had seen it. We were choir number five. We were on the first album. We had two weeks' notice to record the song. That was where it all began. It was absolutely amazing to be in on it. I have been up to London and recorded a music video, Gareth Malone was there and Aled Jones from *Daybreak*. I auditioned and was lucky enough to sing at the Festival of Remembrance. I have met an amazing group of women. We just all get it.

My Military Marriage

Mine is not a typical military life. I don't live on a patch. We have never lived in quarters. I am not living in anyone else's pockets. True, he does not go away for six months at a time.

I have stayed near my family and not moved with him, other than the short time in Yeovilton. They are the three things that most do as a military wife. We had children and we said we would look at how old they were and what John's next job would be as to whether he left or not. The closer we are to his twenty-two years the bigger the pay out and the more pension we will get – we will get an extension on the back of the house and take the children to Vegas. It would seem silly for him not to do his twenty-two years.

Fundraising

I ran the London Marathon in 2012. I have done the Great South Run a couple of times. Once for Cystic Fibrosis Kids, which is a charity my sister-in-law set up for kids in Portsmouth. They give kids PlayStations and things like that. I go to the gym and don't do quite as much running – I am not in the zone, I need to get back into it – it was something I had always wanted to do, a marathon. I didn't expect to do it quite as quickly as I did.

I missed the deadline to apply normally, so I contacted the Cystic Fibrosis Trust – we give to them monthly – and just emailed them and said I was interested in running. They said that all their places had been taken but I could fill in a golden bond place. This meant that you filled in a form, told them what previous fundraising you had done and the best form won. I didn't think I stood much chance as I hadn't done much for them. I had been involved in organising a street party, but it wasn't my idea, and the Great South Runs. I had an email and they said I hadn't been successful but to try again.

Then in the January, I had just got over a chest infection, a lady rang me and said that they had a couple of people drop out due to ill health and would I still like to run it?

'When do I have to let you know by?'

'By five o'clock today as, if you are not going to do it, I will ring someone else.' I had to raise £2,000. That was their ball-park figure.

'What if I only raise, say, £1,600?'

'We will need you to raise another £400 after the event. That is the amount.'

I put the phone down and called John. He said, 'I don't think you can, Charlotte. You can't put that much pressure on yourself.'

'I really want to do it.'

'Well, I think you will be really silly.'

'OK.'

I put the phone down. My friend was training with a friend who had a normal place. I wondered what training week number they were up to. I gave her a ring and said, 'What do you think? Do you think I can do it?'

'Course you can! We are on week six, doing 13 miles this Saturday. Come and join us.'

I had not done 13 miles for two months: the Gosport half-marathon in November. Walking into Fareham with my mum and Evie, we discussed it, and I rang the lady back at five o'clock and said, 'Yes, I'll do it. Thank you very much.'

I rang John back and he said, 'I think you are really stupid.'

'Right, you have said your piece. I am doing this because I want this. It is a big thing for me. It is a big charity. It is close to my heart and I am doing it. So, support me or don't talk to me.'

'OK, OK.'

So that was that. I had a mission. Ten weeks. I did a cake sale at school. I was in the *Portsmouth News* twice. My sister-in-law did a cake sale at my nephew's school as well. I had a coffee morning at home. Loads of patients sponsored me and I raised £3,542 in ten weeks. I could not believe it.

Then I had to run it. That was five hours and forty seconds. I was over the moon. Every now and again John will say to me, 'Can you believe you ran that?'

'No, I can't! I couldn't do it now. I would have to start the training all over again.'

I was on Wave Radio. They came and did an interview on the Friday before I travelled up on the Saturday. They played snippets of it all through the morning 'cos they didn't have anyone else local who was running it. That was part of the story – I had ten weeks.

Patients sponsored me – they just threw tenners and twenties at me at work. I had a pot up on the reception desk at work as well. I emptied that once a week and had £9 one week, £3 another and it all adds up. I had a 'Just Giving' page and kept putting it up on Facebook all the time. I had quite a few donations that were anonymous, and I know that the *Portsmouth News* put my Just Giving number in the articles.

Some of my training runs were in January, February, and March, and one was 15 miles in three hours and it was torrential for the whole three hours. I got in, and was due to go to a friend in Lee-on-the-Solent, and John said, 'Oh my God look at you. You must be freezing. Come and get in this bath I've run for you.' I felt really humble.

I was plodding it in vile conditions and I just had to keep going because it is not me that has a life expectancy of 32. I kept thinking, 'It's not me that has to get my back punched every day to get the phlegm loose', and that is how I got through it. It was a very emotional day. I cried at 9 miles and 19 miles. At 9 miles we went through an industrial estate with no people and all we could hear was plod, plod – people's feet. It was awful. Really eerie. I just thought, 'Oh my God, there is no one here. Just keep going, Charlotte.' It was horrible.

Luckily it was only for about half a mile. Then we were back on the normal streets again. At 19 miles I was just tired, really. I was at the wall. My longest training run was 20 miles and I thought I couldn't do it, but I could. I tried to eat something and had a cereal bar, and I stopped and stretched and said to another runner, 'Oh my God!' I had my name on my vest and they said, 'Come on Charlotte, come on.' I got to 20 miles and the last 6 miles I jogged and walked. I wanted to do it in four and a half hours. If I had not jogged and walked I would have done it quicker than that. I was only half an hour slower, so, if I do it again it will be on time. It was the achievement – I only had ten weeks and I made it. John said, 'You nailed that!'

'Yes, I did. You didn't think I would, did you darling?!'

The charity that Charlotte is involved with is Cystic Fibrosis Kids of Portsmouth, which raises funds to help children affected by the disease in Portsmouth and Southampton. More information is available on: www. cfkids.org.uk.

❧ Nicola Laing ❧

Nicola is married to weapons engineer Iain, a lieutenant commander in the Royal Navy. She is the carer for their disabled son, Regan, and she herself is living with the effects of being knocked over by a lorry nine years ago. Nicola and Iain have been married for twenty-nine years and have recently renewed their wedding vows, at Whale Island, Portsmouth.

Ballroom Dancing

At fourteen I used to teach Scottish and ballroom dancing, which is what they learn at their first term at Dartmouth Officer Training College. So I went to my first ball at that age and met Iain when I was teaching dancing there. There were six couples who got married the same summer as we did and we're the only two that are left. We renewed our wedding vows a couple of years ago, which was really lovely.

Martial Arts

My martial art is Choi Kwang Do (CKD) and is a modern martial art developed by Grandmaster Kwang Jo Choi as a non-competitive form of self-defence. It uses the body's natural movements to develop powerful blocking, striking and kicking techniques without the harm to joints and muscles caused by the over-extension used in some traditional martial arts. Grandmaster Choi developed the form after becoming seriously injured demonstrating Tae Kwon Do around the world.

We study with the Hampshire CKD schools [see www.hampshireckd. com, where both Nicola and Iain are listed on the 'Head and Chief Instructors' page] mostly here in Portsmouth, but they have grown over the last ten years and now have fifteen venues around Hampshire.

My son, Regan, and I started and then Calum, but then Calum quit. Sam, our daughter, also started, but our other daughter had no interest. Iain came back from sea and said, 'If I am ferrying you lot around, I might as well start.' That is how it went on.

Our martial arts are based on self-defence and there are no competitions in it. I think this was where we were lucky with the children. There is no contact. If we hit anything it is a great big shield. I have grown in confidence. I wouldn't say 'boo' to a goose before, now I can go out on my own and wouldn't worry, and I take a class.

We teach to ability. The eldest person I have ever done martial arts with was 89. She had wrist braces on. We talked to her and she said her bone density had improved by 30 per cent through doing martial arts. It is all biomechanical, so you don't hurt your joints.

I was terrified doing my black belt as I was in plaster. Sam said, 'I'm doing mine', and I'm not going to be outdone by her, but I thought 'I can't go on my toes'; I would be in a lot of pain. We turned up, and we did it. Then I started working on my Second Dan and got it. Now I am working towards my Third Dan. Although it took six years to get to second degree black belt, I have been waiting to finish my third degree black belt for two years, because of the time I now commit to the Military Wives Choir. We are hoping to open our own school. When you get to Third Dan you get into examining. It means you can do a lot more yourself.

To be honest, with my ankle, my consultants say, 'How can you do it?'

'If I am having a good day, I can do it. If I don't then I just take it easy.'

I've done a grade exam in a wheelchair before. It improves bone density and flexibility. I think, if it hadn't been for martial arts, I would have been permanently in a wheel chair. It's what has kept me out of it. As much as the pain is … At the end of the day, do I give up? Sit and do nothing? I wouldn't have it any different. On a good day I will send you flying across the room. I actually managed to throw Master Biophy on the floor. He is ex-army and he knows exactly what we are going to do. That was probably my most memorable thing in martial arts.

Family

We have four children, Samantha Margaret, the eldest (1987), is the only one who went full term and was born in Torquay during Iain's break from the Royal Navy between leaving in 1986 and re-joining in 1988. Samantha is now a full-time supervisor and special educational needs co-ordinator at Shadwell Playbox Nursery in Portsmouth.

Danae Louise (1989) was born while Iain was Officer of the Day on HMS *Shetland*, alongside in Newcastle for a stand-off during fishery protection duties. Danae was born at twenty-nine weeks, weighing 2lb 10oz. Iain was able to get compassionate leave to travel down to Plymouth the next day, where we had her christened by the Naval Chaplain because she was very poorly and in the Special Care Baby Unit. Danae is now married and living with her husband, John, in their new home. She works as an administrator for Hampshire Constabulary.

Calum Robert Iain Leslie (1991) was also born at twenty-nine weeks, weighing just 1lb 10oz, in Plymouth while Iain was studying for his engineering degree at the Royal Naval Engineering College, Manadon. Unlike Danae, he had cerebral palsy caused by a bleed on the brain. While he had developmental and motor skill delays, two years of Peto-style inductive training at the Trengweath School and a lot of support through school have enabled him to lead a normal life and he is now a semi-skilled technician working for GKN Aerospace here in Portsmouth.

Regan Connor (1995) was born at thirty-four weeks, but suffers from periventricular leukomalacia and is permanently confined to a wheelchair and needs full personal care. Regan lives at home and since leaving school last year he has enjoyed a life of gaming, reading and playing on his laptop.

I had Sam when I was 18. I had my family young and now we can do so much. A couple of times Iain has been flown home from different things. We were in Plymouth when I miscarried. We had been there for a party. I left Calum with a next-door neighbour. I had to go to the hospital and when I got there it was, 'Sorry'.

Iain drove all the way up to HMS *Collingwood*, got a shower and a shave and picked up mail and drove all the way back. The next morning they did a scan to make sure, and Regan was still there. I lost four sets of twins in all.

Calum had a bleed on his brain when he was born and I wasn't told. He was born in Plymouth at twenty-nine weeks. Eventually, they told us. Iain was in Newcastle when one of our other daughters was born early, at twenty-nine weeks, too. My uncle was phoning around every dockyard [to find the boat]. Eventually, he contacted the police and they turned up at the sub. It was five in the morning, and they said to Iain, 'You have a daughter.'

'Yes, I know I have a daughter.'

'No, another one.'

Then she stopped breathing, and I had to rush her into hospital. It was hours before we managed to get hold of Iain. He was out doing a NATO Military Committee Sea Day with the Chief of the Defence Staff of all NATO. Unfortunately, the submarine got stuck on the bottom of Portland Harbour in an emergency. He got to the phone as soon as he could, and the navy couldn't do enough to get him home, but when he is not instantly available it is just ... When I was told the boat was stuck at the bottom of the harbour I was thinking, I have a child I have just had to resuscitate and there's Iain miles away, for all I knew stuck for I-don't-know-how-long.

There are times when it's difficult when they are away. In some ways emails are lovely – for minor things. For major ones, you're letting them know, but there is probably nothing they can do.

Regan

I was paranoid when I had Regan. 'You've got to test!'

Everything was clear. He was very poorly at Christmas and Iain was away in February. I went to see a new health visitor because I was away on holiday. She accused me of not looking after him properly because he wasn't growing and wasn't feeding. Eventually, we were referred to a neurologist who then found out that what he's got is quite rare. The consultant had never seen it before. I was told to 'go home and Google it'. When we went home we were ticking symptoms off the list. They don't know what will happen long term. With a lot of children they say that their learning tails off at a certain point. With my other son, he had a stroke. Regan is a different kettle of fish. That has been difficult.

Routine

Iain hasn't been at sea for a couple of years as he is doing naval recruiting now. We've been out with him. We went to the Good Food Show and the Mountbatten Festival of Music three times. It's nice [to have him home] but also quite nice when he's away! You can do what you want! You have your routines and set everything out, and then they come home and the kids don't want to know. It's 'Dad can I have …?', knowing that, a week before, I had said 'No'.

Roots

In Mutley Plain, Plymouth, it was much more of a community. You go and help each other, you don't have to make a phone call. We moved to Portsmouth for six months after two different quarters in Plymouth. We had all the help for Calum – wheelchair, shoes – and wanted to stay put for a little while. We did not know about Regan then. He is now 19 and our roots are here, although Iain's family are in Scotland and my mother lives in Plymouth. The house has been adapted for Regan.

Wives Go Too

When we first got married there were lots of things that wives would go along to and I think, over the years, they have cut back. There is not that amount of things to go to. Even when Iain was doing the Mountbatten Festival, it got to the stage when the Second Sea Lord could go and have his food, but his wife couldn't because the navy wouldn't pay for it. We've not been to a function for seven or eight years. We follow the Royal Marines Band around instead. Eight bandsman came to our wedding. My uncle was head of the band service at Dartmouth Naval College. We go down to the annual Regatta Week at Dartmouth, which is where I am from.

The Military Wives Choir

We watched the Military Wives on TV and I jokingly said to Iain, 'Oh, wouldn't it be lovely?' I used to be in the school choir.

It was advertised in the newspaper, and so I emailed and I started the following week. We met at the leader's house and there were twenty-five or so of us who turned up. One day she said she had a surprise for us – we were recording an album in two weeks' time! We said, 'Two weeks? You're having a laugh!' Most of us hadn't sung. I don't read music.

Since then, Sam, my daughter, has joined too. I was on *Surprise Surprise* when Gareth Malone proposed to his girlfriend. We went to their wedding in Southampton. Sam has been on *Songs of Praise*. We have launched the Portsmouth Poppy Appeal. We've had some experiences that we would never have had without the choir and it has become a big part of our lives in the last eighteen months. In a way, it has brought Iain and me closer together because he can sometimes get time off to join us.

Medal

Iain was in the Gulf for eight months. I didn't know much about it. The kids were quite young so I had my hands full, anyway. It wasn't until a couple of years later that he said, 'Oh, I'm going to get a medal.'

'What for?'

'We were out in the Gulf.'

'And?'

'I didn't tell you we were involved in some stuff ...'

'Oh, my God!'

Actually, I think I was quite grateful he hadn't said anything at the time. We've lost friends in the Falklands and were friends with the guy who was shot on the submarine a little while ago in Southampton. That was probably one of the worst days of my life. Our best friend was the captain. All you heard at the time was that somebody had been shot. Iain phoned the helpline, and they said they couldn't help. Iain asked if the captain was involved. They said 'no', so that was all we needed to know then. The next day we heard who it was. It was hard.

EPILOGUE

The experiences recounted in this book show the varied lives that military wives have led over the last century. As you would expect, domesticity has prevailed for many, with wives bringing up families in the safety of their homes or following their men as they are posted to all parts of the world.

For some women, talking about their experiences has been painful, particularly if loving their man has led to their losing him in conflict. For others, talking has been a release. Most seem to look back on their time as a military spouse with nostalgia and a smile.

Josephine (Jo') met Peter Ball while he was serving his National Service in the RAF. They were married two years later, had a son Kenneth and have two granddaughters, Tina (now serving as a bandsman in the Coldstream Guards) and Julie, an air hostess. In 2013, Jo' and Peter celebrated their diamond wedding anniversary and were thrilled to receive a congratulatory message from the queen. Both talented artists, they now live in Hampshire. Poet Pam Whittington wrote the following poem for Jo' to give to Peter as a gift. It is reproduced here by kind permission of Pam Whittington and Jo' Ball.

TO PETER, FROM JO' ON HIS BIRTHDAY

Dear Peter
Few people can recall a love like you and I have shared.
The moment that you met me you made it plain you cared.
A Devon man in uniform, so handsome and so smart,
Dancing there in Cardiff you stole this Welsh girl's heart.

The day you left the air force, you helped me, baking bread.
But airwaves were your passion and would shape our years ahead.
Our flat was near The Oval when we married in '53,
Watching the famous arriving; and you made our first TV.

Waltzing at the Service Clubs; 'Too Young' our favourite song,
But you were never that impressed when I would sing along.
Moving out to Clapham, and then our little son.
Times weren't always easy, but still we had some fun.

Changing jobs you had a car to travel far and wide.
And I was often lonely without you by my side.
Our time we've had together was spent in many ways.
And some seem just like yesterday, our own warm velvet days.

Pembrokeshire and Hereford, the Beacons and my Wales,
Were canvasses for happiness where the colour never pales,
And water colour sea waves, where stones were deftly skimmed.
Parchment sketches, kept and loved, by me have never dimmed.

Talking to the world at dawn, your paintings of the sea.
Your wicked sense of humour and your patience dear with me.
And now we have granddaughters, seeds that we have sown,
For all these things I've loved you, so much. I hope you have known.

By Pam Whittington – who met her husband, Tony, three days after he was demobbed from National Service. (First published in *Sunshine and Showers: Poetry and Prose* by Pam Whittington, printed by Hobbs Printers Ltd, Totton, Hampshire, 2011. www.pamwhittington.com.)

THE FINAL WORD

The last word goes to Steffi Hughes, who sums up the military wives in this book, and the thousands who did not make it into print:

One thing is for sure, and this applies to ALL military wives out there: They are all very special, brave and strong women, who support their husbands throughout their often very difficult careers, regardless of what it brings for them and their families. They all, therefore, deserve a lot of respect, coupled with lots of understanding and support!

BIBLIOGRAPHY

BOOKS

Moreau, M. (project manager), *This is my Home Now* (Southampton: This is my Home Now, 2011).

MAGAZINES

Jottings, Avenue St Andrews United Reformed Church magazine, April/May 2006 edition.

WEBSITES

BBC – www.bbc.co.uk
HMS *Ambuscade* – www.ambuscade.org.uk/AmbVis1981.htm
HMS *Ambuscade* – www.ambuscade.org.uk/amb_dits81.htm
HMS *Irresistible* – Wikipedia: http://en.wikipedia.org/wiki/HMS_Irresistible_ (1898)
The Society of Old Priceans – www.sop.hampshire.org.uk
Victoria Institute – www.viweb.freehosting.net/badminton.htm

INDEX

1st and 2nd Parachute Division 71
4th Royal Tank Regiment 87
7th Royal Horse Artillery 68
8th Army 48
33rd Airborne Division 71
45 Commando 199
815 Squadron 108
Aberdeen 63
Acton 81
Aden 11, 66, 79, 80, 87, 88, 98, 164
Afghanistan 9, 11, 125, 131, 143, 147, 152, 154, 155, 157, 158, 159, 165, 166, 167, 172, 188, 194, 195, 196, 197, 198, 203, 204
Africa 43, 48, 49, 109, 162, 174, 191
Aldershot 50, 68, 69, 70, 71, 85, 98
Algeria 46
Alton 83, 84, 85, 86
Amesbury 153
Anguilla 134
Anstey 8, 23, 25
Arborfield 87
Arbroath 66, 198
Armed Forces Christian Union 114
Armstrong, Jay 7, 121, 185–9

Army Commando 44
Arras Offensive 16
ATS 50
Auction 67, 77, 83, 94
Australia 103, 175, 196

Backhouse, Carol 7
Badminton 51, 62, 217
Baghdad 132, 179
Bahrain 47, 78, 79, 150, 196
Bailey, Stella 26
Ball, Jo' 7, 213
Balkans 95, 121
Balneil, Lord 97
Barlow, Gary 128, 194
Basingstoke 42, 83
Battle of Britain 80
BBC 15, 128, 185, 217
Beirut 110
Belfast 118
Belize 115
Bemand, George, 2nd Lt 24
Bethune 24
Big Ben 128
Bishop's Waltham 24, 25

Blandford 116, 126, 127, 130
BLESMA 143
Bombay 39
Borneo 64, 72, 90
Borstal 75
Bournemouth 49, 126, 155
Bosnia 105, 123, 130, 202
Bray, Lauren 7, 164, 170
Bremervörde 54
Bristol 38, 39, 190
British Council 196
Brize Norton 78, 99, 100, 106, 197
Brunei 191, 192, 193, 194
Buckingham Palace 135, 184
Buckinghamshire 80
Bulford 116, 117, 126, 128, 130
Burma 20

Cameron Highlands 52
Canada 47, 92, 97, 145, 154, 155
Cape Town 162
Caravan 62, 82, 83, 84, 87
Cardiff 214
Catterick 116, 128, 186
Charing Cross 77
Chatham 55, 56
Chelsea Pensioners 143
China 20, 26, 69
Civvy Street 108
Choi Kwang Do 207
Churchward, Kate 7, 190–5
Coffee with God 114
Coldstream Guards 48, 213
Cook, Frederick Alexander 23
Corsham 119
Cosham 200
Cuffe, Jenny 7, 44
Curtis, Gladys 7, 27, 28–38
Cyprus 71, 117, 125, 127, 131, 146, 157
Cystic Fibrosis Kids of Portsmouth 207
Cystic Fibrosis Trust 205
Czechoslovakia 39, 40

Dartmouth 29, 157, 164, 168, 211
Dawson, Rose 7, 39–44
D-Day 38, 46
Deahl, Winifred 7, 27
Delahay, Laura 7, 195–9
DIY 59, 60, 199
Dorset 187 142
Douglas, Gail 7, 136–142
Dover 22
Dresden 40
Dubai 132
Duncan, Antonella 118, 143–5

El Alamein 48
England 31, 40, 51, 52, 54, 55, 56, 88, 97, 160, 167, 173, 174, 179, 192, 193, 194
Eire 108
Exocet 107
Falkland Islands 67, 119
Falklands Conflict 95, 103, 106, 107, 109, 133, 135
Fareham 65, 78, 119, 184, 194, 201, 205
Farnborough 83
Festival of Remembrance 172, 204
Fiji 191
Fillingham, Anthea 7, 87–93, 97–8
First World War 5, 8, 9, 15, 20, 23, 25, 28, 41
Fleet Air Arm 66, 72
France 16, 24, 28, 31, 46, 127
Friend, Wendi 7, 23

Gallipoli 21, 173
Germany 32, 33, 37, 38, 41, 44, 46, 47, 52, 53, 55, 57, 71, 72, 86, 116, 127, 128, 130, 157, 160, 161, 186
Gestapo 40
Gibraltar 99, 109, 110
Gillingham 55
Glasgow 99, 107, 198
Glencross, Alis 7, 106–8

Goose Green 106
Gosport 66, 78, 123, 184, 205
Great Ormond Street 97, 98
Great South Run 204, 205

Hale, Joy 7, 15, 20, 47–52
Hamburg 54
Hampshire 16, 24, 55, 66, 81, 182, 187,
    208, 209, 213, 214, 217
Hampshire Regiment 43
Hasler, Royal Hospital 146
Hattingh, Sarah 7, 125, 151–6
Hawaii 201
Heidelberg 161, 163
Helensborough 78
Hill, Barbara 7, 68–72
Hill Head 65, 160
Hilsea Barracks 48, 50
Hitler 37
HMS
    Ambuscade 102, 217
    Andromeda 109, 110, 111
    Antrim 104
    Anzio 78
    Ark Royal 63, 96, 101, 103
    Ariel 62
    Birmingham 100
    Carlisle 26
    Carysfort 59
    Centaur 66
    Collingwood 61, 78, 142, 170, 178,
        190, 204, 209
    Coventry 107, 135
    Courageous 26
    Daedalus 66, 67
    Daring 170
    Drake 146
    Edinburgh 179
    Endurance 137
    Excellent 149
    Foxglove 26
    Ganges 26

Glamorgan 102, 103, 104
Glasgow 107
Intrepid 108, 134
Irresistible 21, 217
Jufair 78, 79
Maidstone 78
Manchester 181
Newcastle 146
Norfolk 79
Ocean 201
Pellew 78
Penelope 98
Raleigh 121
Sheffield 107
Shetland 209
Southampton 119
St Vincent 78
Sultan 123
Victory I 26
Warrior 169
York 180, 181
HRH The Prince of Wales 78
Holland 41, 119
Holroyd, Phyllis 7, 62–5, 96–7
Hong Kong 105
Horse Guards Parade 134
House of Commons 128
Houses of Parliament 128
Hovercraft 67, 72
Huckle, Alan 134
Hughes, Steffi 7, 160–4, 215

India 19, 25, 47, 52
Indian Army 19, 38
Indian Staff College 38, 39
Iraq 130, 132, 143, 146, 147, 148, 150,
    157, 158, 165, 166, 172, 175, 179,
    180, 182, 188, 194, 202, 203, 204
Italy 31, 32, 33, 37, 49

Jaji 113
Jamaica 24

Jameson, Fiona 7, 172–9
Jarrett-Kerr, Margaret 38–9
Johnson, Boris 128
Jones, Aled 204

Kampen 116
Kano 113
Kenya 157, 158, 164
Kiff, Sarah 7, 119–121, 179–184
Krayfeld 116
Kuala Lumpur 50, 51

Laing, Nicola 7, 207–212
Las Vegas 201
Leahy, Christopher 7, 23
Leahy, Eve 7
Leahy, Jade 7, 156–160,
Leahy, Olive 7, 23, 24, 25
Lee-On-The-Solent 66, 72, 138, 196, 206
Legg, Penny 11, 133–4, 108–112
Lehrmannova, Rusena 39
Leonard Cheshire Home 86
Le Touret Military Cemetery 24
Liverpool 39, 63, 68, 109
Llandudno 58
London 39, 40, 41, 50, 55, 57, 66, 80, 81, 83, 113, 119, 121, 123, 128, 130, 133, 134, 135, 145, 148, 153, 160, 168, 170, 172, 185, 192, 198, 204
London Marathon 204
London Zoo 92, 139
Lossiemouth 63, 66

Macedonia 117, 130
Malaria 113, 176
Malaya 47, 50, 51, 52, 64, 88, 90, 91, 92, 98
Malayan Badminton Championships 51
Malayan Crisis 64
Malaysia 89

Malcolmson, Helen 7, 145–151
Malone, Gareth 126, 127, 128, 171, 184, 203, 204, 211
Malta 58, 59, 87, 97
Married Quarters 26, 62, 65, 68, 81, 107, 109, 119, 138, 159, 183
Marsh, Edith 7, 44–46
Matthews, Lorraine 7, 101–6, 135–6
Mauritius 47, 61
Merchant Navy 36, 101
Meningitis 137
Middle East 79, 196
Middleton-West, Margaret 19–20
Ministry of Defence (MOD) 104, 168, 169, 172
Moreau, Maianna 7, 44, 217
Morocco 99, 110, 176
Mother's Union 85
Mumbai 39
Münster 161, 163
Musgrove, Carol 7, 116–7, 125–133

NAAFI 68, 69, 112, 116, 117, 126, 177
NATO 210
National Service 213
Nazis 41, 46
Newcastle 109, 136, 137, 139, 209
New Zealand 156, 172, 173, 175, 176, 178, 179
Nigeria 112, 113, 114
North Africa 43
Northern Ireland 11, 118, 157
Norway 46, 123, 191, 192, 202
Noyce, Irene 7, 77–9

Odiham 80, 81, 84
Officers Christian Fellowship of America 100
Olympics 197, 198
Ottawa 92, 93
Oxford 55

Pakistan 39, 157

Pakistani Staff College 39

Palestine 71

Payne, Lily Hannah 23–5

Parkinson, Liesel 7, 114–5

Persian Gulf 80

Piper, Sue 7, 19, 38, 93–4, 98–101, 112–3

Plymouth 20, 109, 110, 111, 121, 123, 145, 146, 192, 209, 211

Portcullis House 129

Portland 78, 108, 210

Portsmouth 20, 21, 22, 62, 65, 66, 78, 79, 102, 104, 122, 137,142, 145, 146, 148, 149, 150, 164, 169,170, 172, 184, 185, 194, 204, 206, 207, 208, 209, 211

Portsmouth Military Wives Choir 142, 170, 184

Powell, Dr Jean 7, 72–7, 95–6

Prague 39, 40

Preston 51

Price's Grammar School 65

Purbrook 49

Queen Alexandra Hospital 200

Queen's Royal Lancers 52

Quetta 38, 39

RAF 79, 82, 86, 145, 187, 188, 193, 213

RAF Cranwell 70

RAF Odiham 80

RAF Uxbridge 80

Raj 47

Rationing 35, 51, 52, 55

Reading 37, 119, 191

Red Cross 31, 37, 38

Redundant 141. 142

Rhodesia 115

Roedean 53

Rolls-Royce 48, 52

Rommel 31

Romsey Cathedral 149

Rowner 62

Royal Artillery 28, 68

Royal British Legion 38

Royal Electrical and Mechanical Engineers (REME) 43, 47, 87, 88, 91, 151

Royal Engineers 38, 114

Royal Marines 149, 164, 185, 190, 191, 196

Royal Naval Air Station Yeovilton (RNAS Yeovilton) 65, 112

Royal Navy 20, 26, 62, 64, 66, 77, 79, 93, 98, 101, 102, 105 108, 111, 112, 118, 119,121, 133, 136, 141, 145, 147, 156, 164, 172, 175, 178, 179, 185, 199, 207, 209

Royal Society of Arts 61

Salisbury 36, 118, 126, 127, 129, 130, 143, 186,

Salisbury Military Wives Choir 126, 127, 143, 163

Sandberg, Sheryl 185, 186

Sandhurst 70, 115

Sappers 38

Scotland 45, 66, 72, 73, 78, 80, 161, 197, 198, 211

Second World War 7, 11, 23, 27, 28, 38, 44, 47, 53, 135

Serembang 88

Sergeant's Mess 70, 71

Shaftesbury 67

Shaw, Dr Clare 7, 118–9

Singapore 50, 174, 182, 193

South Africa 162, 174

Southampton 17, 27, 28, 30, 33, 35, 36, 37, 40, 41, 42, 43, 44, 45, 86, 116, 201, 207, 211, 212, 217,

Southampton Blitz 42

South Atlantic 108, 180

South Atlantic Medal 134

South Coast Proms 148, 149
South Shields 109
Stead, June 5, 7, 13, 14, 47, 57–62
Stubbington 72, 182, 183, 184
Suez 11, 71, 182
Sungei Ugong Club 89
Swindon 16, 186
Switzerland 31, 32, 33

Taunton 77, 194
Thomas Cup 51
Tidworth 121, 128, 151, 152, 153
Tilbury 54
Titchfield 184
Tobruk 31, 32, 48
Trieste 49
Tunisia 46, 48
Turkey 21, 80
Twyford 119

Under the Queen's Colours 10
University College London 24
Verona 31, 32, 33, 37
Victoria Institute 51, 217

Waterloo Station 41
Watford 24
Weeks, Jean 7, 65–8
Wells, HG 15
Western Front 16
Weymouth 72, 73, 74, 108
Whale Island 149, 207
White, Jessie Maud 20–3
Whittington, Pam 7, 213, 214
Winchester 155, 164
Winter, Margaret 16–9
Women's Institute 73, 76
Women's Royal Naval Service (WRNS) 62
Woolrich, Charlotte 7, 121–3, 199–207
Woolton, Frederick, Marquis, 1st Earl of 34
Woolton Pie 34
Woolwich 70, 71, 92, 97
Woolworth's 30, 103
Woosnam, Margherita 7, 53–7
Wylie, Kay 7, 79–87

Zimbabwe 192

Visit our website and discover thousands of other History Press books.

www.thehistorypress.co.uk